The Problematic and Conceptual Structure of Classical Indian Thought about Man, Society and Polity

The Problematic and Conceptual Structure of Classical Indian Thought about Man, Society and Polity

Daya Krishna

DELHI
OXFORD UNIVERSITY PRESS
BOMBAY CALCUTTA MADRAS
1996

Oxford University Press, Walton Street, Oxford OX2 6DP
Oxford New York
Athens Aukland Bangkok Bombay
Calcutta Cape Town Dar Es Salaam Delhi
Florence Hong Kong Istanbul Karachi
Kuala Lampur Madras Madrid Melbourne
Mexico City Nairobi Paris Singapore
Taipei Tokyo Toronto
and associates in
Berlin Ibadan

ISBN 0 19 563797 6

Typeset by Rastixi, New Delhi 110070
Printed at Saurabh Print-O-Pack, Noida
and published by Neil O'Brien, Oxford University Press
YMCA Library Building, Jai Singh Road, New Delhi 110001

Dedicated
to
the memory
of
A.M. Ghosh
whose
untimely death
deprived
me of a dear friend
and the 'Jaipur Experiment'
of
one of its most conscientious
and committed supporters

Preface

The genesis of our concern with India's intellectual traditions and their distinctive problematic and conceptual structures has been spelled out by me in the introduction to *India's Intellectual Traditions*.[1] It tells the entire story of the 'Jaipur experiment' as it emerged from a lecture by Professor S.C. Dube sometime in 1983. The 'collective thinking' on the subject by the interdisciplinary group at Jaipur as well as other convergent 'experiments' initiated by Professor M.P. Rege resulted in the publication of *Saṃvadā*.[2] It also led to what I have elsewhere called 'the Sarnath experiment' where, for the first time, more than a hundred Naiyāyikas from all over India met under the leadership of the late Pandit Badrinath Shukla to discuss some modern issues in respect of Nyāya. The 'Sarnath experiment' was later continued in Mīmāṃsā and Kashmir Śaivism at Tirupati and Srinagar respectively under his leadership.

These experiments also led to the attempt at locating traditional Sanskritic scholars in various fields of knowledge all over India and the resultant publication of the *Who's Who of Sanskrit Scholars in India* by the Sahitya Academy, New Delhi.[3]

The Jaipur experiment lost its momentum sometime after 1985, and though occasional meetings of the group continued, we gradually began to realize that we could not proceed significantly beyond what had been achieved so far. I realized then that, ultimately, only 'individual' effort would enable us to take any further steps towards the goal that we had set ourselves. I decided to do some thinking and make an attempt in this regard.

The present work has arisen out of this effort and, however tentatively, presents for the first time the way India's intellectual enterprises appear to those located in contemporary times. It focuses on the problems that they addressed and the conceptual structures in terms of which they articulated their thought. The purpose, as I have repeatedly stated in the book, is to take hold of India's millennia-long attempt at understanding man, society and polity so that one may make *use* of it not only for understanding the present reality about these phenomena, but also for developing them further in the context of the intellectual challenges of the present.

The book was largely written during the grant of a national fellowship by the Indian Council of Social Science Research for which the late Sukhamoy Chakravarti, who was Chairman then, was primarily responsible. The manuscript greatly benefited from the critical and careful comments of Dr Mukund Lath which resulted in significant changes in some portions of the book. Heavy reliance has been placed on the *Dharmakośa* of Pandit Laxman Shastri Joshi, one of the most comprehensive encyclopaedic reference works deriving from the non-Buddhist and non-Jain traditions. However, for the same reason, Buddhist and Jain sources have been completely neglected which, of course, is a great failing of the work. It is hoped that future works in this domain will take into account these sources also and reveal how far the picture built on the basis of the sources in the *Dharmakośa* requires to be modified in their light. The sources in languages other than Sanskrit are a *terra incognita* and have hardly been utilized for the study of the intellectual traditions of India. Equally, there has been little attempt to see the thought relating to the natural sciences in terms of either their problematic and conceptual structure or their impact on thinking in other fields which are more familiar to scholars of Indian thought and culture.

A task for the future, this can only be undertaken if the presupposition that all non-western modes of knowledge have been superseded by the current western thought in these fields is abandoned. This, however, can only happen when the social, political and historical roots of thought arising in the west is realized and its 'intrinsic parochiality' understood in terms of its own contentions elaborated in disciplines such as the 'sociology of knowledge' and the 'paradigms of thought' in recent times. One has to realize the relation between power and knowledge in order that the attitude towards non-western forms of knowledge may be freed from the prejudices in their own civilizations.

Besides this, however, there is another obstacle preventing these traditions from becoming an active presence in the intellectual consciousness of the present. This is the attitude common to most traditional scholars who feel that all the thinking on these subjects has already been done and that nothing more is required except to 'understand' it as fully as possible. Their only dispute, therefore, is with regard to the 'correct' understanding of what the texts say in these matters. The question is not whether the understanding of a concept or of a set of concepts is 'correct' in the light of what has been said in a particular text or a series of texts on the subject, but whether one is creatively *using* and *developing* it to understand one's own experience as did so many of the great thinkers in the past. To be bound by the past intellectual traditions of one's own civilization is as harmful as it is to be bound by the cognitive traditions of the contemporary west. One has to be free of both and 'use' the rich cognitive heritage of both regardless of whether one's current usage is in complete accord with that in the east or west, in the past or present. It is in this hope that this effort at articulating the problematic and conceptual structures of India's thought about man, society and polity is offered to fellow intellectuals in India and abroad.

One cannot but help fondly recalling all those who were involved in the Jaipur experiment. Shri A.M. Ghosh, to whom this book is dedicated, was one of the most committed persons in the project and his untimely death deprived me and the project of one who had been constantly available for any help. Among others, Dr Mukund Lath, Dr Francine E. Krishna, Dr Virendra Shekhawat, Dr R.S. Bhatnagar, Dr N.K. Singhi, Professor R.C. Dwivedi, Professor V.R. Mehta and Dr K.L. Sharma, all in their diverse ways, helped in the unique intellectual experiment and directly or indirectly, and contributed to whatever is really worthwhile in the spirit of this book.

Notes

1. Daya Krishna (ed.), *India's Intellectual Traditions* (Delhi: Indian Council of Philosophical Research and Motilal Banarsidass, 1987).

2. Daya Krishna, M.P. Rege, R.C. Dwivedi and Mukund Lath (eds), *Samvāda: A Dialogue Between Two Philosophical Traditions* (Delhi: Indian Council of Philosophical Research and Motilal Banarsidass, 1991).
3. K.C. Dutt (ed.), *Who's Who of Sanskrit Scholars in India* (Delhi: Indian Council of Philosophical Research, Rashtriya Sanskrit Sansthan and Sahitya Academy, 1994).

DAYA KRISHNA

Contents

Contents

Introduction

Civilizations have seldom been studied in terms of the intellectual and existential problems they encountered and tried to solve in their long history over millennia, or in terms of the answers to the various questions they sought in different fields. We have also not tried to understand civilizations in terms of the conceptual structures they formulated in order to make their own experiences intelligible and the problems created by these concepts for the thinkers of civilizations down the ages. Yet, man as a self-conscious being, inevitably formulates his thinking in terms of concepts which give some form and shape to his experiences so that he can feel comfortable and familiar with them. Such formulations, transmitted and developed over successive generations by diverse thinkers, give an identity to a civilization distinctive from that of others, which have in turn formulated their own experiences in terms of a different problematic and conceptual structure. And yet, because all human beings share something in common, the way that any civilization formulates its intellectual and existential concerns is of abiding interest to others.

Thus the cognitive enterprise of those civilizations which have self-consciously developed concepts in different domains and carried this on for millennia is doubly interesting. For, on the one hand, this gives us an insight into the civilization concerned, and on the other, it makes available to us the conceptual and theoretical richness of an alternative version of similar enterprises carried out in the west.

The availability of these alternative cognitive enterprises and of the conceptual structures in which they are embedded makes us aware of the unconscious parochiality of the intellectual exercises of the present. It also challenges us to unfreeze them from their seemingly finished moulds of the past and develop them further in the light of contemporary situations.

All thought on man, society and polity has a continuing relevance: these are the basic themes with which human thought has been concerned. Indian thought on these matters is embodied in a śāstric form, that is, a self-consciously organized body of knowledge which makes it doubly relevant.

A śāstric form, however, tempts one to think of the cognitive enterprise of civilizations, particularly those that belong to a distant past, as essentially static and final. In other words, the very form in which knowledge is available to us creates the impression that there is no room for it to be critically evaluated in terms of incompleteness or inadequacy. The intellectual format in the Indian tradition also encourages this attitude as it takes the form of writing commentaries and sub-commentaries on the original text, known as *bhāsya*, *vārtika*, *vṛtti*, *ṭīkā*, etc. However, this is a superficial view of traditional literature, even though it seems to be widely shared by scholars and laymen alike. This 'closed' attitude is further strengthened by the usual presentation in historical works of different cognitive disciplines, as they neither take into account the deceptive nature of the format nor do they pay attention to the countervailing fact that the intrinsic intellectual nature of the cognitive enterprise in Indian tradition is immanently presented according to one's *siddhānta* or doctrine.

The intellectual tradition of developing thought through the format of commentaries on the earlier texts, therefore, does not militate against modification, change and even radical departure in thought over a period of time. This is because, first, the tradition pertains not just to one text or school of thought but pervades all of them, and secondly, the very format of intellectual writing, whether in the basic text or the commentaries, is generally in the form of stating counter-positions and counter-arguments and then refuting them to establish one's own siddhānta. Since debate with rival schools continues all the time, the need for writing a subsequent bhāṣya or commentary arises primarily because of fresh objections raised by thinkers and the necessity of answering them. Thus, successive commentaries on a basic text or even later commentaries on earlier commentaries show a gradual modification in the positions held in order to remedy various weaknesses pointed out by critics from other schools of thought, as well as to develop some important sub-schools within the tradition of the main school itself. There have thus been either gradual or sudden modifications in all schools of Indian thought over a period of time.

But in spite of their many differences, they all share a common discourse and address themselves to a common problematic which arises out of the peculiar constellation of specific circumstances, providing the breeding ground for intellectual thinking about man, society and polity. The discourse and the problematic relate to the fact that man, as a self-conscious being, finds himself embedded both in nature and society and yet considers himself apart from them in an essential sense. While he cannot disown them as a part of his being or pretend that they are not there, he yet does not feel that his innermost being can be understood or defined in terms of his relationship with nature and society. A similar situation, though on a subtler level, exists in terms of his relationship to reality as a whole, in both its transcendent and immanent aspects: one 'knows' that one is part of a wider reality which transcends both space and time and yet manifests in space and time, and that one is somehow integrally and deeply related to it all the time. With respect to this wider reality, one has to feel apart from it in order to be related to it, just as in one's relation to nature and society, where, at the empirical level, one feels oneself to be a part of them and yet above or beyond them all, so also one feels defined in an even more radically intimate manner by this transcendental reality. The dilemmas and paradoxes that such a situation give rise to in the socio-cultural being of man as well as at the trans-empirical level have been articulated most in ancient Indian literature which has viewed man primarily in relation to his own ideal self rather than in terms of his relationship to anything else, whether transcendental or empirical. The latter has not been denied but all other relationships have been given a secondary place. This obviously had tremendous implications for thinkers who were primarily concerned with man as a socio-political being or those who were primarily concerned with his relationship to the transcendental 'other', whether conceived personally or impersonally.

However, the problematic situation of man in any of these

areas, if self-consciously articulated, has necessarily to take recourse to a myriad concepts in terms of which the problematic can be formulated. This would allow him to view his situation intellectually so that he could objectively see the paradoxical situation in which he is, where very different and opposite kinds of demands are made on him with equal insistence and from among which, he often finds it difficult to choose. The articulation of the problematic in its various dimensions is thus closely related to the conceptual structures within which a civilization articulates what it considers to be its fundamental problematic.

The present work, therefore, tries first to articulate the problematic of the Indian civilization in its various dimensions and then to delineate the conceptual structures related to each of these major domains. It also tries to distinguish between society, law and polity in the realm of the institutional 'other' in which a human being is necessarily involved and with respect to which he finds himself burdened with different types of obligations. The legal realm specifies the essential conflict of interests between different individuals and groups while the political realm deals with the conflicting interests of polities in terms of power which demands to be tamed and made subservient to moral considerations even though this power seems to be essentially amoral in nature. Man as a social being, however, is not contained in the legal and political realms alone. Rather, his centre of existence seems to lie in the calling of the householder with its different occupations, professions and functions without which social living seems impossible. There is thus an inherent tension between what may be broadly called 'social' on the one hand, and the legal and the political on the other, just as there is an innate tension between the inner obligations of a polity to its own citizens which is epitomized in the notions of justice and welfare and its relations with other polities with which it exists in a state of potential hostility.

The life of the householder shows an ambivalent relation to society in the larger sense as, even though it may be regarded as the primary social unit, it is rooted in a biological nexus wherein the task of bringing up children and acculturating them into society has a primacy over everything else. This generally tends to generate conflict between the norms and values of what may be called public life and the interests of the family which inevitably remains the primary unit of identification for the individual. On the other hand, the life of the householder, being only a particular stage in the biological cycle of an individual, is sandwiched between important phases in which his connection with the life of the householder is secondary and perhaps essentially instrumental. If we add to this the fact that the individual, as a self-conscious being, feels apart from all others, both individuals and institutions, and finds that his ideal self cannot ever be realized in terms of these relationships which are transitory and fleeting, avenues are opened for the realization of the non-centrality of the householder's life and its essential conflict with the demands to be really 'oneself'.

Thus, while the householder has an ambivalent relationship within the social realm comprising both law and polity, the individual who leads the life of the householder, which is primary for him in an empirical sense, has an ambivalent attitude to it not only due to the fact that he has to enter it at a certain stage of his biological life but also because he has to gradually distance himself from it as his children grow up and themselves enter the householder's life, and because in his own self-conscious being, he cannot but feel that it is something imposed on him by the biological cycle and that it is not exactly an essential part of his being. This, of course, runs counter to the accepted psychology of the human personality which sees an individual's identity primarily in terms of his socialization and the socio-cultural experiences which he undergoes during this process and internalizes in terms of his self-consciousness. But such a view of individual identity, though widely held in modern times, is alien to the ethos of the classical Indian civilization, and even if the currently fashionable theory is accepted as correct, it would imply that the idea of the self is implanted in the individual by a culture through the process of socialization. In fact most of the thinkers of ancient civilizations have held such an idea of the individual, even though in India it was carried to its extreme limits and, through socialization and acculturation, made a part of the psyche at the deepest level of those who participated in it. The problematic created by such an internalization is writ large over the history of Indian culture where society, through the creation of norms, proclaims its own secondary character and thus creates in the individual a basic dichotomy between his empirical being which comprises the biological, social, legal and political realms and his transcendental being to which all of this is an 'object', that is, something 'other' than what his own 'real' self is. The former has generally been designated *jīva* in the Indian tradition, while the latter has usually been termed *ātman*, even though the Buddhists do not accept any such substantive ontological reality. It is thus the dichotomy between the jīva and the ātman and the conflicting identification with them which, in the Indian perspective, may be said to define the human situation. The *Sāṁkhyan* terms for these are *puruṣa* and *prakṛti*, the latter comprising not only the *karmendriyas* and the *jñānendriyas*, that is, all the senses which are either instruments of knowledge or of action, but also *manas, buddhi* and *ahaṁkāra*, that is, the mind, intellect and the ego. However, the term 'jīva' seems to convey better the idea of an empirical being than the term 'prakṛti'. The latter, in common parlance, does not convey the same meaning even though, used in its technical sense, it does carry the same meaning, spelt out in a more differentiated manner.

The articulation of what a great civilization thought about man, society and polity is interesting in itself. It becomes even more so when the history of the civilization over millennia is seen in terms of the problematic that such a vision gave rise to both at the theoretical and existential levels, thus giving a distinctive shape to thought, feeling and action over a long period of time. Also, as the problematic created by the formulations is continuously attempted to be solved at the levels of thought, feeling and action by successive generations which have tried to come to terms with it, the history of the civilization itself becomes a history of the problematic and its successive solutions which, in turn, leads to new problems, providing both continuity and change in the understanding of the vision itself. This is reflected in the changes, modifications and extensions of the concepts which formulated the problematic initially encountered in different areas of human experience and the development of new concepts to capture aspects of changing reality and experiences not contained in the concepts formulated earlier. An exploration of the problematic of classical Indian thought about man, society and polity and the conceptual structures within which this problematic was embodied, thus attempts not only to provide an insight into one of the greatest civilizations that the world has produced but also attempts to create a methodology by which all civilizations can be understood. A comparative study of civilizations would then be a study of the diverse problematics that they formulated for themselves and the ways in which they tried to solve them both theoretically and existentially. It would also be a comparative study of the conceptual structures civilizations evolved to articulate and comprehend the problematic and the manner in which these underwent extensions, modifications and changes. However, such a comparative study of civilizations would have to await the formulation of their problematic and conceptual structures on the model that has been attempted here in the case of one civilization alone, that is, the Indian civilization. Also, as the attempt itself is a pioneering one, it will have to be supplemented and modified by others whose own formulations of both the problematic and the conceptual structures may be radically different from mine. This would be a welcome move as it would provide not only alternative insights into the understanding of a civilization but would also indicate the acceptance of the methodology adopted here for the understanding of the Indian civilization in particular, and of civilizations in general.

PART I

CHAPTER I

The Vedic Roots of the Problematic

The beginning of the Indian problematic can only be constructed through reflections on the earliest text available to us–the Vedas. The scanty archaeological evidence of the Mohenjodaro and Harappan civilizations is of little help in the matter. The Vedas, however, though long known, studied and commented upon from diverse points of view, have usually been accepted in the form in which Vyāsa is supposed to have left them after compiling and editing them for his own purposes. The usual four-fold division of the Vedas makes little sense, particularly if we are interested in their contents; for not only does the Sāmaveda have little by way of content, even the other Vedas have a lot of material that is duplicated in more than one text and sometimes even at more than one place in the same text. Also, many of the so-called *śākhās* of the Vedas have substantial differences in the text accepted by them, and hence there is little point in going by the usually accepted four-fold division of the Vedas.[1] However, as our interest is not in the text *per se*, but in the problematic for which it provides the evidence, we may ignore these problems for the present.

The Vedas, as we see it, present a four-fold problematic behind the variety of concerns that are found in the text. These may be designated as: (1) The transcendental reflection on the ultimate origins of things, (2) the immanent-transcendent gods of the visible, the sensuously apprehended universe, (3) the *yajña* or sacrifice linking man to the universe with its multifarious gods in terms of his diverse physical, mental and spiritual needs, and (4) the concept of the body-social or the four-fold *puruṣa* adumbrated in the *Puruṣa Sūkta.* The first finds its most surprising and awe-inspiring expression in what has come to be known as the *Nāsadīya Sūkta* (10.129). The r.c. 10.129 opens with the astonishing statement that 'there was, then neither *sat*, nor *asat*' and closes with the even more astonishing statement that 'perhaps it formed itself, or perhaps it did not. The one who looks down on it from the highest heavens, only he knows–or perhaps even he does not know'. No translation can ever capture the power of the original verse, the deep, reverberating, echoing sound from a distant millennium–the long past of Indian civilization coming to us as if we had put our ears to a conch-shell and heard the sound of the ocean in whose depths it had grown and developed. And who can forget the ever-questioning, opening query of hymn 10.121, asking '*Kasmai devāya haviṣā vidhema*' ('What God shall we worship with oblations, or to whom shall we sacrifice'), even though the question is theoretical in view of the answer given at the end of the hymn. The answer, in fact, is no answer, for the *Nāsadīya Sūkta* is supposed to be a later hymn and suggests that the idea of a lord of creation as the creator God, that is Prajāpati, was found to be highly problematic.

The idea that there is an immanent-transcendent Godhead in everything that we encounter is clearly evident in the hymns of the Ṛgveda. Every *mantra* is supposed to have a *ṛṣi* and a *devatā*, that is, a seer or a visionary and a god specifically associated with it. A sacred enchantment thus encompassed all that man encountered, both outside and within himself. It not only made him feel at home in the universe, but also left intact his feeling of wonder, a feeling that comes so naturally to man when he sees natural phenomena unburdened by the manipulative, causal knowledge that he may have of them. It is not that the causal-functional knowledge was not sought after or valued or acquired. It is not only the well-laid cities of Mohenjodaro and Harappa that testify to this, presupposing as they do the science of engineering, public health, etc., but the performance of the Vedic yajña itself that required all the knowledge specifically referred to as *vedāṅga* in traditional literature, including a knowledge of astronomy and geometry. In fact, some of the hymns of the Ṛgveda have been dated on the basis of the astronomical observations mentioned in them,[2] and the *Śulva Sūtra* is supposed to provide the geometrical basis of building the sacrificial vedic altar. The sacralization of the universe, thus, in no way entailed the neglect of the secular sciences as is usually alleged. This is perhaps so in any culture, for man's empirical life in this world depends, to a large extent, on the successful acquisition of knowledge of the secular kind. The conflict between the sacred and the secular seems to be a recent invention of the western intellect; otherwise, most cultures in the past appear to have happily integrated the two together.

The centrality of yajña and its performance on all occasions and for all purposes is known to even a cursory student of the Vedas. In fact it is supposed to have been created along with the universe and is conterminus with it. But the construal of the yajña as being central to the Vedas led to a whole problematic surrounding the strategies of interpretation to be adopted with regard to them so that such a centrality was ensured. In the process, the other aspects of the Vedas had necessarily to be underplayed. But the strategy adopted forced the protagonists of the yajña-centric interpretation of the Vedas to ultimately deny it any cognitive meaning whatsoever.[3]

The four-fold theory of varṇa which is supposed to be propounded in the *Puruṣa Sūkta* is perhaps even better known than the idea of yajña or the profound reflections on the origin of things, the best known example of which is the *Nāsadīya Sūkta* referred to earlier. In it are supposed to lie the roots of what has come to be called 'Manu's Curse' or the so-called caste system of India. The idea of varṇa propounded in the *Puruṣa Sūkta* became as determinative of the Indian way of looking at social reality as the idea of yajña had been of man's transactions with cosmic reality in general.

However, both the ideas of yajña and varṇa see man as socially interdependent and as essentially a desiring being. The two are also linked, as for most yajñas the distinction between *yajamāna* and *ṛtvika* is essential, and the ṛtvikas, who are specialists in the ritual of the yajñas, may only be brahmins. There are, of course, further restrictions in the case of certain yajñas, such as *sattra* where not only is there no distinction between the yajamāna and the ṛtvikas, but which can only be performed by brahmins belonging to a certain *kalpa* or *gotra*. As the ṛtvikas are paid a stipulated sacrificial fee for performing the sacrifice for the yajamāna who is normally desirous of attaining some benefit through the performance of the sacrifice, yajña is an economic transaction also with all the attendant problems which economic exchanges involve. There is also a hierarchy, along with a specialization of functions, amongst the ṛtvikas, necessitating co-ordination between the different specialists, a function performed by the ṛtvik designated as Brahma for the occasion.

Besides these, the performance of yajña required a knowledge of astronomy to determine the auspicious time for the performance of the sacrifice and a knowledge of geometry for the correct construction of the fire altar where the yajña was to be performed. So, all in all, it was a large festival, a many-sided undertaking with vast implications for the development of knowledge, social relations and economic interchange. And it helped in the development of a class of literati concerned solely with the preservation of the Vedas and developing the techniques of its oral preservation and transmission on the one hand, and the knowledge of the exact ritualistic procedures to be followed in different kinds of yajña, on the other. These two, however, further resulted in an activity which was philosophically more interesting and related to the question of how to understand and interpret a Vedic text.

The yajña-centric interpretation construed the Vedas to consist primarily of injunctions, that is, of prescriptions and prohibitions regarding what was to be done and what was not to be done. Such a way of looking at the Vedas was sought to be buttressed by building a theory of language in which the verb was the primary unit or focus of meaning in a sentence and not the noun. Man was thus seen primarily as an 'action-centred' being, motivated by desires, the fulfilment of which he sought through the performance of diverse types of yajña. But a 'desire-centric' view of action can only result in hypothetical imperatives and not in any categorical imperative, as *dharma* is usually understood to be. Surprisingly, though ostensibly Jaiminī proclaims dharma to be the subject matter of his well-known *Mīmāṁsā Sūtra*, he does not see the necessity of making this distinction which is central to the very notion of dharma. Not only this, he confines himself only to discussing the procedures of the various yajñas as described in the Brāhmana texts. Surely, there could be no greater perversion than this, if we wish to take the notion of dharma seriously. Even the interpretation of yajña as establishing a relationship with the cosmic order which was called *ṛta* by the Vedic seers, is not sustained by the way Jaiminī treats the whole subject in his *sūtras* and the way Śabara explicates it in the *Bhāsya* on it. The whole exercise is full of finicky details and is concerned with the performance of something the declared purpose of which is the attainment of some common worldly good desired by ordinary mortals.

But even the other major text which also claims to be concerned with dharma seems to be equally unconcerned with moral issues. This is the *Vaiśeṣika Sūtra* of Kaṇāda which promises that a knowledge of his six *padārthas* (categories) will ensure both *abhyudaya* (worldly well-being) and *niḥśreyasa* (liberation) which dharma alone is supposed to provide. Perhaps dharma is being used in these texts in a sense which is radically different from the one in which it is used in, say, the Rāmāyaṇa or the Mahābhārata where *dharmasaṁkaṭa* or the conflict of duties and the grounds for its resolution is the heart of dharma. Dharma, of course, is also used, specially in technical Buddhist philosophy, for what may be called 'properties' or 'qualities'. But the Vaiśeṣika use of dharma can hardly be considered as analogous to that use for the simple reason that *guṇa* which comes closest to what is conveyed by the term property or quality is itself regarded as a padārtha in that system.

The close relation between 'desire' and 'action', or *kāma* and *karma* so clearly articulated in the well-known *Mīmāṁsā* injunction '*svargakāmo yajeta*' led, on the one hand, to the almost axiomatic belief that action always leads to bondage and, on the other, to the idea of an action which has nothing to do with desire, or *niṣkāma karma.* But it is not clear why action motivated by desire should always lead to bondage, or even why action which is not the result of any specific desire should not lead to bondage. An action performed from a sense of duty may quite well have unwelcome consequences, just as an action undertaken from desire, say, for a cup of coffee, may result in nothing more than the gratifying of sensuous or non-sensuous desires. Surely, the desire to hear inspiring music or read good literature or see a well-known piece of architecture does not usually lead to anything that may reasonably be called bondage. The *Gītā* contains a sequence which shows why kāma which, according to it, is born of attachment, must necessarily lead to destruction. But there is no necessity in the chain, for it is not obvious why kāma should always lead to *krodha* or anger, or anger to delusion, and so on. Even if we read the modern sequence of desire-frustration–aggression–guilt–repression–neurosis into it, it will not help matters much, for desire need not necessarily lead to frustration or frustration to repression. The modern sequence is contingent upon, and, like the ancient, derives its strength from, the fact that it sometimes happens to be true.

The relation of desire to bondage, thus, is arbitrary and so also is its supposedly inalienable and intrinsic relation to action. The confusion basically arises from the fact that it is not clear as to what is meant by karma or action, on the one hand, and desire or kāma on the other. For example, is the desire for *mokṣa* the same as the desire for, say, money or love or fame or the desire to help others? Similarly, is meditation an 'action' or is it, say, *upāsanā* which is treated by Rāmānuja as karma in his *Śrī Bhāṣya* on the *Brahma Sūtras*. But even if upāsanā is intended to include all the ritualistic actions that might go into it, would it be proper to interpret it as karma in the same sense as, say, walking?

But whatever we may think of these relationships, there is little doubt that different thinkers saw them as a major problem area, and thinker after thinker tried to grapple with them. A problem, ultimately, is what is *felt* as a problem; in its case, its *esse* is *percipi*. And if a sufficient number of persons can be made to feel that there is a problem requiring a solution, we have a historical tradition formed by successive thinkers who take diverse positions that give rise to different schools or *sampradāyas* with their own master texts and teachers.

An analysis of desire and its relation to suffering and bondage on the one hand, and to pleasure, happiness and fulfilment through action whose paradigm was the Vedic yajña on the other, provided one such problematic.

In the Indian tradition, Buddha's overwhelming emphasis on suffering as the essence of human life and desire as being its root cause gave such a slant to the Indian way of looking at man and his empirical life that Indian culture hardly ever recovered from it. The Sāṁkhyans also talked of *ātyantika duḥkha nivṛtti*, the cessation of the very possibility of suffering. Different thinkers vied with each other to provide a diagnosis of the human situation and suggest basic strategies for a radical and permanent cure demanded by the analysis.

The yajña-centric view of life, also saw human life as centred in desire, but did not think that there was anything essentially wrong with it. Rather, it prescribed various types of activities known as yajñas to attain these desires. The procedure of performing these yajñas was, however, not only prescribed by a transcendental authority and known only to specialists who alone could perform them on behalf of people on payment of the prescribed fee, but by a strange twist of logic, yajñas were not allowed to be performed for everyone and thus lost their universality just when they could easily have become widespread.

The denial of the right to yajña by the orthodox interpreters of the Vedas to śūdras deprived the so-called *śruti* of that universal claim which it had made for itself and which was made on its behalf by others. The varṇa-centric theory of society as derived from the Vedas and its construal in such a way as to make it totally and exclusively yajña-centric and deprive the śūdras the right to them, gave a permanent disabling twist to Indian thought about man and society which myriad attempts at rectification by outstanding personalities could hardly succeed in healing, then or later. Even the 'knowledge-centric' thought of the *Upaniṣads* failed to include the śūdras as, in spite of his Brahman-centric interpretation of the texts, Bādarāyaṇa, as much as Jaiminī, stuck to the view that according to the śruti itself, the śūdras could not be allowed access to it. The two divergent streams of vedic interpretation, thus, concurred on the central fact of the social exclusion of the śūdras from the crucial vedic performances, whether conceived of in terms of knowledge or action.

The problems created by such an exclusion were both internal and external. The confinement of the varṇas to just four raised the problem of how to fit the myriad groups existing in society under these four varṇas alone. Even in the context of the vedic yajñas, the question arose as to the exact varṇa of the *rathakāra* (the chariot maker) and the *niṣadapati* (the tribal chief) as, according to the text, they could not be accommodated under the three varṇas, that is, the brāhmana, kṣatriya or vaiśya who had already been assigned the seasons for performing some sacrifice and who could not be śūdras either, for śūdras were excluded from performing sacrifices, whereas these two categories were permitted by designation to perform sacrifices. Under the circumstances, there was no option but to regard them as belonging to a varṇa other than these four, a solution that did not help matters much as, firstly, there was no generalized name for such a varṇa and, secondly, it was only an *ad hoc* solution to an *ad hoc* problem created by certain passages in the *Brāhmaṇa* texts which were regarded as a constituent part of the Veda because of its yajña-centric interpretation by Jaiminī and his followers. They, however, failed to notice that by doing so they were introducing an inner contradiction between the *Mantra* and the *Brāhmaṇa* portions of the Veda as there was no mention of any varṇa other than the usual four in the *Puruṣā Sūkta* on the basis of which the theory of varṇa seems to have ostensibly been formulated. In fact, one can have serious doubts about the genuineness of the commitment to the so-called *śruti-prāmāṇya* of both Jaiminī and Bādarāyaṇa, the founders of the two schools of Vedic exegesis. Both the *Brāhmaṇas* and the *Upaniṣads* which are respectively accepted by Jaiminī and Bādarāyaṇa as the fundamental śruti texts for the systems they built had sufficient material to permit different positions to be taken on the question of the śūdra's access to śruti. The well-known story of Kavaṣa in the *Aitareya Brāhmaṇa* and that of Satyakāma Jābāla in the *Chāndogya Upaniṣad*[5] provide sufficient warrant for this. Not only this, a careful reflection on the *Puruṣa Sūkta* itself reveals a different interpretation more in consonance with the text than the usual one offered by orthodox scholars. First, the cosmic puruṣa divides himself not only into the four varṇas mentioned in it but also into the other things comprising the universe such as the sky, etc.; second, it quite clearly says that he dwells only with one-fourth of himself in the visible universe; the other three-fourths of himself transcends this universe, or rather is contained within it as its invisible, transcendent essence. Now, this organic and immanent-transcendent view of the cosmic puruṣa in which all reality is rooted could easily have given rise to a view of society as constituted by all the four varṇas together, where no one was intrinsically superior or inferior to the other and where each was not only complementary to the other, but required all the others for its own completeness in as essential a manner as society required nature in which it was embedded. Besides this, each participated and dwelt within the invisible puruṣa, the transcendent Brahman which exceeded the visible universe by three-fourths of his reality and sustained the latter only by one-fourth of it. All the varṇas, like everything else, were thus an integral part of his being. Such was the clear message of the *Puruṣa Sūkta* and the fact that even Bādarāyaṇa, who did so much to propagate the Brahman-centric interpretation of the Upaniṣads, succumbed to the theory of the exclusion of the śūdras from access to śruti speaks volumes for the social determination of the interpretation of the Vedic texts even in ancient times. In fact the *Śukla Yajurveda* gives a whole list of persons and professions in *Adhyāya* 30, persons it designates as *abrāhmaṇāḥ*, *aśūdrāḥ* and yet whom it considers *prājāpatyāḥ*, that is, the children of Prajāpati.

The exclusion of the śūdras from any access to the Vedas either through the performance of yajñas or through the knowledge of Brahman was challenged from a strange quarter. Bharata, the author of the *Nātya Śāstra* or the *Nātya Veda* did not only claim for it the status of a fifth Veda, but also called it *sārva-varṇika*, that is, as belonging to all the varṇas in contrast to the four Vedas which were accessible only to the three varṇas. Not only this, the śūdras probably occupied the centre stage in the show where all the other varṇas were relegated to the pit as spectators. The rivalry contained in the *Nātya* with yajña is proclaimed by Bharata by calling it *sarvaśilpapravartakam*, that is, providing the incentive for the development of all the crafts. Not only this, it is claimed to be *sarvakarmānudarṣakam* as well as *dharmakarmānudarṣakam*, that is, it mirrors or portrays all human actions and their moral dimensions in all aspects. Besides this, it is what Bharata has called *lokayātrānugāminaḥ*, *lokasvabhāva-nugāminaḥ* and *lokasvabhāvasaṁsiddaḥ*, that is, it is concerned with the 'this-worldly' life of the human individual in all its variety and not with some transcendent aspect of it alone with which the Vedas are supposed to deal and which only the Vedic specialist, whether he is a follower of Jaiminī or of Bādarāyaṇa, knows about. But however much one may critically question the accepted orthodoxy in art or even create a topsy-turvy world opposed to it, the real world of social relations embedded in the institutions which perpetuate and sustain it remains unaffected except in some marginal, imaginative sense which might become historically effective at some later time, given favourable circumstances.

The challenge to Vedic authority, particularly the exclusion of the śūdras from any legitimate access to it, continued to be made in diverse forms and from many quarters. The Buddha and the Mahāvīra explicitly rejected the authority of the Vedas and the theory of varṇa supposedly supported by it. However, as they were primarily oriented to the *śramanic* form of life in the *saṅgha*, it is not quite clear what sort of lay society they envisaged, and in what way they wanted it to be different from the orthodox Vedic conception of it. A more serious challenge arose from the *Bhagavad Gītā* which not only explicitly criticised the desire-centric nature of the Vedic yajñas and their extreme ritualism, but also entitled all, including śūdras and women, to seek the divine.[6] The Mahābhārata in which the *Bhagavad Gītā* is embedded, in fact, declared itself to be a fifth Veda just as Bharata had done earlier if we accept the date of the *Nātya Śāstra* to be earlier than that of the Mahābhārata.

But the *Gītā*, like Buddha and Mahāvīra, seems interested only in opening the doors to the divine, as was the case with the later saints who led the various Bhakti movements in India. It has little to say about the social system and the one statement it makes in this connection has been taken by the orthodoxy to support the theory of varṇa as it has interpreted it in the perspective of the theory of *karma* and the theory of rebirth.[7] The Mahābhārata, like the Rāmāyana, seems to have openly supported the orthodox interpretation of the theory of varṇa in its ideal form as propounded in a large part of the *Smṛti* literature deriving its inspiration from the Vedic sources as traditionally presented by Jaiminī and Bādarāyaṇa. The *Smṛti* literature of the Jains and the Buddhists is hardly known, and the various Bhakti saṁpradāyas are not known either, for having any separate special *Smṛti* texts of their own. Still, whatever the problems were regarding the thought about social organization which these non-vedic or even anti-vedic movements envisaged, there is little doubt that they provided a common point for the coming together of people from different varṇas who were attracted by the thought of access to the 'spiritual' or 'divine' path in contrast to the restricted and closed avenues proudly proclaimed by the orthodox interpreters of the Vedic śruti. The Ārya Samāja and the Brahma Samāja seem to have played a similar role in modern times. In any case, the formation of a new saṁpradāya where people from different varṇas could come together and form a new social group that cut across old varṇa divisions would provide an effective social dimension to the 'spiritual protest', and consolidate it over a few generations in case the movement had the momentum to keep its élan and last that long.

The challenge of 'open access' to 'spiritual truths' was met by orthodox interpreters of the Veda by the declaration that though the Vedas and the Upaniṣads were closed to the śūdras, the same truth was accessible to them through the *Itihāsa* and the *Purāṇas*, texts dealing with history and mythology. But then, the *Itihāsa* or the *Purāṇas* were not exclusively meant for those varṇas alone which were denied access to the śruti. Rather, people of all varṇas had access to them and, over time, they became as, or even more, popular amongst the three varṇas for whom the so-called śruti was exclusively meant. It is also not clear how yajña, which is supposed to be the heart of the Veda, according to Jaiminī, could have been made accessible to the śūdras through the *Itihāsa* and the *Purāṇas*, as is normally alleged by apologists of the orthodox Vedic tradition. Yajñas were usually performed by ṛtvikas, the ritual specialists, who were specifically hired for the job and paid a fee stipulated in the text itself. Thus 'access to it' on the part of the non-śūdra varṇas did not mean anything except having the requisite wealth to hire ṛtvikas and defray the other sundry expenses involved in performing the yajña. This, obviously, is no access to the śruti even in Jaiminī's sense, and could have easily been made available to anyone who had the means to afford it. In a sense, as we shall see later, this actually happened, specially when, through military conquests, some of the śūdras became kings, or through other economic activities, became affluent. Even in the case of kṣatriyas or vaiśyas, it is not clear what their so-called access to śruti would mean in Jaiminī's framework, besides the right to hire Brahmanical priests to perform yajñas for them. They themselves could not perform the functions of the ṛtvik and hence any knowledge of the Vedic ritual would have been useless to them, even if they had access to it. Perhaps the crucial question in this context would be to enquire about the proliferation of people into the Brāhmaṇa varṇa through the acquisition of certain kinds of knowledge. Social mobility is always through knowledge or valour or wealth. But while the latter two are relatively easier to acquire through one's own ability and effort, the former seems to be far more dependent on personal apprenticeship which makes it easier for a society to restrict access to knowledge, if it so desires. But, however closely guarded the secret of knowledge is, there are always teachers willing to instruct bright students from any varṇa. There are also students who, because of need or the desire for adventure or both, migrate to other lands where there are less restrictions on gaining knowledge.

It may be thought that the problem of providing access to the truth contained in the śruti through the *Itihāsa* and *Purāṇas* to the śūdras arises only for the yajña-centric interpretation of the Veda and not for the Brahman-centric interpretation of Bādarāyaṇa. Unfortunately, this is not true. It is one of the central contentions of Bādarāyaṇa, as well as Śaṁkara, who wrote his famous commentary on the former's work, that the knowledge of Brahman cannot be had independently of the śruti, that is, the Upaniṣads, and specially of the three *mahāvākyas* contained in them.[8] Now, if śūdras are denied access to the śruti, according to the śruti itself, and if the knowledge of the Brahman can be had only through the śruti, then it is obvious that the śūdras can, in principle, never gain knowledge of the Brahman, which alone is true knowledge, according to them. Recourse to the *Itihāsa* and *Purāṇas* is of no help whatsoever, as nothing but the śruti, that is, the Upaniṣads in this case, can provide this knowledge.

This is the hard core orthodox position on the subject, though it was continuously suggested that the *Itihāsa* and *Purāṇas* were meant for all those who could not grasp the subtle truths of the Upaniṣads meant for the *buddhi* which was ratiocinative, abstract and intuitive at the same time, But then there is little point in saying that the truth of the Upaniṣads was accessible to the śūdras through the *Itihāsa* and the *Purāṇas*, as it was assumed that the śūdras congenitally did not possess that kind of buddhi or conversely, that anyone who found the Upaniṣadic truth more easily accessible through them, was a śūdra.

Both alternatives, if seriously entertained, would lead to unpalatable consequences. No one would ever be sure of who was congenitally a śūdra, except under very severely restricted conditions of reproduction, and that too only in those generations on whom restrictions were imposed. In actual fact, such conditions have never obtained, not even in the so-called times of the śruti, if the story of Satyakāma Jābāla is to be believed. The other alternative holds that even the authors of the *Itihāsa* and *Purāṇas* would have to be credited with at least some sort of a śūdra buddhi as presumably they enjoyed reading what they had created. Most members of the so-called non-śūdra varṇas ostensibly enjoy reading them and probably derive some profit from them, thus revealing the śūdra buddhi that is in them. There is the added problem of accounting for the fact that the *Bhagavad Gītā*, which was meant for the śūdra buddhi, according to this view, has needed elucidation through commentaries by some of the great *ācāryas* on the same pattern as the Upaniṣads. If something was really meant for the śūdra buddhi, it should be intelligible without mediation or elucidation by anyone else. Besides this, one would also have to explain how the Rāmāyana, which is neither an *itihāsa* nor a *purāṇa*, has performed the same function better.

The orthodox interpretation of the Veda, whether in the tradition of Jaiminī or of Bādarāyaṇa, denies their *sārvavarṇic* character which is claimed by other texts, such as the *Nātya Śāstra*, *Bhagavad Gītā*, *Itihāsa*, *Purāṇas*, the various texts of the different Bhakti saṁpradāyas, as well as of the Buddhists and the Jains who openly rejected their authority in both the secular and non-secular contexts. The Veda however, as we have already noted, provided not only a vision of the sacred but also what may be called a theory of ṛta or of cosmic order, the theory of yajña or of man's interaction with cosmic powers through sacrifice and the theory of varṇa or of society, and thus set the background for the debates and developments that took place later.

The theory of ṛta or of cosmic order subsequently divided into two parts which may be called (1) the theory of dharma and (2) the theory of karma in the human context. Dharma has a wider meaning in which every entity is supposed to have its own dharma or nature or *svabhāva* which itself may be understood both in actual and ideal terms. In actual terms, a thing is what it is, different from everything else; in ideal terms, a thing is what it ought to be, something different from what it actually is, that which makes it feel dissatisfied and attempts to make different. The latter characteristic is found most clearly only in beings who possess self-consciousness, though it can be observed to some extent in most living beings, particularly those which appear nearer to human consciousness. As for the inanimate world, the distinction seems to be forced and the two appear to coincide except in the context of a consciousness which observes them and finds them beautiful or ugly. Svabhāva and *svadharma*, thus, seem totally fused or merged at the level of inanimate nature. But even in their case the reference to consciousness immediately introduces a bifurcation in terms of good or bad, pleasant or painful, beautiful or ugly. And, as in self-consciousness, consciousness itself becomes an object to consciousness, the bifurcating predicates are felt to apply to it in an even more pre-eminent manner.

There is, however, a problem here: besides the fact that an individual human being finds himself self-conscious and thus applies all these dichotomous predicates to himself, he also finds others whom he regards not merely as conscious but also as self-conscious, that is, as beings who apply these predicates to themselves. Thought about dharma in India, thus, builds up a dual theory, one which is concerned with one's own consciousness and the other which is concerned with others who are either only conscious or are both conscious and self-conscious. Dharma, as concerned with one's own self, seeks to achieve a state of consciousness which is completely bereft of any negative element in it. Dharma, as concerned with others who are only conscious, such as animals, for example, is thought of primarily in terms of *ahiṁsā* which is usually translated as non-injury, but which perhaps should be taken to mean as 'not causing any pain or suffering to others'. The Mahābhārata suggested another dharma vis-à-vis all conscious beings on the part of a being who is self-conscious, that is, *ānṛśaṁsa* or non-cruelty in place of, or along with, ahiṁsā. Perhaps the reason for the substitution was that while it is impossible not to cause suffering to others in some form or the other, it is always possible not to be 'cruel' to others.

Dharma towards a being who is self-conscious would not only involve that which is expected from one towards all conscious beings but also all that one can possibly do to help the other in attaining that consciousness which has no negative element in it. That is the deepest obligation that one may have to another self-conscious being, just as ahiṁsā or ānṛśaṁsa is the obligation which a self-conscious being has to all conscious beings, whether self-conscious or not. And this is in a sense what all saints and realized souls feel towards all self-conscious beings. It is what is known as the *mahākaruṇā* (the Great Compassion) of the Buddha, or of all those who have attained Buddhahood in some form or the other. In fact, it may even be regarded as the deepest obligation of all those self-conscious beings who have moved even slightly in the direction of achieving a non-negative consciousness. But the discharging of such an obligation is the most difficult of all as it relates to the fundamental freedom of another to move or not to move towards the achievement of a state of consciousness which is utterly non-negative in character.

Moreover, besides this deepest obligation which a self-conscious being has to another who is self-conscious, there is another obligation which is almost equally fundamental. This is what may be called 'trustworthiness' or 'reliability', denoting the fact that others can count on one's word and deed. The traditional name for this in the context of a discussion on dharma is *satya* which is usually understood as truth. But truth has too much of a semantic import and leans too heavily towards the idea of a correspondence with reality, to be very meaningful in this context. This meaning is of course included to a certain extent, particularly where the imparting or seeking of information is concerned. But basically what it means is the quality of consciousness and being from which words and action emanate, and suggests that they should have such a quality about them that others may naturally rely on them. At the deepest level this is what *śabda pramāṇa* means, and it has to do not only with what is technically known as śabda but includes, or should include, karma and to some extent *bhāva*, that is, feeling, also.

Now that we have tried to understand and formulate the traditional meaning of dharma which incorporates ahiṁsā and satya, it may not be amiss to try and understand the other three, usually known as *asteya, brahmacarya* and *aparigraha* in the context of the notion of dharma as a 'demand' or 'obligation' felt by a self-conscious being towards others who are conscious or self-conscious, as the case may be. Asteya, usually translated as 'non-stealing', is basically only a form of satya in the sense that we have understood it to be. As for brahmacarya, usually translated as 'chastity', it should perhaps be more properly understood as the virtue of ahiṁsā in the sphere of sexual activity. It has usually been interpreted as the denial of sexuality which itself has been taken as paradigmatic of all desires. But this interpretation conflicts with what has almost always been treated as the paradigmatic 'debt' in the Indian tradition, that is, the debt to one's forefathers which may only be discharged by having a progeny of one's own. On the other hand, sexual desire was also seen as the paradigmatic cause of dependence, bondage and involvement in the world, thus giving rise to that basic tension between the life of the householder and the renouncer, the *grahastha* and the *sannyāsin*, the *śrāvaka* and the *muni*, the laity and the monk in the Indian tradition. *Tantra* tried to bridge the gap, but without facing the problem of family life which normally involves both a wife and children. Later, some of the Bhakti saṁpradāyas began the tradition of having mahantas with families as their gurus and preceptors, particularly amongst the followers of Vallabhācārya. But this gave rise to one family succeeding to the headship of the saṁpradāya with all its attendant evils, including litigation.

If brahmacarya may be regarded essentially as ahiṁsā in the sphere of sex, aparigraha may be regarded as related to asteya which we have treated as a form of satya. Aparigraha is usually translated as 'non-accumulation' of material goods, generally designated as wealth. But perhaps what one wants to avoid is 'miserliness' or not seeing that the wealth one accumulates is for the good of others. Traditionally, it was dāna or 'giving in its myriad forms' which was supposed to be aparigraha, and not desisting from accumulating anything at all, in which case dāna would not be possible. In fact, the accumulation of non-material goods, such as knowledge or merit, has never been considered undesirable.

Parigraha, of course, has another characteristic which may be said to affect consciousness in ways that are undesirable. It not only creates 'dependence', particularly with respect to the material goods one accumulates, but also fosters in one's consciousness an attitude which considers all transactions in terms of profit and loss, advantage and disadvantage along with an ever-increasing desire for more and more. A bent of mind that is given to calculating and desiring, however, is regarded as worth having only if these qualities do not begin to dominate the mind and eclipse everything else. And this is perhaps what is meant by aparigraha, that is, the non-domination of the psyche by the calculus of gain and loss, specially in the material domain.

The foundational dharma, particularly with respect to other beings who are conscious or self-conscious, thus consists only of ahiṁsā and satya, and the rest follow as a matter of specific application. But the usual five-fold formulation of dharma in the human context is too negative in character and hence may be treated as only minimal in nature. Dharma as a positive desire to create a joyful world for all conscious beings and a world in which creativity and innovation in the pursuit of infinite values in unending time is encouraged and facilitated amongst all self-conscious beings, has not been adequately explored by thinkers in India or elsewhere.[9] In fact, the creation of a world of imagination in which human beings may live and find significance, which has been the chief function of art and religion, has hardly been the subject of reflection. Beyond this is the problem of the parameters within which dharmic obligations may obtain, or the limited group within which the obligations arising from the consciousness of dharma should be entertained or legitimately applied. A problem which is still more intractable is how to deal with those who do not observe dharma or wilfully violate it or merely state that they follow a different dharma.

These and many other problems need to be explored in the light of past reflections on this concept and the way other cultures and civilizations have thought about it. But in the perspective of the problematic that Indian thought raised and encountered in this context, the issue seems to have centered on its relationship with the theory of ṛta, that is, cosmic order, on the one hand, and with the theories of yajña, varṇa, karma and puruṣārtha, on the other. The theory of dharma or moral order faces a problem vis-à-vis the theory of cosmic order in that the former necessarily depends upon human effort and will, while the latter is independent of it and is conceived of either as immanent in the universe itself or as dependent on God's will. Even in the latter case, it is not clear as to what it would mean for His will to have produced a non-orderly or disorderly universe. In fact, we do not even know what it would mean for the universe to be without order except in relation to some idea of order which, according to human conceptions, would alone be regarded as 'order'. It is interesting to note in this connection that while the opposite of dharma is adharma which is perpetuated by human beings, the opposite of ṛta is anṛta, that which is spoken by man and which is opposed to that which is truth. But truth is that which *is* and hence denotes ṛta itself. Anṛta, therefore, can only come into being because of man, and hence is a part of adharma, which also is brought into being by man. But man does not, and cannot, know what this ṛta or cosmic order is.[10] The only way he knows it, and can know it, is as dharma, which may then be understood as ṛta in the human realm. Yet dharma can be violated, and in fact, is continuously being violated, while ṛta can never be violated for the simple reason that it is the sort of thing whose violation is inconceivable in principle.[11]

This, then, is the dilemma and the problematic. Ṛta and dharma have to be identical, and yet they cannot be identical. They have to be known; yet they can never be known fully or completely. Dharma is always plural and multiple in character; ṛta perhaps can never be so.[12] The dilemma and the problematic emanate from the fact that the roots of dharma lie in a consciousness that is turned both to itself and to the 'other', the many 'others'. This deep cleft at the heart of self-consciousness and the problems it gives rise to has been so well understood and articulated by ḍharmic thinkers in India that it is surprising that it has so far not been paid sufficient attention. The conflicting claims of the multiple 'others' result in what has usually been characterized as 'dharmasaṇkaṭa' in the tradition, and both the epics and the *Purāṇas* are full of situations of dharmasaṇkaṭa. But the deepest dharmasaṇkaṭa is between the conflicting claims of self-consciousness, at every level, to be different from what one is and the claims of others which one's consciousness is aware of all the time. The well-known adage '*atmārthe prithivīm tyajet*' epitomizes this literally and metaphorically, while Buddha's *mahābhiniṣkramaṇa* paradigmatically illustrates it for all time. But in both these the unquestionable superiority of the claims of self-consciousness over the claims of others has been assumed, while in life as well as in the epics, the reality seems to be the other way around.

The relative balance of the claims of the higher possibilities of one's own consciousness of which one is vaguely aware in one's consciousness and the claims of others on oneself has been a perennial problem in the Indian tradition and has usually been formulated in terms of the spiritual versus the moral or, to use the classical Indian terms for these, mokṣa versus dharma. The theoretical thinker in the Indian tradition had, by and large, no doubt about the superiority of mokṣa over dharma, whereas the dharma-centric thinker generally paid only lip service to the superiority of mokṣa, concentrated on exploring the complexity and diversity of dharma, and emphasized that one may not attain mokṣa without dharma, dharma being a necessary, if not the sole, condition for the attainment of mokṣa.

The dilemma between dharma, understood as the claims of other conscious and self-conscious beings on oneself and mokṣa, understood as the claim of a pure consciousness to be actualized and possessed as a permanent state of one's being without the admixture of any negative element in it, may be resolved by taking recourse to a distinction made by Nicolai Hartmann in the realm of values. According to him, values are distinguished not only in terms of the 'lower' and 'higher', but also in terms of the 'weaker' and 'stronger'. The stronger values, according to him, are those which do not need to be realized by the actualization of any other value or at least need a lesser number of values than do the weaker values. The higher values generally happen to be weaker also, as they presuppose the realization of other values for their own realization or actualization. Mokṣa, in this perspective, would be a higher value than dharma but also a weaker value in relation to it. But this reading of the relationship would be to accept the view of those dharma-centric thinkers who have argued for the prior practice of dharma for the realization of mokṣa. However, there are a substantial number of mokṣa-centric thinkers in India who deny the necessity of such a priority and argue for a tangential relationship of mokṣa with all the other puruṣārthas, which is accidental in nature.

There is, however, another aspect to the problem which seems to have escaped the attention of both Nicolai Hartmann and the traditional Indian thinkers. For, as far as the seeking of values, and the demands and claims thus generated, are concerned, there are other dimensions besides the spiritual and the moral, or the mokṣa-centric and the dharma-centric. There is, for example, the pursuit of knowledge in the ordinary sense of the word, or the seeking involved in embodying an imaginatively apprehended concept or a significant meaning which is felt to be of relevance to the life of man as lived through the experiencing consciousness of man. Art is, of course, the generic name for all such seekings towards the embodiment of that which is imaginatively grasped and felt as vitally significant for man.

But whether it be the seeking for knowledge or for embodying the imaginatively apprehended myriad forms of beauty which are satisfying, significant and meaningful for their own sake, they find no place in the thinking of either the dharma-centric or the mokṣa-centric thinkers of classical India. Not only this, the development and display of multifarious skills, so conspicuous in sports and other domains of life, are equally absent from the horizon of either the dharma-centric or the mokṣa-centric thinkers of India. It may be said that these come under the other puruṣārthas and hence have not been paid attention to by those who have concentrated on either dharma or mokṣa exclusively. But this does not help matters, as it becomes difficult to bring these either under artha or kāma, as I have argued elsewhere.[13]

The theory of the puruṣārthas, however, is not our immediate concern here. We are basically concerned with the problematic created for the Indian thinker by the conflicting claims of dharma and mokṣa on the one hand, and dharma and ṛta on the other. From the perspective of mokṣa, dharma is seen not as an other-centered consciousness or even as the fulfilment of categorical imperatives, but rather in terms of the effects it has on one's own consciousness. The 'consciousness-centric' perspective of mokṣa thus turns the 'other-centered' perspective of dharma completely around the discussion of the state of one's own consciousness. Thus, instead of being concerned with the 'consciousness' and 'self-consciousness' of others and how one's actions affect them, one begins to be concerned with the effects that actions have on one's own consciousness. The *Gītā* is the classic example of this. The discussion of action contained in the *Gītā* seems to suggest that the consequences of one's actions on others are irrelevant if they do not adversely affect one's own state of consciousness. And, if perchance one has achieved a state of consciousness either through God's grace or personal *sādhanā* or past karmas or all of these together, it does not matter what one does or how it affects others.

Hartmann has a related, but essentially different, notion. He has argued that the moral quality of an action does not depend so much on the nature, or the superiority, of the value sought to be realized, but rather on the intensity, enthusiasm and commitment of the consciousness that is seeking to realize it. In the mokṣa-centric perspective on dharma, on the other hand, it is what the seeking *does* to the consciousness itself that is the centre of attention and approbation. Also, Hartmann does not distinguish between what I have elsewhere called the 'moral' and the 'axiological' ought.[14] In the context of the present discussion, I think we would have to add another 'ought' to these two, i.e. the one that arises from the awareness of a self-conscious being that his consciousness is not what it ought to be. This is different from the other two 'oughts' that arise from the claims of other beings who are conscious or self-conscious and the claims of values which have no direct relation either to one's own consciousness or to that of others.

The problematic of dharma with respect to ṛta arises from a different direction. Dharma is always, in principle, that which can be violated, while ṛta is that which in principle can never be violated. What, then, is the relation between the two, and does dharma fall outside the domain of ṛta? How is the latter alternative possible, if ṛta is really universal and applies to all beings? The question relates to man's place in the scheme of things and has troubled thinkers everywhere, but it has taken a peculiar turn in India, as we will see later.

The notion of ṛta, in fact, is subverted by the notion of yajña in the Vedic corpus itself. The performance of a yajña is a willed, voluntary activity, whether undertaken for the achievement of a desired end or for the prevention of something undesirable, technically known as *pratyavāya*. The performance of a yajña in both cases is a human intervention, as happens with all other human actions. It is the dharmic action *par excellence*, at least for the orthodox *Mīmāṁsaka* interpreters of the Veda who hold such a position by virtue of the fact that the śruti, consisting of the mantra, and the Brāhmaṇa texts, say so. The yajña, for them, was what these texts declared to be a yajña, and nothing else could legitimately claim that title. One could not add to, or subtract from, the list mentioned in these texts, or the procedures prescribed in them. Most of the discussions in Jaiminī's *Mīmāṁsā sūtra* and Śabara's *Bhāṣya* on it are concerned with deciding what exactly is the correct interpretation of the sentences prescribing the procedure for performing a particular yajña according to these texts.

However, as always happens, there were others who were more interested in the idea of yajña and wanted to extend it. For them, the extensional definition of the orthodox mīmāṁsaka as presented by Jaiminī, or the *Śranta sūtras* was not only too restrictive but also too literal in intent and inspiration. The Upaniṣads, for example, clearly evince this tendency. For them, not only is the inhaling and exhaling of breath a continuous act of yajña, if properly perceived, but so also is the sexual act where something is offered as an oblation, if it is felt as such, seen in the proper perspective and done in the proper way.[15] The *Gītā* condemns the Vedic yajña as too ritualistic and concerned with obtaining the objects of worldly desire in its well-known ślokas 42–46 in Chapter Two. Yet, it also tries to widen the notion of yajña and treat it almost as conterminus with creation, as in 3.10.[16] In fact, if one sees the sequence of the ślokas from 3.9 to 3.15, one would perceive that the idea of yajña is being widened to include all actions provided they have been preceded by a renunciatory *saṁkalpa*, analogous to the *dravya tyāga* in the Vedic yajña which is sealed and consecrated by the well-known utterance on the part of the yajamāna, '*Agnaye idaṁ, na mama*' (This is for Agni, not for me).

Professor Staal has tried to conflate the two usages, forgetting that the *dravya tyāga* of the Vedic yajña is not the *phala tyāga* or the renunciation of the fruit of action of the *Gītā*.[17] Also, that the *niṣkāma karma* of the *Gītā* comprises, besides phala tyāga, the tyāga of *svatva* and *kartṛtva*, that is, renunciation of the ideas of ownership and agency with respect to action. But there are grounds for Staal's confusion, as is evident from śloka 3.10 in the *Gītā*. Here yajña is supposed to be *kāmadhuk*, that is, the means of fulfilling all desires, on the condition that such a fulfilment of desires be preceded by an act of giving up to the gods and receiving from them something in return. But though the gods are present and the yajña is kāmadhuk, the similarity with the Vedic yajña is illusory and need not deceive anyone. For, firstly, this yajña has no śruti-prescribed *vidhi*, and secondly, it is not confined to any particular varṇa. Basically, it does not believe in any prescribed vidhi, whether by śruti as interpreted by Jaiminī or anybody else, or in any other way. Further, as the argument develops, the *Gītā* drops not only the kāmadhuk character of the yajña which is considered so essential to it here, but also the giving up for the sake of the gods who cease to be essential to the yajña, even in the formal sense in which they are understood in the strict orthodox *Mīmāṁsā* tradition. The straight contradiction between ślokas 3.9 and 3.10 can perhaps only be resolved in some such way. Yajña, in the *Gītā* framework, cannot simultaneously be kāmadhuk and 'not be the cause of bondage', as is asserted in these two verses together. Any action undertaken with the knowledge and the desire for a particular result cannot but lead to bondage, is the way the *Gītā* seeks to analyse the situation. Yet, in these verses, the *Gītā* takes the essential components of the Vedic yajña, ignores the vidhi and the *pātra* restrictions, and universalizes the situation.[18]

The extension of an idea to different contexts and its continuous reinterpretation over a period of time provides a basis for continuity and change without which no culture can live or grow. But the spurious identity given by the use of the earlier term, that is, yajña not only hides the deep differences in the new meanings attached to the term, but also suggests the wrong idea that yajña in the *Gītā* means the same as yajña in the Veda. The Vedic yajña was primarily concerned with the fulfilment of diverse kinds of desires, while its various extensions in the Upaniṣads or the *Gītā*, or even in later periods, have either nothing to do with desire and its satisfaction or have only a marginal and tangential relation to desire. The Vedic yajña also involved a theory of action or karma which was in conflict with the way the theory came to be understood later in the tradition, as it necessarily involved the attainment of the fruits of the yajña by the yajamāna even when the actual yajña was performed by the ṛtviks, that is, the priests, on the ground that they had been hired for the purpose on payment of the usual fees (*dakṣiṇā*). This, in fact, may be regarded as the precursor of the practice even today of hiring a brahman or a priest to perform a *pūjā* or undertake any other religious ritual, with the fruits of the pūjā or the ritual accruing to the lay person.

The theory of action exemplified in the Vedic yajña, or rather as arising out of the attempt to defend the practice along with such practices as the performance of *śrāddha*, that is, the sacred ritual ceremonies for one's dead ancestors, treats the hard-core theory of karma as its *pūrva-pakṣa* standing in need of refutation. And Jaiminī in fact does so. Both in practice and in theory, therefore, yajña stands in opposition to the equally widely accepted theory of karma which, since ancient times, has held that no one can reap the fruit of another's actions. The law is a straightforward formulation of the demand for the 'moral intelligibility' of the human world, just as the demand for the intelligibility of the natural world gives rise to the idea of causality which tries to understand a thing in the context of that which brings into being what has occurred. It is not that the idea of causality is excluded from the human world; in fact, it is continuously employed for understanding what happens in the human realm, but it is modified to include both the voluntary initiation of action by human agents as well as its determination. The demand for 'moral intelligibility', however, is more than this. It arises from the self-conscious nature of man and makes a radical difference between that which is done by the 'self' and that which is done by 'others'. It is prepared to accept responsibility for one's own actions. If something happens to one because of what one has done, it can be regarded as 'morally justified'. The causality here is not being denied; rather, it is being restricted to one's own self. The drama of cause and effect is confined to the arena of one's own self. Elsewhere, I have described it as 'moral monadism'.[19] It is a necessary consequence of the way moral intelligibility has been understood in the law of karma. But it also assumes that there are separate, individual, atomic and self-conscious persons, who are exclusively and completely responsible for changes in their own selves, at least in the moral sphere. There is, therefore, a *svatva* or ownership of both agency and action which is necessarily involved in the notion. Along with this there has, of course, to be the svatva of effects without which the theory would not be complete.

But as the demand for moral intelligibility does not annul the general requirement of causality for rendering the universe with its alteration and change intelligible, and as the general notion of causality does not require any such restrictions as are imposed on it in the context of moral intelligibility, it may be expected to apply to those 'morally monadic' beings who are not monadic in their non-moral aspects. The relation between the morally monadic action and the non-moral non-monadic action should, then, have been the focus of attention in the classical Indian reflection on action. But, as far as I know, this has not been the case. Equally important are issues relating to svatva or ownership of action. In other words, what exactly are the criteria that would determine the correctness of such a description? Further, as there are large numbers of self-conscious human beings who are also aware of each other as self-conscious beings, there is the added problem of determining the criteria for the correct application of 'his' or 'her' action and the differences, if any, between these criteria and those which each one applies when he or she uses the term 'my action'.

The svatva of action, whether of one's own or of another, however, presupposes that there is a distinctive 'self' of each which is capable of independently initiating action. But there are a large number of schools of thought which either do not admit a 'self' at all, as in Buddhism, or do not admit any real agency in it, as in Sāṁkhya, or do not admit their independent plurality as in Advaita Vedānta. But Indian thinking about dharma or *vyavahāra*, that is, about morality and law, does not seem to have been aware of this problem which lay at the very foundation of thought in these realms. Perhaps the issues that troubled thinkers were too specific and concrete to be much affected by the deeper concerns of thinkers dealing with ontological issues related to the nature of ultimate reality itself. But before I deal with the specific problematic relating to each of these realms, I would like to consider the one raised by the śramaṇa traditions of India which has played a crucial role and given the Indian civilization such a distinctive stamp of its own.

Notes

1. See, on this whole issue, my article, 'The Vedic Corpus: Some Questions' in *Indian Philosophy: A Counter Perspective*, New Delhi, Oxford University Press, 1991, pp. 63–94.
2. K.V. Sharma, 'A Survey of Materials' in S.N. Sen and K.S. Shukla's *History of Astronomy in India*, New Delhi, Indian National Science Academy, 1985, pp. 4–5; Hymns 1.164.1 and 3.99 give the date of their composition as 2350 BC. Also, 5.40.4.9. is supposed to give the date given by a hymn as 6200 BC.
3. The Vedas themselves display a diverse understanding of the notion of yajña as indicated, for example, in the opening of the *Jaiminīya Brāhmaṇa*. However, it is the later orthodox *Mīmāṃsaka* interpretation that came to be accepted as the real hard core interpretation of the Vedic yajña. Also, the centrality of the yajña in the Veda was established by the *mīmāṃsaka* and all other elements treated as ancillary to it. There has been an extension of the meaning of yajña in later literature but the central model for the metaphorical extension has always been built on the literal manner in which the *mīmāmsā* understood it.
4. *Aitareya Brāhmaṇa*, 'Story of Kavaṣa', Ānandashram Sanskrit Series, No. 32, Poona, p. 216.
5. *Chāndogya Upaniṣad*, 'Satyakāma Jābāla', 4.4, fourth edition, Gorakhpur, Gita Press, Samvat 2019.
6. *Gītā*, 2.42–6, 9–32.
7. *Gītā*, 4.13.
8. There is some dispute about the exact number of the *mahāvākyas* and though tradition usually mentions the number as twelve, it is only these three that occupy a prominent place in Vedāntic thought.
9. The concept of *abhyudaya* which may be considered to come closest to it, however, does not seem to capture the notion either centrally or marginally.
10. Satya, as the opposite of anṛta, has also been regarded as identical with ṛta, but then it will almost be the same as ṛta in the human realm, that

is, dharma, for it will have an opposite of itself. In such a context, it would mean 'being in accordance with the cosmic law'. My main interest, however, is to emphasize an aspect of the concept which has not been noticed and which, in my opinion, is more related to other living beings, both human and non-human, and thus becomes central to the domain of morality, that is, dharma.

11. Anṛta may, of course, be taken to a cosmic level, but this will lead to an ultimate dualism of Good and Evil, a position which Indian thinkers seem disinclined to accept. The *devāsura saṅgrāma* or the battle between the gods and the demons came closest to this conception, but while it played a critical role in mythology and epics, it hardly became the subject matter of serious philosophical reflection in India.

12. The relation of ṛta and dharma is of course as problematic as the relation of the cosmic order and the cultural order, for the former is supposed to be independent of human consciousness while the latter is not only supposed to be dependent on it but also has the perennial possibility of being disturbed by the freedom which man has to do *adharma* either because of ignorance or because of wilfulness born of desire. There is a wider sense of dharma in which it is identical with the essential nature of anything and thus perhaps of the universe also. However, when I distinguish between rta and dharma, I am using the latter in a restricted sense only.

13. Daya Krishna, 'The Myth of the Puruṣārthas' in *Indian Philosophy: A Counter Perspective*, New Delhi: Oxford University Press, 1991, pp. 189–206.

14. Daya Krishna, 'The Moral and the Axiological "Ought": An Attempt at a Distinction' in *The Journal of Philosophy*, USA, October 1956; included in the *Art of the Conceptual*, New Delhi: I.C.P.R. and Munshiram Manoharlal, 1989, pp. 196–204.

15. It is true that the Upaniṣads are also regarded as an integral part of the Vedas but the very fact that they themselves reject the previous portions of the Vedas, considering them to be *aparā-vidyā*, and regard themselves as the purveyors of *parā-vidyā* shows the radical difference in the way the latter part of the Śruti looked at the former part. Not only this, in the famous story of Narada and Sanata Kumāra in the *Chāndogya Upaniṣad*, knowledge of the four Vedas along with other knowledge is not supposed to give enlightenment as it is not concerned with that 'real' knowledge which is the subject of the Upanisads alone and not of any other part of the Vedas.

16. There seems to be some evidence of the extension of the idea of yajña even in the *Brāhmaṇas*, but there can be little doubt that the way the yajña was understood in the Vedas in the sense of the various sacrifices enjoined for the attainment of different fruits, including that of heaven, and the daily *agnihotra*, were the basic models for understanding what a

yajña meant. This was also the reason why the Vedas were condemned by the *Gītā* as consisting primarily of those kind of yajñas and that even such a late commentator as Sāyaṇa considered them to be central to the understanding of the Vedas. Not only this, the whole controversy about *hiṃsā* in the Vedic yajña would be meaningless if the Vedic yajña was to be regarded as essentially metaphorical in nature. Even today when people perform the different yajñas they obviously are performing not the metaphorical yajña but the yajña proper as enjoined by the Vedas.

17. Fritz Staal, *Agni: The Vedic Ritual of the Fire Altar*, Delhi: Motilal Banarasidass, 1984, pp. 4–5.

18. The idea of yajña in the *Gītā* undergoes successive transformations which do not need to be delineated here. The problem with respect to ślokas 3.9 and 3.10 which have been referred to here is that in 3.9 it is explicitly stated that except for actions done for the sake of yajña all other actions are the cause of bondage, while śloka 3.10 states that the yajña was created along with creation itself by Prajāpati, that is, the Lord of Creation, who said to the people he had created that the performance of a yajña would lead to the attainment of whatever they desired. There would be no problem with the two ślokas if the *Gītā* had not held in general that action done for the sake of the fulfilment of desire always led to bondage. One may say that yajña is action which is done not for the sake of the fulfilment of any desire, but that, in fact, it does fulfil desire, and hence there is no contradiction between the two ślokas. But the performance of yajña is being commended *because* it is kāmadhuk, that is, the means of fulfilling desire, which is what creates the problem. The turns and twists in traditional literature regarding the interpretation of these and many other ślokas in the *Gītā* would surprise non-scholarly readers. Śaṁkara, for example, interprets the term yajña not in the usual sense of sacrifice, but as meaning 'Viṣṇu' as it happens to be one of the meanings of yajña in the *Nighanṭu* or the lexicon of Sanskrit words in the Vedic language. But, obviously, we cannot go into these details here, nor is it necessary for our purpose.

19. Daya Krishna, '*Yajña* and the Doctrine of Karma–a Contradiction in Indian Thought about Action' in *Indian Philosophy–A Counter Perspective*, New Delhi, Oxford University Press, 1991, pp. 172–88.

CHAPTER II

The Śramaṇa Traditions and their Problematic

Tradition has divided the sources of ultimate authority more or less into Vedic and non-Vedic. It has called the former *nigama* and the latter *āgama*. The term āgama seems to comprise those texts which are considered authoritative by some saṁpradāya or the other in the long history of India encompassing at least three millennia of recorded history. The term āgama, then, is an omnibus, all-embracing term which includes not only the Buddhist and Jaina texts but also the texts of, say, the *Pāñcarātra*, *Śaiva*, *Śākta*, *Vaisnava* or *Śaiva Siddhānta*, the *Trika* and even the *Cārvāka* schools.

There was earlier another term to designate the non-Vedic, or even the anti-Vedic, streams in Indian thought and that term was 'Śramaṇa' which was applied to followers of non-Vedic texts in contrast to the term '*Brāhmaṇa*' which was applied to the followers of the Veda, whether in its Yajña-centric or Brahman-centric interpretation as epitomized in Jaimini and Bādārayaṇa. The Śramaṇa tradition, thus, has been the 'other' to the Vedic tradition, even though there have been deep internal differences within it, as also in the Vedic tradition. The Buddhists and the Jains are the more well-known followers of the Śramaṇa tradition, but presumably *Sāṁkhya*, *Yoga* and *Pāñcarātra* also belonged to it. The word 'Śramaṇa', in fact, comes from the Buddhist lexicon. The equivalent term in the Jain canon is *muni* which is already found in the Vedas where it is contrasted with the word ṛṣi which is supposed to designate the *mantra-dṛṣṭā* or the seer of the Vedic mantras. *Sāṁkhya* is usually not included in the Śramaṇa *paraṁ-parā* or the Śramaṇa tradition. Nor is *Pāñcarātra*, for that matter.

But both are regarded as non-Vedic in character. Sāṁkhya, in fact, is specifically refuted by Bādārayaṇa for claiming Vedic authority and lineage for its doctrines. As for the *Pāñcarātra*, it does not seem to have been taken seriously in Vedic quarters. It was never regarded as part of the Śramaṇa tradition and is supposed to have been the precursor of the Bhakti tradition in India whose relations with the Vedic tradition have always been ambiguous and problematic in nature.

The hard core Śramaṇa traditions have always viewed man's familial, social and political life as not only secondary in character, but as basically inimical to his spiritual life. The Buddha's *Mahābhiniṣkremaṇa* or 'the Great Going Away' is the paradigmatic example of it, though Jain tradition has always been far more austere and renunciatory than the Buddhist. In the long history of Buddhism and Jainism there has, as far as I know, been no saṁpradāya which accepted the idea of married *bhikṣus* and munis, though the Buddhists were more tolerant of the idea of a bhikṣu leaving the monkhood and re-entering the life of a householder. Neither of them, however, justified their position theoretically. This was done by Sāṁkhya, though not perhaps at a self-conscious level. Rather, it was its view of consciousness and the human personality which entailed such a position, though not necessarily of the Buddhist or the Jain kind. Sāṁkhyan thought influenced and permeated all the traditions in such a substantive manner that no tradition seems to have remained unaffected by it, except perhaps Buddhism.

The main aspect that appears to have influenced almost all schools of thought is its doctrine of the threefold nature of *prakṛti* and the contention that except for pure consciousness everything belonged to prakṛti, including anything that appeared as an object to it, in any form whatsoever. As prakṛti is *acit* or *jaḍa* or unconscious, the strange consequence is that not only is matter regarded as part of prakṛti, according to Sāṁkhya, but also such things as mind and intellect or *manasa* and buddhi which are usually not treated as part of inanimate nature, but rather as elements of the conscious self which is supposed to have desires, feelings and the power to reason and initiate action through the *karmendriyas* on the basis of the knowledge provided by the *jñānendriyas*, both of which are located in the body. The dissociation of manasa and buddhi from the centre of consciousness, that is, the self or puruṣa, in Sāṁkhya means that the whole life of the mind and reason has been seen to belong to the 'not-self'. In fact, Sāṁkhya goes even further and relegates the 'I' or *ahaṁkāra* to the realm of the 'not-self', even though it argues for the ontological plurality of centres of pure consciousness or puruṣas. Not only this, 'consciousness' is just seen as being 'conscious of', that is as pure *dṛṣṭā* and in no sense a 'doer' or 'enjoyer' of what it is 'conscious of'. In traditional terminology, it is neither a *kartā* nor a *bhoktā*, and if it does think of itself as such, it is only because it illusorily identifies itself with what it is not, that is, the 'not-self' or prakṛti.

There are a number of problems raised by the Sāṁkhyan analysis, but the problematic that we are interested in here is to view the self in such a manner that all its social and political life on the one hand, and its affective-volitional life, on the other, become non-essential to it in an essential sense. Its main spiritual task thus is to dissociate itself from any illusory identification and the resulting consequences. Yoga developed as the transcendental praxis for the achievement of such a complete de-identification not only from all external objects, but also from one's own bodily and psychic life including the affective, the ratiocinative and the volitional parts of it. In fact, the *Yoga-Sūtras* include *pramāṇa* as a *vṛtti* whose *nirodha* is intrinsically required for the practice of Yoga.[1] The whole of the ratiocinative enterprise, therefore, is in vain, at least from the perspective of the author of the *Yoga-Sūtras*, and a very large part of the Indian philosophical enterprise has consequently conceived of itself in a negative way as removing the false opinions which obstruct one from pursuing the path that leads to the attainment of that state of consciousness which alone is real as it coincides with reality itself.

Yoga as transcendental praxis, along with its meditative practices, spread far and wide and had a pervasive influence on almost all the spiritual practices in India. Such a wide-ranging acceptance of its praxis resulted in its indirectly influencing the world-views of even those schools which, at least at the metaphysical level, may be regarded as totally opposed to that of Sāṁkhya. The Vedānta of the *Upaniṣads*, for example, may be regarded as one such view if we take seriously its contention that 'All this is Brahman' (*Sarvaṁ Khalvidaṁ Brahma*). Here is a call to not reject anything, but to see everything as Brahman, to see the self in everything and everything in the self, or rather to see the two as the same. Taken seriously, this might lead to a de-de-identificatory spiritual direction resulting in a sādhanā or a transformatory practice of a spiritual kind, both in the field of knowledge and action. The consequence would be an ideology which would otherwise have looked askance at any differentiating or discriminatory behaviour in personal, social or political life and asked for justifications for submitting such behaviour to critical scrutiny. But, instead of this obvious direction which the Upaniṣadic insight could have taken, and which it developed in such concepts as *bhumā* and *vaiśvānara*, Bādārayaṇa closed the doors to any such attempts by explicitly excluding a large part of humanity, that is, the śūdras from access to the knowledge of Brahman through the śruti and Śaṁkara. He sealed the doors completely by opening his *Bhāsya* on the *Brahma-sūtras* with the declaration that any identification of the self with the not-self at any level whatsoever was the fundamental illusion and that the task of spiritual sādhanā was to overcome it as completely as possible. Indian thought never recovered from this Sāṁkhyan influence, buttressed as it was by the Śramaṇa traditions of Buddhism and Jainism on the one hand and the Bādarāyaṇa-Śaṁkara interpretations of the *śruti* on the other. There were of course, valiant attempts to counter the tidal waves from the two directions, and the encounter between all of them and the problematic it gave rise to, is one of the most interesting stories we will deal with later on.

The three-fold division of everything which the not-self, that is, nature or prakṛti could be said to be composed of, perhaps had even greater influence as it affected all the empirical sciences in India. *Sāttvika*, *rājasika* and *tāmasika* became household words and were applied as much to food as to mental processes. Intellect or buddhi was classified accordingly, and so were varṇas or social classes. The *Gītā*, in its closing chapters, particularly the seventeenth and the eighteenth, has classified almost everything, including *yajña*, *tapas*, *dāna*, *tyāga*, *jñāna*, *karma*, *kartā*, *buddhi*, *duḥkha* and *sukha*. In fact, verse 18.40 declares explicitly that there is nothing in all the three worlds which escapes the three-fold characterization in terms of the three Sāṁkhyan attributes of prakṛti.

Surprisingly, however, the *Gītā*, after giving such a detailed and thorough classification which, in a sense, cuts across the usual formulation of most of these concepts, reverts to the four-fold varṇa classification and the type of social actions assigned to them in the orthodox Vedic tradition. It does not take cognizance of the fact that if there are only three guṇas there can not be four varṇas and that, in any case, characterization in terms of guṇas is primarily of the individual and not of classes and that according to the classical Sāṁkhya theory there cannot be anything which is purely sāttvika or rājasika or tāmasika in nature. In fact, this aspect of Sāṁkhya thought seems to have been missed by all later thinkers who accepted its three-fold classification but failed to see that, according to Sāṁkhya, everything that belongs to the 'not-self', that is prakṛti will have all the three guṇas in it, the only difference being that some guṇas will be predominant in some things, while others will be predominant in other things. But even this situation, according to Sāṁkhya, cannot last long, for the guṇas that are in the background are bound to gain ascendancy in due course.

Taken seriously, such a theory would have had social consequences of a revolutionary nature in India, but, unfortunately, the whole concept was given a static twist and instead of a dynamic interpretation it ascribed even to individuals fixed and unchanging qualities of sattva, rajas and tamas and, what was even worse, ascribed these qualities on the ground of their being *born* in a particular varṇa. The conservative apologists took recourse to the theory of karma to explain why they were choosing birth as the criterion of varṇa and developed extremely subtle theories of perceptual knowledge, as in Kumārila's *Tantravārtika*, to argue that *Bhāhmaṇatva* was as much a *jāti* or a universal class of a natural kind as, say, *vṛkṣatva* or treeness. But these very apologists forgot that in the strict theory of karma, there could be no such thing as a yajña for *kāmya* purposes as most of the yajñas were performed by ṛtvikas who were paid a prescribed fee by the yajamānas who obtained the desired results from the yajñas. Jaimini, in fact, treats the theory of karma as the pūrva-pakṣa, according to Śabara, in this context. The theory, therefore, cannot obviously be invoked to provide support for advocating birth as a criterion for the determination of varṇa by anyone who believes in the yajña-centric interpretation of the *śruti*, as Kumarila obviously does.

A culture, of course, is not all of a piece, neither diachronically nor synchronically, and it is tensions between the different conflicting and disparate elements that give rise to diverse problematics, both at the theoretical and the practical level. But it is the *use* to which the theoretical resources available to a culture are put by its intellectual elite that gives a direction to society at crucial junctures of its history. The Indian intelligentsia in the Vedic tradition somehow could never get rid of the restricted, narrow, rigid and fixed interpretation of the varṇa theory in the social context, even when they tried to rebel against the same type of interpretation in the spiritual sphere. Perhaps this has been characteristic of intellectuals in every culture, and a comparative study of the intellectuals' role in these spheres in different societies would not reveal the traditional Indian intellectual in a bad light. After all, even Aristotle who is supposed to have defined man as a 'rational animal', not only defended the institution of slavery but denied slaves the possession of any 'deliberative rationality'. In fact, the persistence of the pūrva-pakṣas in this regard and the increase in their diversity and subtlety is evidence of a countercurrent which has not been sufficiently articulated and highlighted. The Buddhist and the Jaina traditions are well known in this connection, but little is known about their impact on the structure of civil society even in the days of their dominance. And Sāṁkhya, in any case, had little interest in the understanding of man as a socio-political being.

Such was perhaps also the situation with *Pāñcarātra* along with the other non-Vedic āgamic traditions of India. But as each of these drew followers from all the varṇas, they would have played a role in breaking the barriers between the varṇas, specially in the context of ritual intermixing and dining during religious festivals. Moreover, as members of some of the sects are supposed to have had ritualistic sexual intercourse on special occasions during religious practices, it may be assumed that there was some relaxation in the prohibition of inter-varṇa marriages. All the āgamic traditions, as a matter of fact, proclaim themselves to be sārvavarṇic, even though in practice they may have made some compromises with the prevailing varṇa structure in society. However, relations between persons belonging to different āgamic traditions seems to have been modelled on the pattern of inter-varṇa relations, theoretically formulated in the Vedic tradition and embodied in the various *Smṛti* texts. This, in fact, may have been one of the reasons for the rise of new jātis or castes in India. However, it is not quite clear how the Vedic tradition itself would classify persons belonging to the different āgamic traditions within its varṇa scheme or how the āgamic saṁpradāyas would socially classify persons belonging to varṇa systems of the Vedic tradition, on the one hand, and persons belonging to other āgamic traditions, on the other.

But, whatever the answers are to questions regarding the diverse interrelationships between the different Vedic and āgamic traditions both at the theoretical and the 'lived' social level, there can be little doubt that they largely contributed to make India the pluralistic society that it is, and kept the orthodox protagonists of the varṇa system continuously under siege so that they had to devise new strategies for defence and in doing so, had to sometimes even modify their positions a little. The development of the purāṇic tradition may be seen as evidence of this, along with the apologetic position taken in the orthodox camp that even though access to the *Śruti* in the strict sense was not open to śūdras, access to the truth embodied in them was not denied them, as it was available through the *Itihāsa* and the *Purāṇas* to which they were duly entitled.

The story of the Śramaṇa challenge to the varṇa structure of the Vedic tradition is fairly well-known, though not so well documented or historically recorded over time. The repeated āgamic challenge which was essentially non-Śramaṇic in character as it did not emphasize the necessity of the renunciatory path for achieving the ultimate end of life, is, however, neither so well-known nor so well documented. Nor do we have a history of the response of the varnic orthodoxy to the repeated challenges to it from different sides. Yet, there is at least a vague awareness of these, particularly amongst those who have paid some intellectual attention to the Bhakti traditions in India. The denial to women of knowledge contained in the *Śruti*, irrespective of the varṇa to which they belonged, and the diverse responses this gave rise to has, however, hardly been paid any attention. Yet, it is as, or perhaps even more, important than the exclusion of the śūdras, for women cut across all the varṇas and formed a varṇa outside the varṇa system, suffering disadvantages because of biological differences. In fact, the male-female divide cuts across the varṇa-divide, yet it has not been the subject of any detailed study so far.

Women, of course, were supposed to partake in the Vedic yajña as it was meant only for the householder, and this she did as the wife of the yajamāna. She thus had to belong to one of the non-śūdra varṇas. The non-śūdra women, then, had a certain participatory privilege in performing the yajña which, according to one school of Vedic interpretation, the *Mīmāṁsā*, was its central concern. Yet, according to the same school, she had no right of access to the *Śruti* in the sense that she could not study the Vedas. But in case she did recite the mantras herself, it would mean some sort of an active involvement with the Veda, even if formal access to it was closed to her through explicit prohibition of its study. The Upaniṣads, of course, have in them examples of women seeking knowledge of the ultimate reality, that is, Brahman, the most famous amongst them being Maitraeyī and Gārgī. The former is one of the two wives of Yājñavalkya who asks him about that which would give her immortality.[2] Gārgī, on the other hand, engages him in an active debate in the court of King Janaka and asks him pointed questions.[3] Both these examples should suffice to prove that, at least in Upaniṣadic times, women were not debarred from seeking the knowledge contained in the Śruti. It is, of course, true that Yājñavalkya had earlier threatened Gārgī and said that if she continued to ask further questions, her head would fall off. But then there was no gender discrimination in this, as he had threatened other male disputants in the same manner, and it seems to have been a prevalent practice in those times, as evidenced by other such incidents in the *Bṛhadāraṇyaka Upaniṣad*.

But just as the story of Satyakāma Jābāla in the *Chāndogya Upaniṣad*[4] did not give any right to the people not of the three upper varṇas in the strict sense of the term, to have any access to the *Śruti*, so did these explicit counter-instances not stand in the way of the orthodox Vedic tradition taking the formal position of denying women any access to the *Śruti*. The orthodox position on these issues was obviously not being dictated by mere considerations of textual exegetics or of *adhyātma-sādhanā*. What is, however, more surprising is that even in the āgamic and non-Vedic Śramaṇa traditions, the attitude to women does not seem to have been very different in spite of the fact that they did not formally deny them access to spiritual truth. Buddha's reluctance to admit women into the saṅgha and his remark after having acceded to Ānanda's importunate requests in this regard, is well known. So also is the denial of the possibility of salvation to women by the Digaṁbara sect of the Jains. The *Sāṁkhyans* seem to have identified women too much with prakṛti in their system, and thus the role assigned to prakṛti became the paradigmatic model of the role that women were supposed to play in the spiritual seeking of man. She was the temptress *par excellence* leading man astray from the path of liberation, as if she herself were not a seeker on the same path. The various Bhakti sects following the *Pāñcarātra* tradition seem to have been no better, as the well-known stories of Caitanya and Mīrā seem to attest. Only Lallā in Kashmir seems to have been an exception.

The situation was complicated by the fact that the *Nātya śāstra* had developed a theory of *rasa* as the core of aesthetic emotion and *śṛṅgāra* as the rasa *par excellence* amongst all the rasas. The erotic, thus, became central to all art and women began to be conceived of in this context almost exclusively. Man became the bhoktā and woman the *bhogya*, as Kalidāsa describes the way Duṣyanta sees Śakuntalā in *Abhijñānaśākuntalam*, and that became the model depiction of the man-woman relationship in literature in India. The Bhakti tradition did nothing to change the situation. Jayadeva's *Gīta Govinda* only made the situation worse and, from then on, Bhakti literature became even more śraṅgāric than before and influenced all the other arts accordingly. The epics, of course, did create a different spirit, but they were as male-centric as anything else.

The situation, however, did not go unchallenged and, as in the case of the śūdras, there is evidence of a counter-position, with its own ebb and flow over time and with regional differences over different parts of India. The worship of various forms of *Śakti* headed by Durgā, and epitomized in the *purāṇic* story of

Mahiṣāsurmardinī, brings this out as clearly as possible. Lord Śiva, lying prostrate with the foot of the uncontrollable and indomitable *Śakti* over him symbolizes this completely. It is true that the moment she realizes this, she comes back to her mild and submissive form. But the point has been made, and the widespread celebration of Navarātra and the daily recitation of Durgā-Saptśatī during this period mainly by men, testifies to this. Even Sītā in the Rāmāyaṇa is transformed in the Adbhut Rāmāyaṇa into the analogue of Mahiṣāsurmardinī who alone can fight and kill the thousand-headed Rāvaṇa when Rāma fails to do so. There must obviously have been deep resentment against the male-dominated universe for such a version of the Rāmāyaṇa to have been written, and that too in Sanskrit. If we also remember that this version was written by a man, the significance cannot be underestimated.

For a perspective on sex from the point of view of women, one would have to go to *prākṛta* literature where presumably the voice of the rural, down-to-earth folk is more easily heard. *Gāthā-Saptśatī* is not bereft of such verses where the male is often seen more as an *object* of desire rather than its subject, as he is almost invariably shown in Sanskrit literature. There is, of course, the story of Urvaśī in the Mahābhārata where the woman is the protagonist in the drama of desire, and even curses the male for not acceding to her wishes. There are, moreover, even open challenges to the Sītā-like ideal of marital fidelity in the poems of Cūḍāmaṇi and Śaraṇa recently brought to our notice by Mukund Lath through his translation of the poems into Hindi.[5] The former goes even as far as to call the non-voluntary relationship with the husband as essentially sinful, a sinfulness that can be washed away only by the willed and voluntary embrace with the beloved. The lovely bower is explicitly called *tīrtha*, that is, the holy place where people go to wash away their sins or earn fresh merit. Rādhā and the gopīs had, of course, already opened the way for not only the legitimization, but also the celebration, of love outside marriage. But that was in the context of the Lord himself who in the Indian mystical tradition, as pointed out by Mīrā to Tulsīdāsa, is the only male in the universe. What Cūḍāmaṇi is saying, on the other hand, is something totally different, and in a completely secular context. Furthermore, even the author of *Śrīmadbhāgavad* or of the *Gīta Govinda* had not gone so far as to describe the relationship of Rādhā or the other gopīs with their husbands as sinful. There is, of course, a lot of discussion on *parakīyā-bhāva* or that real love is always for someone who is socially bound to somebody else, though the discussion has mostly been from the male point of view. Here, on the other hand, it is the woman's point of view that has come to the fore and as Dr Lath has rightly pointed out, this should more properly be called parakīya-bhāva.[6] The deeper problem, however, is why love is supposed to achieve real intensity and flavour when the 'other' is enmeshed in restrictive bonds of a social kind and has a prohibited, illicit character, a point so well illustrated by the famous śloka which Caitanya is supposed to have sung so often.

The issue, however, is not of eroticism or asceticism, as has been supposed by many, but of the equal and independent 'subject-hood' of women in the social and cultural life of a people. It is true that in hardly any society, past or present, has this been achieved to any significant extent. The recent feminist critique has made us all aware of the enormity of the problem just as the Marxist exposé had done earlier in the case of all the oppressed and exploited classes in history. The ideals and ideologies of a society may support or subvert such a situation; what I have tried to highlight is the counter-current in Indian culture protesting against the dominant position of men with regard to women and of the higher castes *vis-a-vis* the śūdras. Even today there is evidence of women enjoying a relatively better social status in regions such as Bengal, the coastal belt of India and the South in general, where counter-ideology with respect to women was more prevalent in classical times. The matter obviously requires more detailed study, but there is substantive evidence of a counter-position regarding both women and the śūdras in a culture that fluctuated over time and varied over different regions at different periods of history.[7] The ambivalence in this regard can be found even in a text such as the *Manusmṛti* where women are simultaneously exalted and treated as being unfit for independence.

The problematic centring around varṇa and the position of women took a distinctive turn under the *Śramaṇic* and āgamic impact in the Indian tradition. So also did the evaluation of the life of the renouncer as against the life of the householder, and the contrast between them increased under the impact, breaking the continuity and the balance between them which is so evident in the Upaniṣadic part of the Vedic tradition. The yajña-centric part of the Vedas was obviously tilted more towards the life of the householder; society and polity were in the centre, particularly as many of the most important yajñas, such as the *rājasūya* and *aświamedha*, were primarily meant to be performed by a king.

Besides these, the non-Vedic traditions had another peculiarity. Most of them were founded and promulgated by human beings who had attained enlightenment through personal seeking and effort. The Buddha and the Mahāvīra are, of course, the best known examples. The other traditions also had either a human being who had achieved perfection or become a *siddha* through sādhanā, and could thus lead others on the path to realization, for in the process he had also become *sarvajña* (omniscient), or was a divine being who was already omniscient and was thus entitled to impart instructions which would help others to attain release from bondage and achieve liberation. In contrast, the Vedic tradition developed the doctrine of *apauruṣeyatva* and claimed that the Vedas were neither the word of God or man, but were themselves uncreated and eternal. Along with this, they also denied the concept of *sarvajñatā* and claimed that neither God nor man could ever have that characteristic as it was self-contradictory in nature. The debate around apauruṣeyatva and sarvajñatā resulted in one of the strangest problematic in Indian culture. It related to the ambivalent and ambiguous position of God in Indian tradition. God was never expressly denied, except by the *Cārvākas*, but was also seldom explicitly posited. It is not the strict votaries of the Vedic tradition, the Mīmāṁsakas or the Advaita Vedāntins who talk about God or try to prove His existence, but the Naiyāyikas who have little to do with the Vedas and have come to be associated with the so-called orthodox mainstream tradition only by courtesy. Yet, though the Naiyāyikas are famous for coming to the defence of God and for trying to prove His existence and sometimes even boasting about it, as did Udayana, they have seldom been *bhaktas* (devotees), as is found in other āgamic, and even non-advaitic Vedāntic traditions. In fact, there is hardly any well-known *stotra* which is ascribed to any Naiyāyika.

But Naiyāyikas apart, the fate of God or *Īśwara* seems highly problematic in classical Indian thought. The Mīmāṁsakas were forced by the logic of their position to treat the Vedic gods as 'nothing' apart from the function or role that the terms designating them have in the Vedic yajña. They are like syncategeromatic words in a language which have no meaning of their own and yet are necessary to give meaning to other words in a sentence. Or, to give a more respectable example, they are like the 'theoretical constructs' in science which are only instrumental in getting the cognitive work of science 'going' but which are not required to have any independent reference of their own and whose verification is thus neither sought nor done. The Brahman-centric interpretation of the Veda, at least in the advaitic tradition, treats Īśwara as the *adhiṣṭhāna* of *māyā* and the illusion born of primal *avidyā* or ignorance to be overcome. In Nyāya of the *Nyāya Sūtras*, He is not even important enough to be separately mentioned as one of the *prameyas* in the system. The latter commentators, in order to avoid embarrassment, treat Him as included under *ātmā* mentioned as first of the prameyas, forgetting that according to sūtra 1.1 10, ātmā is an entity inferred on the basis of desire, aversion, effort, pleasure, pain and knowledge. But, except for knowledge, how can Īśwara be ascribed all these properties in order to be included in the generalized prameya which has been termed ātmā? As to the Vaiśeṣikas, they do not seem to have any special status for Īśwara among their padārthas. In *Sāṁkhya*, he can at best be a *puruṣa-viśeṣa* who presumably never gets deluded, but then he can never be the creator of the world, as not only is he not an agent or kartā but also because it is the deluded identification of the puruṣa with the prakṛti that is the cause of the transformation of prakṛti into this world or *jagat*. In yoga, he is only an alternative way through whom the same goal may be attained, but which can also be reached *without* him.

Basically, it is in the schools of non-advaitic vedānta that Īśwara comes into his own, though they are greatly influenced by the *Pāñcarātra* and other non-śramanic āgamic schools of India. The drama, in fact, had begun earlier without the knowledge of the professional philosophers who came into the arena only later, *after* becoming conscious of what had already happened. It was the writers of the epics who had created counter-personalities to those of the Buddha and the Mahāvīra, the two most outstanding personalities to have created new religions after attaining enlightenment through sheer effort. Rāma and Kṛṣṇa are the answer to Buddha and Mahāvīra, men who are God incarnate on earth, come to save humanity by fighting and destroying evil through action and not by merely preaching as the Buddha and the Mahāvīra did. They were examples of a different sort, examples through the life they lived, the life of not only a householder but of a king who had always to fight evil-doers on a more concrete and external plane than anyone else, and in a more sustained way as well. Buddha and Mahāvīra do not fight external representatives of evil, the actual wrong-doers in society; rather, they fight inner psychic temptations and that too only before enlightenment.

The counter-reply, however, did not unambiguously establish the idea of God or Iśwara, as it emphasized not so much the idea of a creator-God or even of a God who judges people and rewards or punishes according to what they have done in life, but rather of a God who is born into this world, lives the life of man, fights the entrenched forces of evil and establishes the rule of righteousness or dharma on earth. He does not preach so much, though he sometimes does that too, as in the *Gītā*, as enacts on the stage of the world what ought to be done in all human situations and relationships. He even displays weaknesses and faults, and considers them an integral part of being born a human being. He is a child, a friend, a brother, a lover, a husband, a king, a warrior —all rolled in one. Such a conception of God has never been attempted in any civilization, and the replacement of God by God-incarnate in human form is the distinctive character of the Indian civilization.

The situation is further complicated by the fact that there are not one but two major incarnate gods, each with a distinctive personality. There can perhaps never be two such different ideal personalities, both sketched and filled in by a series of great writers and poets, as Rāma and Kṛṣṇa. Vālmīki and Vyāsa, the authors of the *Rāmāyaṇa* and the *Mahābhārata*, created in Rāma and Kṛṣṇa the perfect counterparts to Buddha and Mahāvīra who over-shadowed the latter by the sheer fullness, splendour and magic of their personalities. The *Śrīmad Bhāgavad* from the South, gave a new twist to the personality of Kṛṣṇa which almost completely obliterated the one developed in the *Mahābhārata*. Jayadeva's *Gīta Govinda* and, following him, hundreds of poets in all the regional languages created idyllic pictures of the eternal child and the eternal lover which has since then haunted the Indian imagination. In fact, such was the power of the new Kṛṣṇa image that there were a number of attempts to cast even Rāma in the same mould. Thus there came to be written the *Bhuṣuṇḍī Rāmāyaṇa* which tries to portray Rāma on the pattern of Kṛṣṇa in the *Śrīmad Bhāgavad*; but the stamp that Vālmīki gave to the personality of Rāma resisted all attempts at change, as in the popular mind he continued to be the ideal king who upheld dharma and was the model of dharmic behaviour in all human relationships, and could not be the loveable transgressor that Kṛṣṇa was. The remodelling of Rāma on the pattern of Kṛṣṇa could not succeed for the simple reason that if people wanted the other model, they already had it to perfection in Kṛṣṇa and did not need a pale imitation of it.

There cannot be two more different incarnate models of God on earth, yet the classical Indian tradition adopted both without caring for the problematic that it gave rise to, as the exemplar models whom human beings were supposed to follow and approximate in their lives happened to be poles apart. This is not the place to explain and dwell upon the two radically opposed models of dharma presented to the imagination of the Indian people; but it may be pointed out that while one is almost the perfect embodiment of dharma conceived of in completely externalized formulations, the other dharma consists of the attitudes of the mind which transcend any fixed, external formulations. There are so many other divergences but they all follow from this central difference of what dharma essentially is.

Buddha and Mahāvīra were not such colourful personalities as were Rāma or Kṛṣṇa, and even though Aśvaghoṣa wrote *Buddhacarita* presumably on the pattern of the *Rāmāyaṇa*, he could not rival these creations at the borderland of the Vedic and āgamic traditions. Buddhism did resort to outstanding creations in the field of architecture, sculpture, relief panels and even painting, but somehow it did not achieve the same creativity in the field of literature. Its influence in the field of art and architecture is enormous and visible even to a non-perceptive eye and the image of the Buddha became the ideal model for the depiction of anyone in a meditative posture. In fact, the Buddha was even accepted as an *avatāra*, the God-incarnate, and included in the expanded list of incarnations. But having renounced everything, he could never provide the rich material for literary creations as could Rāma and Kṛṣṇa. Mahāvīra, on the other hand, does not seem to have provided even that much motif for literary and artistic creations. This was probably due to his being an extreme ascetic, a position that Buddha had rejected as he had practised it and found it wanting.

In any case, as the two outstanding personalities of the Śramaṇic tradition, they put the life of the ascetic renouncer at the heart of the Indian tradition and left it with the central problematic of how to reconcile the life of the householder with all its duties and obligations, with the ideal of the ascetic renouncer with no social or political obligations, who alone had access to the ultimate truth. The conflict between karma and jñāna, or action and knowledge of the ultimate or the transcendent, and the various attempts to reconcile them, reflected the deep schism at the heart of the Indian tradition which still remains unsolved, in spite of Gandhi's radical attempt to demonstrate the reconciliation in practice and of Aurobindo's herculean effort to do so in theory.

The concept of the *Jina* or the *Buddha*, on the one hand, and those of avatāra and apauruṣeyatva or rather *aīśawaratva* on the other, thus constituted the three-fold perimeters within which the traditional Indian psyche developed its models for seeking the transcendent. The apauruṣeyatva or the aīśawaratva model, however, receded into the background and even though a large number of attempts were made to dissociate the two and treat the Vedas as the creation of Īśwara, that is, God, they did not recover their central position as against the avatāras or the Gods Incarnate such as Rāma or Kṛṣṇa, on the one hand, and the ideal renunciatory models of human perfection, such as the Mahāvīra and the Buddha, on the other. The fight against the renunciatory model never ceased, but it never succeeded either. The ideas of the *parivrājaka* and the muni are as old as the Veda itself, but Śaṁkara provided an institutional framework for them which the Buddha and the Mahāvīra had done long before him. Surprisingly, Śaṁkara did not provide for female ascetics in his organization, even though both the Jains and the Buddhists have always had women as regular members in their saṅgha. Yet, I am told by Komal Kothari, one of the most knowledgeable persons of the folk traditions of Rajasthan, that many of the *sannyāsī* orders established by Śaṁkara have divided themselves into two halves–one, consisting of renouncers proper who have left family life and the other, of those who have a regular family life. If true, this would be a strange development indeed for, unlike Buddhism, the return to the life of a householder by a sannyāsī is considered one of the worst things in the Śaṁkarite tradition. That this could happen is a clear evidence of the influence of that old Vedic tradition which was more centred on the familial and social life of man and sought his spiritual development primarily in that context, a tradition which was later developed by many of the Bhakti and Tāntra schools. However, the creation of *maṭhas* on the pattern of the Buddhist saṅgha led to myriad problems of succession and ownership which became even more compounded with the adoption of the hereditary principle of succession by many of these saṁpradāyas which tried to marry the householder's life with spirituality in their traditions. The institutionalization of charisma, to use a phrase of Max Weber, is not the problem in such contexts, but rather the transmission of charisma to successive personalities who occupy the position after the Master has left. A spiritual position, it should be remembered, is itself charismatic in character and whoever occupies it possesses it to some extent. This is, of course, true of most positions of authority, but in the case of positions designated as 'spiritual' it is preeminently so.

The status of the householder's life in the context of the spiritual seeking of man was thus the great unsolved problem left by the diverse Śramaṇa traditions of India. And, as the householder's life involves the whole social, political and sexual life of man, including the bringing up of children, their education and the transmission of culture to them over generations, these traditions posed a basic continuing challenge which forced the thinkers concerned with man in society and polity to reformulate and redefine their positions. The result, by and large, was the elaboration of the theory of the puruṣārthas and the theory of *āśramas*, that is, the theory of the stages and aims of life which tried to give a due place to all the aspirations of man and to reconcile them within a total, holistic framework. We will examine the attempt, in its variegated and diverse forms, in the next chapter.

Notes

1. *The Yoga Sūtras*, 1.6.
2. *Bṛhadāranyaka Upaniṣad*, 2.4.1.
3. *Ibid.*, 3.8.1. and 3.8.11.
4. *Chāndogya Upaniṣad*, 4.4.
5. Mukund Lath, *Svīkaraṇa* (New Delhi: National Publishing House, 1991) (Sanskrit–Hindi), pp. 107–8.
6. *Ibid.*, pp. 152–65.
7. There is also an interesting correlation between the lower caste status of women and their relative freedom *vis-a-vis* their counterparts in the upper castes, but this is not just the case with women as even men are supposed to be freer, a fact recognized by the *Smṛtis* themselves. Also, the notion of freedom in this context is seen more in terms of laxity in matters of food, sex and drink and not in terms of the 'discipline' required for any higher seekings of men and women, including the ideals of dharma and mokṣa.

CHAPTER III

The Theory of Āśrama and the Theories of Puruṣārtha: The Stages and Aims of Life

The idea of stages of life is written into the very biological cycle of life. Like all other living beings, human beings are born, grow and die. Even those with whom it is an article of faith that there is no such thing as human nature will hardly deny that human beings are born and, whether they like it or not, die, and that during this interval there are fairly well-marked stages of physical and mental growth, decay and decline. This man shares with all the living world, but the fact that he is self-conscious makes him wonder what the meaning of it all is and want to know the why and wherefore of this incessant, uni-directional process in which he finds himself and over which he has little control, except perhaps to end it if he so wishes or to let it happen as and when it occurs.

Each culture is bound to have a theory of āśramas and a theory of puruṣārtha which it formulates as universally valid for all men. These theories which are formulations of self-conscious human beings may, therefore, be found in all cultures and it is strange that Indian thinkers have not asked themselves why the theories of āśrama and puruṣārtha in other cultures are different from those that have been formulated by the classical thinkers of India. One reason for this neglect on the part of scholars, both in India and abroad, is the tacit assumption that all non-western thought has no universal validity or applicability and that, at best, it may be helpful in understanding certain features of those societies in which such thought has arisen. As for the question of cognitive validity and its universal applicability, it is supposed to be confined only to the contemporary west and its intellectual enterprises.

In the classical Indian formulation of the subject, the biological and the cultural seem to have been fused into one. The student and the householder stages of life seem to fall into a separate category from the last two which are only progressive stages in withdrawal from active involvement in worldly life and an increasing absorption in a life devoted to the transformation of consciousness and the establishment of a relationship with the transcendent. The *vānaprastha* and *sannyāsa* are the two stages in this withdrawal process; in the former, man is supposed to live with his wife if she also agrees to a life of withdrawal, while in the latter all relationships are supposed to cease and man seeks a life of 'aloneness' as far as possible. Just as *brahmacarya* is supposed to be a preparation for the life of a householder, that is, *grahastha*, so also *vānaprastha* may be seen as a preparation for the life of the sannyāsin. It is obvious that basically the stages of life have been seen only in terms of preparation, involvement and withdrawal with predominant ends prescribed for each of them.

The theory of ends, as is well known, revolves around the notions of dharma, artha, kāma and mokṣa–terms which are difficult to translate into English and which even in the tradition are ambiguous and have a diversity of meaning attached to them. Yet, they may roughly be understood as norms or rules governing human behaviour with respect to wealth or power, desire and freedom or release from bondage. Desire or kāma may thus be taken as the generalized term for all that man may aim for, except the desire to get rid of all desires, or rather, of the act of desiring itself. But artha, then, may be thought of as all that which in a generalized way is the means of satisfying kāma, that is, whatever man may desire. But as the distinction between the 'instrumental' and the 'intrinsic' is relative, so also will be the distinction between artha and kāma. That which is artha in one context may easily become kāma in another, or vice versa. Similarly, that which is kāma for one person may not be so for another, or even for the same person at another time. And, if there is no kāma, there is no artha either, for the latter is, by definition, parasitic on the former.

The traditional theorist devised a way out of the above difficulties by concentrating on the phenomenology of 'desiring' and reducing the infinite variety of 'what is desired' to just one, that is, pleasure or happiness. This strategy has been adopted by myriads of thinkers in all cultures, but the Indian thinkers added one further restriction to this reduction which, though implicit in the formulations of other cultures, is generally not explicitly stated. They confined kāma to the seeking of pleasure or happiness through some object or the other. Kāma thus, is not just *sukha* or pleasure, but *viṣaya-sukha*, or a sukha that is dependent on some viṣaya or object for its being. And, as objects are independent of oneself, one needs to acquire their svatva or ownership or possession for achieving kāma or pleasure through them. But even possession does not lessen dependence on something else for one's own state of pleasure, not only because one cannot 'own' everything but also because objects have, more fundamentally, a being of their own, both at the ontological and the empirical level. Hence, it was contended that the svatva of artha is necessary for the fulfilment of kāma and if one did not want to be dependent, one should try to forego kāma altogether. The abandonment of kāma, however, did not lead to a non-pleasure-centric thought about values, but only to the seeking of that type of pleasure or sukha which was not necessarily related to, and thus dependent upon, objects. What was recommended as worth being given up was not sukha, but viṣaya-sukha, that is, pleasure arising from objects and hence necessarily related to them. In its place there was posited the idea, and the ideal, of a sukha that had nothing to do with any object whatsoever: *nirviṣaya sukha.* The way to this had already been paved by the famous assertion of the philosopher-sage Yājñavalkya in the *Bṛhadāraṇyaka Upaniṣad* that nothing was really *pleasure-giving* and hence dear to the self, except the self itself. The viṣaya-sukha, it was argued, was an illusion born of the false view that objects could be the source or cause of pleasure or happiness. When this false view was removed, then the illusion also vanished and what remained was the nirviṣaya-sukha which was the very nature of the self. Kāma which arose out of the false orientation of the self towards the object was replaced by *ānanda* which was the very nature of consciousness when it was independent of objects.

However, if one does not want to depend on objects to achieve the self-sufficient state of ānanda, then one also makes the whole pursuit of artha with its relation to svatva irrelevant to the human situation, and thus nullifies its place in any legitimate theory of the puruṣārthas. But all viṣayas or objects are not pure objects. Some of them are also subjects to whom one is an object. In fact, one should distinguish between objects and object-subjects or viṣayas, which are *viṣayīs* also. Besides these, another distinction has to be made amongst the so-called viṣayas at least in the context of a pleasure-centric analysis of relations between the subject and the object, for one may be the occasion or the cause of pleasure or pain to certain kinds and classes of objects. All living beings are presumably capable of feeling pleasure and pain and, if so, one's relationships with living beings is, at least in one dimension, determined by the fact that one can be the possible cause of pleasure or pain or even of happiness or suffering for them.

The distinction between ātman and *anātman* and the discrimination between them is, then, not very helpful as it obscures or even obliterates the relevant distinction amongst the anātmans from the view-point of their being 'subjects' rather than just being 'objects', or of their capacity for feeling pleasure or pain even if they have not achieved the capacity of 'subjecthood' which we tend to ascribe to ourselves and also to other human beings. In practice, of course, the distinction has always been made, but unless it is also made at the theoretical level and its implications explored, both in terms of theory and practice, the practice itself would not only fail to have a theoretical foundation, but would be devalued and seen in the wrong way or at least close the way to their being seen in their own way and on their own terms through a consciousness that is centred on them rather than on itself.

Once the distinction is clearly realized and the consciousness begins to see the 'other' as a subject in his or her own right and capable of being affected by one's actions or behaviour in terms of pleasure or pain, one will begin to see the self as 'responsible' to the 'other' and not just be concerned with the state of one's own being. Yājñavalkya's ātman-centric analysis of the human situation and his contention that everything is 'dear for the sake of the self' would, then, be seen to result from a one-sided analysis which completely ignores one's own capability of making others suffer or happy.

The debate around action is fairly well known in the context of Indian tradition, but its real significance did not emerge as it arose in the context of the Vedic yajña, particularly as understood in its Mīmāṁsaka and Yājñika interpretations. The *Gītā* did try to widen the notion of action and see it in a social and even a political context. But it enmeshed the discussion too much in the context of the devotional relationship to the Lord on the one hand and its effect on the agent's psyche, on the other. It seems to have completely forgotten that action is, and ought to be, primarily concerned with others, their happiness, their freedom, their abhyudaya and their niḥśreyasa. It is true that some saints defined a *vaiṣnava* as one who was aware of, or rather who cared for other people's suffering, a view that Gandhiji reminded himself and his listeners of everyday by getting the relevant verse recited at his prayer meetings. But this was an exception. Most of the vaiṣnavas were more interested in following Caitanya and preferred to dance and sing in the glory of the Lord.

Dharma was the puruṣārtha which was concerned with the 'other' in the moral context. All the other puruṣārthas, that is, kāma, artha and mokṣa were basically self-centric, though they were concerned with different levels of the self. But even dharma came to be construed as primarily concerned with the self, albeit in a roundabout manner, that is, through the performance of one's duties towards others. Both the *yama* and the *niyama* of the Vedic tradition and the *śīlas* mentioned in the Buddhist tradition are evidence of this. It is true that there are absolutizations of such 'other-centric' virtues as 'promising' or 'speaking the truth'· or 'giving to others what one has and what one is asked for'. The cases of Daśaratha, Hariścandra and Karṇa are supposed to function as exemplars in these respects. But, not only are these examples exceptional even in the tradition, they are still predominantly self-centric as they do not take into account the consequences of their actions on others in deciding what is dharma and what is adharma. Kṛṣṇa's behaviour in the Mahābhārata may be construed as a move away from dharma as it is conceived of in the Rāmāyaṇa, that is, as the fulfilment of some absolutized, external norm of action. However, even there action is not concerned with the consequences of one's action on other individuals, but on the generalized establishment of a righteous state of affairs. And, even in this context, it is never clearly established that Duryodhana was not righteous in conducting the affairs of his kingdom. Also, the behaviour of Yudhiṣṭhira is a throw-back to the absolutized external norms propounded in the Rāmāyaṇa. For a real other-centric delineation of dharma, one would have to go elsewhere in the Indian tradition. And these are the hard core other-centric areas of dharma, the realms of vyavahāra or law and *daṇḍanīti* or the science of politics, where the norms related to the conduct of individuals and collectivities *vis-a-vis* other individuals and collectivities are articulated, debated and discussed.

But before we explore the problematic of Indian thought in the realms of law and politics, I would like to see how the culture grappled with the conflicting demands of dharma even in the minimally other-centric or rather other-oriented forms which I have described earlier and mokṣa which has been regarded by many as the ultimate puruṣārtha or end of human pursuit. It is, of course, true that mokṣa has been conceived of in many ways in the Indian tradition and also that in later times it was sought to be replaced by bhakti as the highest or even as the only puruṣārtha. But in whatever way mokṣa may be conceived, it is always a stage of the self in its aloneness and unrelatedness except, of course, when the ideal of mokṣa itself is formulated in terms of bhakti. But even in bhakti, the other-centricity is only in relation to the Lord, and not in relation to other living beings in their empirical existence. In bhakti, the others are primarily seen as being mediated through the Lord and that too indirectly. The gopīs, for example, are only concerned with Kṛṣṇa and not with the other gopīs, except in the context of the distinctive or exclusive favours given to them by the Lord, thus evoking the jealousy of the others who feel discriminated against by him.[1]

Dharma, even in the most minimal sense, involves some awareness of the 'other' and his or her claims on oneself. This invariably not only takes one away from oneself, but also disturbs the equanimity and equipoise of one's being, even to the little extent that one may have it. If one only thinks of one's own state of consciousness or considers it of the highest value, then one cannot but treat anything that disturbs it as standing in the way of realizing that which one regards as the highest end in life. Now, moral consciousness *is* a troubled consciousness, the guilty consciousness *par excellence*, for it makes one continuously *feel* that one is not doing all that one could or ought to do for others. Even in the pursuit of knowledge or the creation and appreciation of works of art, or while engaging in sheer fun or play or social get-togethers or sport, one has to *forget* the immense misery in the world, and the only way one *justifies* it to oneself is that these activities are perhaps indirectly helpful in alleviating the misery of mankind to some extent and that, in any case, one cannot do much to help mankind. Moreover, many of these activities seem worthwhile in themselves and, in fact, have been so regarded in most cultures and civilizations.

The moral consciousness, however, need not necessarily be seen in such an abstract manner. It may be seen as an integral component of all activity involving the determination of consciousness by the 'demands' of the object with which one is concerned and of the type of activity one is engaged in. Perhaps, it is what is conveyed by the term 'honesty' in the context of one's dealings with the world. But mere object-centricity or honesty do not help as there are, by and large, conflicting claims on oneself where whatever one may choose to do, one is bound to hurt someone or the other, or violate some value or the other. This has been known as dharmasaṅkaṭa in the tradition and both the Mahābhārata and the Rāmāyaṇa contain numerous examples of it.

An even more entangling and deeper problem that all action presents to consciousness is that it involves the latter in time and the essential uncertainty of the future, exposing it to the contingency of the result for which the action has been undertaken and yet which depends on a fortuitous combination of many factors over which one has no control whatsoever. To be involved in action is to be involved in a causal nexus where one is only one factor amongst others, and where one has to seek the co-operation of others by persuasion, enticement or coercion, each of which has at least some element of adharma in it in so far as it infringes on the freedom of others. The traditional thought formulates these as *sāma*, *dāma*, *daṇḍa* and *bheda* which respectively mean argument or persuasion, bribery through wealth, punishment, and the threat to make public unpleasant secrets. Moreover, for the achievement of large ends, one has to create complex, enduring institutions with hierarchical structures and specialization of functions on the basis of rules which have to be mostly impersonal in nature. This leads, by and large, to an instrumental use of other persons which normally is regarded by most moral thinkers as immoral in principle. The realm of artha, that is, of industry and trade on the one hand and of politics and government on the other, is the realm *par excellence* where this dilemma is felt by everybody. A question that haunts every genuine seeker of values is whether one can legitimately enter the realm where wealth is created through the production or sale and distribution of goods and services or the realm of the political, where power is sought or efforts made to retain or expand it, and not be immoral even in the accepted sense of the word.

But spirituality is not the same as morality, particularly a spirituality that defines itself in terms of a state of consciousness, whether attitudinally or emotionally related to God conceived in some imaginable form or other, or even as formless though related to consciousness. The moral may coincide with the spiritual to a large extent if morality itself is seen as a command from God, in the fulfilling of which one lives as one ought to, that is, not living so much *in* God as *doing* His will. This is how Judaism, Christianity and Islam tend to understand spirituality. There are, of course, mystical traditions in each of these religions, but they have always been generally subterranean and looked at with suspicion, if not hostility, by the orthodox church. The Indian tradition, on the other hand, treats the transcendental praxis as central, around which everything revolves. It is, of course, true that the Mīmāṁsā tradition, which may be regarded as the most orthodox school in the Vedic stream in India, did not emphasize spiritual experience. But then it did not conceive of the Vedic instructions as consisting of moral observances, but rather of the performance of the various yajñas, whose details are meticulously prescribed in the *Brāhmaṇa* texts and interpretatively fixed by Jaimini in the *Mīmāṁsā-Sūtras* and by Śabara in his *Bhāṣya* on it. The Mīmāṁsakas were the only powerful school in the Indian tradition which, as I have pointed out earlier, developed a verb-centric interpretation of language and propagated the radical view that the primary meaning of the Veda lay only in its injunctive sentences. Here was an opportunity to make morality central to the Śruti in at least one of its major interpretations. But as the injunctions primarily related to the performance of the various yajñas, this became the central concern rather than any other injunctions related to human behaviour in general.

It may be urged that yajña *is* the prototype of all moral action as it not only involves a sacrificial transaction between the world and the gods, but is also supposed to maintain the moral equilibrium of the world which is the central task of dharma. Unfortunately, most of the Vedic yajñas are *sakāma*, that is, performed for the sake of achieving a desired end, including even such things as the killing of one's enemy. Even those that are not done for the sake of achieving any specific purpose, have the added rider that if they are not performed something untoward may befall the person who has neglected to perform them according to the correct method laid down in the texts. Moreover, as most human beings are debarred from performing the yajñas as they happen to be śūdras or even below the śūdras, it is difficult to see how the yajñas could become a paradigm for all moral action or fulfil the task of maintaining the moral equilibrium of the universe. The idea of yajña, of course, underwent a sea-change in the *Upaniṣads*, but then it was more in the direction of what has been regarded as the seeking of mokṣa in the Indian tradition than in what has been regarded as dharma, or the moral realm *par excellence*.

The *Gītā*, of course, took the cause of action in a nonritualistic, that is, non-yajña context. It even drew attention to the fact that one cannot live even for a moment without engaging in some action or the other. But it emphasises so much the maintenance of the tranquility of one's consciousness while doing one's actions and dwells so much on the attitude to be adopted so that actions are not binding, that one wonders if it is really concerned with the type of moral action that is other-centred rather than self-centred. All in all, it reinforces the self-centric and consciousness-centric aspects of action at the expense of its other-centric and end-centric aspects which are central features of all moral action. The *Gītā*, in fact, seems to repudiate all dharma and advises its wilful transgression in its last message which is also proclaimed as the deepest secret. Normally, this is seen as a call to total devotion to the Lord, unhindered and undistracted by any other pursuit or commitment. But a close look at the text discloses a truly perplexing and bewildering message, for the call is to *give up* all dharmas and take shelter in the Lord *alone* who, in turn, so the assurance runs, will release one from any and every sin that may have been incurred as a consequence. The word *sarva*, meaning all, is used twice in the śloka, first as qualifying dharma and then as qualifying *pāpa* (sin). It is obvious that the pāpa or evil that is being incurred is due to the giving up of all dharmas, both *sādhāraṇa* and *viśiṣṭa*, that is, general and specific. In other words, what has been committed is adharma and that is why pāpa has been incurred. Nothing could be further from the moral perspective than this last, most secret, message of the *Gītā* and thus this great attempt at rehabilitating action against the śramaṇa denigration on the one hand and its pure yajña-centric interpretation, on the other, ends in an exhortation that is distinctly amoral, if not immoral, in character.[2]

The distinction between the moral and the immoral, or between dharma and adharma is subverted from another side in the Indian tradition, in its belief that there is no ultimate distinction between the two and that as an expression of duality, the distinction is fundamentally born of avidyā and thus has to be transcended to attain truth. The denial, of course, is only at the transcendental level; at the phenomenal level all distinctions remain real till the level itself is transcended. But to reduce the moral dimension to the phenomenal level and restrict its validity to that level alone is to deny the ontological reality of other beings, both human and non-human, at the deepest level. And it also implies that if one works to transcend avidyā, one should try to minimize one's concern and involvement with moral action. In fact, as far as the realm of values is concerned, Indian thought is predominantly non-dualist, at least at the transcendental level, while subscribing to pluralism at the phenomenal level. The Judaeo-Christian-Islamic thought, on the other hand, seems to tend more towards a strict duality in the realm of values even though it proclaims belief in one God alone at the transcendental level, and yet is dualistic with regard to values both at the transcendental and the empirical level.

The conflict between dharma and mokṣa, thus, sets that basic problematic for the Indian tradition which it has tried to solve in various ways. The first and foremost attempt in this direction has been to see the latter as a culmination of the former. The two form a continuum where the former leads to the latter. After all, dharma transforms and purifies one's consciousness. But this is only to see dharma in the context of the *yama* and the *niyama* as given, say, in the *Yoga-sūtras* or the śīlas as given in the Buddhist texts. But this is to ignore the dharma of, say, the kṣatriya who has to fight and wage wars and conquer other kingdoms for the sake of glory and establish his sovereignty or suzerainty over them. Or, even if one does not go on a conquest, one has to be *prepared* to defend oneself against possible attacks from others. And even to maintain peace and order within the realm, one has to punish those who break the law or try to create disorder and harm others through their activities. The dharma of daṇḍa cannot be subsumed under the dharmas that are recounted under yama or niyama or śīla or *aṇuvrata* as mentioned in the Vedic, Buddhist or Jaina canons.

The dharma of the kṣatriya has, of course, been widely discussed in the tradition, but most discussions assume that every kṣatriya is a king or is someone very close to the king. Equating 'kṣatriya' with 'king' continues among contemporary students of Indian society and culture. A book of essays edited by T.N. Madan, entitled *Way of Life: King, Householder, Renouncer, Essays in Honour of Louis Dumont*,[3] exemplifies this perfectly. As the dharma of a king cannot be the same as that of a householder even though he happens to be one, the problem arises as to what exactly his dharma as a king is. Since everybody is a *grahastha* unless he is a renouncer, the dharmas of a grahastha cut across all the other dharmas which follow from being of a particular varṇa or another such group. The so-called *varṇāśrama dharma* is a misnomer, as every varṇa is not entitled to all the āśramas. As is well known, the śūdras are not entitled to sannyāsa and vānaprastha and presumably not to brahmacarya if it is interpreted in the technical sense of going to the *guru* and living in the *gurukula* after the *upanayana* or the *yajñopavīta* ceremony. Interpreted in a wider sense, the last, that is the *brahmacarya*, may be treated as a necessary stage for all human beings as they all have a period of 'studentship' of some sort, whether formal or informal. But vānaprastha and sannyāsa are not usual states in a person's life, and even in the tradition not many persons of the kṣatriya or the vaiśya varṇa are supposed to have taken to them. Even the brahmans did not usually opt for vānaprastha or sannyāsa, though the majority of the people who took to these two āśramas did belong to the brāhmaṇa varṇa. The brahmans, of all the varṇas, were perhaps most haunted by the ideal of these two āśramas being the desirable last stages in the cycle of life. But even amongst them, it was primarily a male-centered aspiration. One seldom reads about women taking to sannyāsa or taking the initiative of persuading their husbands to leave the family to join them in retirement in vānaprastha. Nor are there many instances of women taking sannyāsa. The so-called āśrama vyavasthā and the dharma corresponding to them are neither theoretically available to all human beings nor are they practically relevant to most of them.

The problematic of puruṣārtha, thus, has primarily been seen in terms of the conflict between dharma and mokṣa, symbolized by the conflict between the brāhmaṇa and the kṣatriya at the varṇa level and the grahastha and the sannyāsa at the āśrama level. And both of these are marginal in nature, at least at the level of varṇa and āśrama in the context of mokṣa. The conflict between the brāhmaṇa and the kṣatriya, for example, has nothing to do with the primacy of dharma or mokṣa. Nor, for that matter, is it concerned with the claims of saṇnyāsa against grahastha as an āśrama. The conflict is more akin to that found between the church and the state in the western tradition or, at a more generalized level, between the wielders of knowledge and the wielders of power in any society. Here 'knowledge' relates more to the exercise of the political function and the purpose for which it is used. There is, of course, a vested interest in exercising knowledge to acquire state power. But besides this, at least in most traditional societies, the exercise of knowledge helped to restrict the arbitrary exercise of the king's power which was analogous to the powers of the judiciary and the legislature in modern times. It is this restrictive function of the brahmans that is a source of conflict and not their espousal of mokṣa or of the ideal of the renouncer, as many writers seem to argue. The use of varṇa terminology in this context is, in fact, more confusing than enlightening. Everyone who is a kṣatriya need not be a king; in fact he cannot be a king in a particular polity which already has a king without depriving the incumbent of his kingship. The number of kingships available is bound to be far less than the number of kṣatriyas in any society. Hence, to include kṣatriyas as a varṇa in the conflict between the functions of a king and the functions of brahmans who, in classical Indian society, mostly exercised the knowledge function is to totally misinterpret the situation. The conflict between the king or one who carries out the functions of a king and all the other groups in a society is not a varṇa conflict in any meaningful sense of the term. In fact, as is well known, persons who were not kṣatriyas did become kings and were recognized as such, and often were given the status of kṣatriyas or treated as such. Even at the theoretical level, though it was the preferred view that only a kṣatriya should become a king, there were *smṛtikārs* who held that any one who possessed the requisite virtues could become a king.

The kṣatriyas, it should be remembered, were as much subjects as any other varṇa or group in the society. They were thus as much a part of the *prajā* in relation to the ruler as anyone else. They were not all members of the ruling class just by virtue of the fact that they belonged to the kṣatriya varṇa, nor was it that all non-kṣatriyas were excluded from the ruling class. Membership of the ruling class and the exercise of the ruling function were always fluid. Heredity and caste affiliation were advantageous to members of royal families and high castes, but this also exposed them to dangers from potential rivals from the same background. Moreover, the field was always open to persons of military genius or superior talent who could seize the throne if the incumbent was weak, or could seek their fortunes elsewhere and establish some sort of overlordship through brigandage. And, while a person of the kṣatriya varṇa may have had some advantage, presumably because of his training in the use of weapons of war, there is little to suggest that only members of the kṣatriya varṇa received such training. And, if tradition is to be believed, many of the great teachers of the art of weapons such as Paraśurāma or Droṇācārya were brahmaṇs and not kṣatriyas. Just as in the case of rulership, there is little to suggest that access to the knowledge of the art of warfare was restricted to kṣatriyas.

The conflict that inevitably rises between a ruler and those who determine in some way or the other the norms of governance, thus has no relation with the so-called brāhmaṇa-kṣatriya conflict in the Indian tradition. There is, however, another conflict which is equally structural, but which has not been paid much attention either in the Indian context or elsewhere. This is the conflict between the wielders of power and the creators and possessors of wealth in a society. The kṣatriya, in the sense of one who exercises the ruling-function, is in as much an ambivalent situation with respect to the vaiśyas, that is, those who are engaged in the production and distribution of wealth through agriculture, industry, trade and commerce, as he is *vis-a-vis* the brahmans. It should be remembered in this connection that agriculture was the accepted occupation of the vaiśyas in Indian society. The king was supposed to provide favourable conditions for generating and amassing as much wealth as possible and for taking part of it from the vaiśyas in the form of revenue for personal and state expenditure. In fact, the relation of the brāhmaṇa or even the mendicant-renouncer with the vaiśya is as ambivalent as that between the kṣatriya ruler and the vaiśya, except that the latter could use coercive measures to extract wealth from the vaiśya while the brāhmaṇa and the mendicant-renouncer had a feeling of dependence on the vaiśya whose role and function had not merely been denigrated, but had theoretically been propounded as inimical to the ideal which all men ought to pursue, that is, mokṣa. The ambivalent relationship of the brāhmaṇa *vis-a-vis* the kṣatriya, primarily in the context of the latter being a ruler, has been noted by scholars, but the same relationship has been ignored *vis-a-vis* the vaiśya. The intellectuals as a class seemed to want to safeguard their independence from both those who wielded political power and those who possessed wealth, and yet they were dependent on them for their livelihood in some form or the other. The situation of the intelligentsia, the Fourth Estate and the Judiciary in modern times is analogous and they appear to face the same dilemmas as did the brāhmaṇas of classical times in India. The dilemma and the ambivalence of the renouncer, however, is of a different order as, unlike brāhmaṇas, he has rejected the world and yet has to be in it, a paradox symbolized by the begging bowl of the sannyāsī and the sanctity of the formal institution of 'begging' by the renouncer in traditional India. The usual form in which the request for alms was made almost as a matter of right and with no sense of shame, epitomizes this completely and is perhaps the only institution which may be regarded as totally distinctive of India.[4] It should, however, be distinguished from the similar 'begging' of the student-brahmancārin who was preparing for a full-fledged participatory role in the world and in whose case it played the role of a social support system of a completely different kind, though in its economic aspect it appears the same.

The conflicting relations between knowledge, power and wealth have not been explored in their psychological, social, political and institutional aspects to the extent needed. Still, it is strange that the sheer dependence on the labour of a vast number of others has never evoked the ambivalence or the type of feelings that the relationship amongst those who wield power or possess knowledge or wealth usually evokes. The śūdra has been out of the picture, even though on him or rather his function everyone *depends* more basically. This absence of the feeling of dependence in a situation where dependence is so obviously present may perhaps be attributed to the fact that one takes it for granted as a part of life. It is analogous to one's dependence on the body of which one becomes aware only during sickness, and that too only for a short while till one gets accustomed to the constraints and limitations imposed by the illness. The body is itself seen as a bondage in the context of certain perspectives of 'freedom' which are well known in the Indian tradition, and one who seeks freedom does try to minimize the needs of the body which make him dependent on others.

The deeper reason for this, however, may lie in the fact that the functions of the śūdra are more physical and can be performed by almost every human being. Hence there is nothing to *distinguish* between the abilities of one person and another, except in cases where a person is physically stronger. There is thus no scarcity of the type of labour which could be valued above other skills not found so uniformly distributed in a population. Beyond this, however, is the fact that the achievement of intellectual, ratiocinative and organizational skills, along with many other skills associated with them, must have been so tenuous in the early stages of civilization and so valuable to the community at large that such skills came to be valued above all things. The valuational hierarchy of those times has come down to us and all attempts by thinkers, reformers and revolutionaries to put labour at the centre of things or even bring it on par with other values in society have not been successful.

But whatever the reasons, the fact remains that there has been no problematic about the śūdra function in the Indian tradition. Nor, as far as I know, has it been a subject of reflection or thoughtful concern in any other society or civilization. In fact, there are various aspects of life which have not been reflected upon and it is surprising that their 'absence' in thought has not been a subject of reflection itself. The world of 'living' and the world of 'thought' seem not only to be worlds apart but also hermetically sealed from each other, even for those who have talked of *lebensphilosophie* or *existenz philosophie*. The absence in thought, however, does not mean a lack of significance and presumably only implies the desire on the part of all those who engage in thought or enjoy its products to get away from the daily business of life for a little while. But even this could be true only of philosophers and thinkers of a certain sort; those who were concerned with the problems of statecraft, of war and peace, of law and order, of adjudicating perennial conflicts between individuals and groups could hardly afford to be unconcerned. And this is what we actually find in the treatises concerned with polity, society and law. They are concerned with man, the problematic of man as an embodied being having interests and values that conflict with those of others. The relations between individuals, groups and polities form the central concern of this thought, and the divergence between 'is' and 'ought' is the heart of the matter. Beyond this is the problem of the formulation of the 'ought' itself, particularly when it concerns the behaviour of groups or polities in actual or potential conflict with others. The way this problematic was seen and formulated in the traditions of classical Indian thought is the subject matter of the next chapter.

Notes

1. The possibility of feelings of bhakti between human beings has not been explored in the tradition, except in a very recent movement known as svādhyāya in western India, primarily in Maharashtra and Gujarat. However, the concept of *bhakti-pherī* is very different from the way Caitanya conceived of bhakti and is more in keeping with the famous lines of Narsī Mehtā which Gandhiji was fond of: *Vaiṣṇava jana to tene kahiye je pīra parāi jāṇe re*. The problem of jealousy may also arise among the objects of bhakti if they want exclusive devotion, as is the case in Islam, Christianity and Judaism. In the Indian context, the idea of exclusivism never took root even though there was the claim by Kṛṣṇa in the *Gītā* of *māmaekaṁ śaraṇaṁ vraja* (let me be Thy only refuge) or *ananya bhakti*, that is, exclusive devotion. There are also stories of disputes about who is the greatest among the three ultimate Gods: Brahmā, Viṣṇu and Śiva. In fact, the *Gītā* itself shows an ambivalence when at one level it explicitly permits plurality and, at another level, seeks to deny it.
2. *Gītā*, 18–66.
3. T.N. Madan (ed.), *Way of Life: King, Householder, Renouncer, Essays in Honour of Louis Dumont*, New Delhi: Vikas Publishing House, 1982.
4. *Bhavati, bhikṣām dehi.*

CHAPTER IV

The *Smṛti Śāstras*, the *Vyavahāra Śāstras* and the *Arthaśāstras*: Their Conflicting Perspectives and Problematics

I

The basic perspective of social, political and legal thinkers in India has been determined by the Vedic and Āgamic traditions with their conflicting approaches to the understanding of human reality. Traditional thought created a framework of ideas, concepts and values relating to man which the empirical theorist had to come to terms with. These were the ideas of varṇa, yajña, dharma, karma, saṁsāra and puruṣārtha. The interplay between these, the concepts needed to understand the reality at the ground level, and the problematic generated by tensions between concepts and reality, forms the subject matter of this chapter. There is, thus, a triple problematic. The one *within* the basic conflict provided by the Vedic and the *Śramaṇa* heritage; the second, within concepts elaborated to articulate and capture the reality at the empirical ground level; and the third created as a result of the interplay between these two.

But, what were the concepts elaborated to articulate the social and political reality at the ground level? As everyone knows, conceptualization profoundly affects and influences reality, for human beings begin to think of themselves in terms of the concepts and act as if they constituted their reality to a large extent. To give an example, at the practical level what perhaps existed was only *gotra* and lineages while at the generalized theoretical level, the Vedic tradition with regard to the structure of society contained the notion of varṇa, though it could not take into account all the different groups which *claimed* to belong to the same varṇa or which did not even claim or know to which varṇa they belonged. Normally, only the brahmans or the kṣatriyas proclaimed their varṇas; the vaiśyas and the śūdras hardly ever.[1] The primary identity of the former, it may be said, was with the varṇa to which they claimed to belong, while that of the latter was with the clan or the group to which they felt themselves to belong socially and to which they owed specific obligations. If one asked, for example, a brahman or a kṣatriya as to who he was, the answer in all likelihood would be that he was a brahman or a kṣatriya and not that he was this kind of a brahman or that kind of a kṣatriya. On the other hand, a vaiśya or a śūdra, if asked the same question, would reply in terms of the group or the clan to which he belonged or the profession in which he or his family were engaged and which he identified himself with.[2]

Faced with the problem, the theoretician co-opted a term which earlier was used interchangeably with varṇa to denote the phenomenon. The term was *jāti*, used to designate the concrete social groupings actually found operating at the empirical level; the use of the term in the earlier sense, that is, as identical with varṇa continued, but only occasionally and sporadically. The use of the term by the social theorist, in turn, influenced individuals to see and define themselves socially in those terms. The social history of India thus became a history of the proliferation of jātis and not varṇas. The legacy of the earlier history of varṇa, however, persisted and created the problem of accommodating the new jāti classification within the old varṇa scheme. Since the older scheme was interpreted in a hierarchical manner, the varṇa a particular jāti was ascribed to assumed importance. Surprisingly, many of the so-called castes were differentiated *only* on the basis of the place their ancestors had migrated from or migrated to, or by the profession which they had sometimes pursued, as in the case of the *saryūpārīya* brahmaṇs. But just because jāti was the only other appellation the theorist could give them, they could think of themselves only in terms of their jāti, and as the varṇa model of social interaction was the only one available to them, they tried to mirror it or approximate to it in their social interactions as closely as possible.

The relationship between social theory and social reality is thus different from the relationship between theories regarding the non-human realm, particularly the realm of non-living matter, and the phenomena pertaining to these realms, as the latter are not supposed to entertain any conceptions about themselves which could be affected by the theorizer's conceptualizations. Past theories tend to become social realities of the present and thus to understand the social realities of any particular culture or civilization one has to go back to the concepts of the earlier theorizers of that culture. This is, of course, true for both the transcendental and phenomenal aspects of reality, but as the latter tends to be more embedded in a matrix that is closer to non-living reality, it reflects more clearly in the interplay between intellectual form and recalcitrant matter, at least in its grosser aspects, than does the so-called transcendental realm. In any case, the realm of the legal, the social and the political cannot but take into account the conflicting interests of a plurality of embodied beings and the groups they tend to form with which they are primarily identified. The problem of differential identification and potential conflict comes into sharper focus when thinkers address themselves to political and legal issues, as one cannot underplay the element of conflict when trying to articulate the nature of society, for society has to overcome conflict and achieve some sort of unity to perform even its minimal functions.

Classical Indian thought about law, society and polity contains a peculiarity in that it introduces two complementary notions that apply primarily to the individual human being and seeks to bridge the gap between the empirical and the transcendental. These are the concepts of *saṁskāra* and *prāyaścitta*. The former occupied an even larger space than the one devoted to *vyavahāra* or law in the *Dharma Kośa* edited by Pandit Laxman Shastri Joshi. The emphasis on these two suggests that the idea of the social thinkers of classical times was to give such overwhelming importance to the processes of acculturation, socialization and spiritual realization of the individual that the need for legal and social control was minimized and if a person happened to transgress what was considered right, he would be able to cleanse himself by performing a penance rather than be punished by society or some legally constituted authority. The institutions of social and legal restraint and punishment were of course there, but the attempt was to minimize their need as far as possible. The various rituals and processes of saṁskāra continuously inculcated in the individual a sense of being a trans-natural part of a trans-natural society. Similarly, by performing a prāyaścitta for a transgression oneself, one not only felt responsible for one's actions but was also an active agent in one's own redemption and transformation.

The idea of prāyaścitta, however, did not remain confined to individuals alone. Rather, it spilled over into the realm of vyavahāra or law and was recommended as a prescription for offences whose legal cognizance was taken by the state. This can only mean that the legal thinkers in India preferred an individualistic solution to the problem of social transgression more than in most other cultures. The impulse in this direction may have arisen from the essentially pluralistic nature of Indian thought about man and society in its empirical aspects on the one hand and its individual or ātman-centric character in the context of adhyātma or spirituality, on the other. The problematic constraints, however, seem to arise from another source, and that is the acceptance of the given varṇa-jāti structure of society which was determined largely by the social thinkers belonging to the Vedic tradition. The hierarchical and differential way of thinking about society in terms of varṇa and jāti which the social theorists had underwritten had to be accommodated by the legal theorists who were supposed to develop a legal system which recognized this hierarchy and differentiation and give it a legal sanction. The demands of justice in the universal, egalitarian sense of knowing no distinction between persons clashed with the theoretical acceptance of an essential difference amongst human beings at the empirical social level which demanded that they be treated differently as their nature, rights and duties happened to be different in society. Strangely, even non-Vedic traditional thought, such as that of the Buddhists and the Jains paid an indirect homage to the Vedic view of the varṇa-vyavasthā by allowing the Buddha or the Jina to be born only in a certain varṇa and not in others. The Buddhists in this respect were a little more liberal, at least at the theoretical level, as they allowed the Buddha to be born either in the brāhmaṇa or the kṣatriya varṇa. In fact, as the act of being born on the part of the Buddha was a matter of choice, it may be taken that he chose to be born a kṣatriya and rejected the idea of being born in a brāhmaṇa household. The Jains, on the other hand, were more forthright and declared straightaway that a Jina could only be born a kṣatriya and emphasized the point by the story that Mahāvīra was first in the womb of a brahman woman but had to be transferred to the womb of a kṣatriya by Indra when he discovered the mistake.

The vaiśya and the śūdra are explicitly excluded both by the Buddhists and the Jains as unworthy of being a Buddha or a Jina, just because they happen to belong to these varṇas. The brāhmaṇas are explicitly excluded by the Jains, while the Buddhists seem to exclude them in practice only. The orthodox Vedic tradition, it should be remembered, had excluded only the śūdras from access to the knowledge of the *Śruti*, that is, the Vedic texts, and had been ambiguous about the varṇa in which the perfect being would incarnate himself. The two major avatāras, Rāma and Kṛṣṇa, are supposed to have been born in the kṣatriya varṇa, though there is nothing to indicate that they ought to have been born in that varṇa alone. Paraśurāma was a brāhmaṇa, but he is regarded only as a partial incarnation or *aṁśavatāra*. However, as the incarnation is supposed to have taken place in the form of various animals, half-animals and half-humans there is little to indicate that the Lord has any specific preference for any varṇa amongst human beings or any particular species amongst other living forms. This should perhaps help to dispel the view that the theory of avatāra or divine descent was formulated to counter the privilege which Buddhism and Jainism claimed by possessing living founders who were perfect in every way and who showed humanity the path to liberation. But even if one were to accept the theory, one would have to acknowledge that the idea of the perfect human being into which the divine embodies itself is far different from the one exemplified and illustrated in the lives of Mahāvīra and the Buddha. Rāma and Kṛṣṇa are different models of perfection and the way they teach through the lives they live is very different from the one lived and preached by the Mahāvīra and the Buddha. The śramaṇ ideal as exemplified in their personalities and in some of their other well-known contemporaries is countered by an ideal of a different kind, the ideal of a person who lives in society and is of society in the sense that he has to perform the functions of a son, a brother, a husband, a friend, a fighter against evil and above all, a righteous ruler. There is nothing of the renunciatory attitude to the world and its obligations, nothing of the *nirveda* that is so prominent in the life of the great renouncers and little of the preaching that is such an important feature of the lives of both the Buddha and Mahāvīra. Kṛṣṇa does preach once, but it is almost as if by accident, and does not return to that role again. Besides this, both Kṛṣṇa and Rāma show a willingness to suffer, if necessary, and Kṛṣṇa even prefers the most frustrating and difficult work of running the quasi-democratic polity of the Yādava clan to being its king and engages continuously in the peace- and war-making operations of the major existing polities of his times.

The moral dilemmas in the social and the political realm and the problematic they give rise to have been the theme of the two great epics which also contain self-conscious reflections on the problematic. The constraint produced by the varṇa-jāti framework of the social theorists continues to plague them also. Rāma who has no hesitation in eating wild berries out of the hands of a tribal woman who has already tasted them to find out if they are tasty enough to be given to him, has to kill a śūdra who has dared to do what only a brāhmaṇa is permitted to do by the tradition. And Kṛṣṇa, though brought up in a community of cowherds, has to leave it to assume his kṣatriyahood and play his rightful role on the stage of Indian polity and society. The author of the *Śrīmadbhāgwad* had to resurrect the Kṛṣṇa of the cowherds and delink him from the great warrior-statesman of the *Mahābhārata* so much so that the Indian psyche has not yet fathomed how to integrate the two.

The legal thinkers, thus, try to come to terms with a notion about society that sees it primarily in terms of varṇa and jāti and attempt to do this by formulating a notion of *daṇḍya* and *adaṇḍya* which helps in differentiating the quantity and quality of daṇḍa or punishment according to the role and function expected from the different varṇas. The central issue in this context relates to the amount and kind of immunity which the intellectual class, that is, the brāhmaṇas should be allowed as they performed not only advisory, but also critical and monitoring roles in the socio-political system. Besides this, they also legitimized the functions of the polity and its ruler. They had, therefore, to be safeguarded from the whims and vagaries of the ruler and his possible vindictive stance towards them; this was done by treating them as adaṇḍya or unpunishable by virtue of their functions in the society and the polity. This, however, went against the principle of justice which demanded that anyone who was found guilty of transgressing the law should be punished. The story of the successive compromises between these two conflicting demands by the legal thinkers of India is interesting in more ways than one. Justice required that those who had greater privileges in society should have greater responsibilities, a principle that appears to lie at the basis of the income-tax policy in modern times. This however, would result in awarding more severe punishment to those with greater privileges and responsibilities for certain offences. And this was exactly the turn that legal thought took in India. The vyavahāra theorist engaged in the strangest of exercises, that is, to determine the kind of offences least excusable on moral grounds from a person of a particular varṇa and hence deserving of more severe punishment than prescribed for others for the same offence from whom less was expected.

But the need to provide some sort of immunity to the intellectual class which was both the guardian of culture on the one hand, and of social and political norms, on the other, remained. This was achieved by deciding that no capital punishment should ever be given to a brāhmaṇa. From adaṇḍya to *avadhya* is the great story of legal thought in India, at least with respect to the intellectual élite of society. And, as the legal thinkers or the creators of the vyavahāra śāstra themselves belonged to this class, it should help dispel the usually prevalent opinion that the brahmans, the intellectual class, formulated the rules to their own advantage. The protection of intellectuals has been the perennial concern of all cultures, including the modern one, and the dilemmas flowing from that concern have been tackled differently by different societies. Even contemporary society has not been able to find a satisfactory solution to the problem.

The brahman, however, was not the only adaṇḍya person for

the legal thinkers of India. The king or the person exercising the sovereign function could himself, obviously, not be punishable in the ordinary sense of the word. Being the ultimate source of the rightful exercise of daṇḍa in society, he could not himself be subject to it, except in a metaphorical sense. The difficulty here was, unlike the one in the case of the brāhmaṇa, both theoretical and practical. At the theoretical level, any such attempt would lead to infinite regress, as the same problem would arise with respect to any other authority set up or postulated to punish the transgression of the ruler. At the practical level, it was difficult to see how this could legitimately be done, except by some sort of a revolt which itself would be a subversion of the system. Yet, the demands of justice, or what may be called dharma in the Indian context, were as insistent as they were in the case of the immunity and safeguards needed for the brāhmaṇs. The dilemmas and the problematic that these conflicting perspectives gave rise to and the attempts at solution are of interest to any student of legal thought in India.

Seeking a solution to the problem of possible transgressions by a ruler appears to have taken a number of forms. The first concerned the training of the ruler in such a way that the possibilities of his transgressing the law were minimized to the greatest possible extent. This explains why so much attention has been given in both the legal and the political texts of India to the moral qualities and training of a king. But as this alone was not sufficient, a whole series of institutional safeguards was created, such as the essential role of the council of ministers in the functioning of the polity, the formulation of the norms in accordance with which the king was expected to rule and the values he was expected to uphold and foster. Yet, if these safeguards against the possibility of misrule by the king proved inadequate, what was the solution? The ultimate solution was, of course, the removal of the king and some of the political writers argued for the legitimacy of such a move. But the legal thinkers, by and large, held that the king was adaṇḍya, that is unpunishable, at least as far as the legal process was concerned.

The king also exercised the judicial function, besides the ruling or the political function of which he was the visible symbol. In the exercise of the judicial function, two problems seem to have arisen. The first was primarily the result of practical exigencies, as it must have been difficult for the king to personally listen to all the disputes that were brought before the court. Also, if the king himself rendered the legal decision on any dispute, there could be no further appeal regarding it. The enlargement of the council constituting those who listened to cases brought before them and passed judgements, and the delegation by the king of his judicial authority to such a council so that he need not be present, were the two developments that followed from this exigency.[3] The other, perhaps, arose from a peculiarly Indian idea relating to the exercise of the judicial function combined with the adaṇḍya character of the king, referred to earlier. As the judicial function was a type of karma, its correct performance would earn one merit or *puṇya*, while if it were incorrectly performed, one would earn demerit or *pāpa*. Now, as human nature is fallible and a wrong judgement could be given, it would have to be atoned for. This was done by providing for the performance of prāyaścitta on the part of the king. The reasons for prāyaścitta in the case of the king, as in the case of a brāhmaṇa, seem to be motivated partly by similar considerations and partly by different ones. The king was adaṇḍya or not punishable for reasons which, as we have pointed out, were basically practical in nature. But if the principle of culpability was to be applicable to him, and the theory of incurring merit or demerit entailed this, the only way out of the dilemma was that he should acknowledge his share of the guilt and punish himself rather than be punished by anybody else. This was ensured by recourse to prāyaścitta prevalent in the culture, which implied that as far as possible one should punish oneself for any transgressions.

But if the act of justice was a collective act in which the king was only one of the members, the guilt incurred through a wrong decision was to be shared by everybody involved. The king's share may be pre-eminent by virtue of his central position, but unless the role of all the others was treated as merely advisory by the legal theorists and the king considered the *sole* decision-making authority in all legal disputes brought before him, the others would have to share in the merit and the guilt equally and be expected to also perform prāyaścitta. Since, in the later period, the legal texts not only enlarge the membership of the council of judges but also make it optional for the king to be present therein, it is pertinent to enquire if prāyaścitta was prescribed for all members of the council.

The extension of the notion of prāyaścitta to the realm of daṇḍa brings together two different areas of concern in Indian legal and social thought, the first concerned with the individual and the ideas of puṇya and pāpa relating to the actions that one does and the second concerned with others, particularly when it violates their rights and comes under the category usually called *aparādha*. This attempt to bridge the realms of dharma and vyavahāra is, in fact, part of a wider attempt to resolve the tension between the two. On the one hand, the very need for vyavahāra or the legal context of human behaviour seems to arise when dharma or moral injunctions and ideals fail to govern behaviour. The existence of vyavahāra and the necessity of thinking about it would, therefore, be evidence that dharma has ceased to function and be effective amongst human beings. Vyavahāra would then be a *pratipakṣa* of, or antagonistic to dharma, as Nārada is supposed to have said in his *Smṛti*. According to him, the relation between them is that between sunshine and shadow; where one is, the other is not. On the other hand, the function of vyavahāra may be seen to be one of restoring dharma and, thus, the relation seen more positively. Interestingly, an analogous situation seems to obtain in classical thought about the relation between dharma and mokṣa. The necessity of dharma arises only because mokṣa has not been achieved, and thus the practice of dharma may be taken as a sign of the absence of mokṣa. On the other hand, dharma may be regarded as the preparation for and a prelude to mokṣa. The relations between vyavahāra and dharma on the one hand and between dharma and mokṣa on the other, show interesting parallels and analogous dilemmas for the legal, moral and adhyātma theorists of India.

The realm of vyavahāra in fact provides a model for other domains also where contending parties staked their claims to the possession of something which, by its very nature, could belong to only one of them. Without the *vādī* and the *prativādī*, there can be no vyavahāra. So also, if there is no judge and no accepted rules for deciding issues, there cannot be any vyavahāra. The intellectual debates provided almost a perfect analogue to the legal disputes and the ideas of *pakṣa*, *pratipakṣa* and *samaya-bandha*, or the rules of the discussion, along with an agreement on who would decide on the victory or defeat of the contestants, may be seen as providing the philosophical parallel to their legal counterparts. The formal structure of *nyāya* is supposed to have arisen out of such discussions, as attested to by many of the technical terms. *Vāda*, *jalpa* and *nigrahasthāna* are some of the examples. The format of the formal debate seems to have been carried over to the written texts, as we usually have a presentation of the *pūrva pakṣa* or even a number of pūrva-pakṣas, that is counter-positions which are then systematically refuted to establish one's own doctrine, that is, *siddhānta*.

The centrality of daṇḍa links the realm of vyavahāra to the realm of the political which is specifically called daṇḍanīti or *rājanīti* in the Indian tradition. The notion of *daṇḍa tārtamya* developed by the legal thinkers has, in fact, both legal and political overtones and seems to be rooted in a view of man and society that is essentially pluralistic in character. In the realm of the spiritual or the adhyātma this principle took the form of *adhikārī-bheda* implying that what was right or desirable for one person at a particular stage of his or her spiritual growth was not necessarily right or desirable for another person at a different stage of spiritual growth and development.

The differentiated adaptation of daṇḍa or punishment has already been referred to in the discussion on the problems encountered in connection with brāhmaṇas or persons exercising the intellectual functions on the one hand, and the king on the other. It has also been mentioned that the demands of justice led to the extension of the principle to other varṇas also. Varṇa, however, was only *one* of the aspects which the principle of daṇḍa tārtamya was supposed to take into account. There were others, which Gautama lists as puruṣa, śakti, aparādha and *anubandha*. These may roughly be translated as the varṇa or jāti to which the transgressor belongs, his or her capacity to bear the punishment prescribed, the nature, type and degree of the offence committed and whether the offence has been committed for the first time or whether the person is a habitual offender. The illustrative examples given in the text are interesting in that they reveal both the principles and the intention behind the formulation. The term *śakti*, for example, is illustrated by saying that the physical strength and health of an offender should be taken into account when deciding on the kind of physical punishment to be meted out. Similarly, in illustrating *aparādha* it is said that one should note whether the offence has been directly committed by the person concerned or by someone who is not an independent agent but is acting on behalf of someone, such as an official or a servant.

The requirement that the punishment be adapted to the individual's physical, economic and institutional situation can be extended in different directions. One such direction was the recommendation by some legal thinkers that the śūdras should not be deprived of their means of livelihood or production. However, in the case of Brahmans, it was suggested that an adequate punishment would be to deprive them of the occasions and opportunities to practice their intellectual and spiritual vocations. Perhaps a radical distinction was made between pursuits concerned with physical and material production on the one hand, and intellectual and spiritual pursuits on the other. In any case, the distinction between prescribing prāyaścitta and daṇḍa on the one hand, and between including or excluding *vadha* or the infliction of capital punishment continued to trouble legal thinkers in India. As regards the first, Kātyāyana went so far as to treat them as alternatives. At least that is how Pandit Laxman Shastri Joshi, editor of the *Dharmakośa*, construed his statement as he puts it under the heading *daṇḍaprāyaścittyorvikalpaḥ*.[4] Interestingly, the śloka treats both as two forms of treatment to cleanse the body social of illnesses and to treat the concerned individual as if he or she were a patient. But there is nothing to indicate that the two cannot be combined and have to be treated as alternatives. Also, it is not clear why, if prāyaścitta is prescribed by judicial consensus, it should not be treated as a daṇḍa or a punishment. Furthermore, as the prāyaścittas themselves are prescribed in authoritative texts devoted to the subject, they have a quasi-legal status. For offences of a public nature, prāyaścittas can be enforced by quasi-judicial authorities such as village or caste councils or professional guilds.[5]

Perhaps it would be best to distinguish between prāyaścittas voluntarily undertaken for personal transgressions and those imposed either by a quasi-legal or fully legal procedure to be performed in the manner laid down in the classical texts. But even so a problem arises as to how a prāyaścitta, being primarily a personal observance, would satisfy the claims of an offended party in a legal dispute brought before a court for adjudication. Perhaps an understanding of the exact difference between what constitutes a prāyaścitta in the legal context and how it differs from daṇḍa would help to clarify matters to some extent.

The problem of inflicting capital punishment or vadha emanates from entirely different considerations. The avadhya character of the brāhmaṇa arises from considerations which are, as discussed earlier, different from those that apply to the king. But its extension to all other categories such as is found in the *Śukranīti* can only be based on generalized considerations regarding the sanctity of life and hesitancy in inflicting this ultimate punishment on anyone. The *Śukranīti* contains a statement that supports this interpretation. Roughly translated, it means that 'as long as any being is alive, no one should kill it. The scriptures declare that no one should ever be killed'. This, in fact, is the principle of ahiṁsā spelt out in the legal context. The issues of violence and killing have always been widely debated in the Indian tradition and it is well known that sacrificial killings were defended as being part of Vedic injunctions. The *Gītā*, of course, is a classic example of a religious text that justifies killing, though in the context of a righteous war. Here the context is neither Vedic sacrifices nor a righteous war, but merely personal offences to be punished in accordance with judicial decisions. It may be surmised that as *Śukranīti* is supposed to be a late work, it reflects the increasing concern in social thought with ahiṁsā or non-violence. *Śukranīti* takes the discussion into the legal sphere and justifies its stand against capital punishment on a legal basis. What is surprising, however, is its appeal to *Śruti* to justify ahiṁsā when the Veda itself is supposed to countenance or even require at least the killing of animals for sacrificial purposes. The strategy is fairly common amongst Indian thinkers, most of whom want to appear to be within the tradition by claiming to understand the real meaning of *Śruti*. This should not blind us to the innovativeness of these thinkers. Dr Mukund Lath in his *Svīkaraṇa* has gone so far as to argue that innovativeness in interpretations of the tradition was accepted as the usual way in which creativity was exercised in Indian culture, even though alternative ways were not frowned upon or excluded. In fact, Indian culture even provided a name for such innovativeness, at least in the realm of philosophy–*sarvatantraswatantra*–that is, independent of all established traditional systems. Dr Lath has, of course, argued primarily in the context of the literary and poetic traditions of India and following Rājaśekhara, has called it *svīkaraṇa*. But the idea can easily be extended to other fields, and cultural innovations and creativity be pursued in this way too. Even those who depart from the tradition in a radical manner have to establish a saṁpradāya of their own within which innovation and creativity are pursued in the new manner. The story of India's cultural creativity in diverse fields may, therefore, have to be told keeping in mind both the aspects, as well as the interaction between them.

II

The realm of vyavahāra forms an integral part of the political function; vyavahāra is concerned with the regulation of society and the maintenance of law and order. The concept of daṇḍa around which the discussion on vyavahāra revolves is equally central to the exercise of the political function. The concept of daṇḍa thus provides a bridge between the legal and political schools of thought in classical India. Political Science, in fact, is called daṇḍanīti, the other name for it being *arthaśāstra*, a name given by Kauṭilya to his famous book on the subject. The two terms bring out both the aspects with which the science of polity is supposed to deal–the exercise of coercive power and the management of the economy on which everything depends. The term daṇḍa, however, is no longer used in the traditional sense of punishment for transgression of norms by individuals, but in the wider sense of coercive power or force, symbolized by military might. The two forms of daṇḍa, though related, are essentially different as they concern two different aspects of a polity, the internal and the external. The term *nīti*, however, draws attention to the fact that the realm of the political is primarily a realm of the practical, where skill in handling coercive power for achieving an end is what really matters. Daṇḍanīti or rājanīti is normally contrasted with *rājadharma*. The relation between nīti and dharma is difficult to articulate, though the former seems to emphasize the practical and pragmatic aspects, while the latter seeks to highlight the normative ones. There is, of course, the notion of *āpaddharma* or acts permissible in a situation of extreme emergency which comes close to the idea of action governed by pragmatic considerations, but then the perspective of nīti is not confined to emergency situations alone. Also, while the concept of a *śāstra* leans more towards the primacy of theoretical considerations, it does not always do so, as is evident by the existence of such śāstras as the *Kāma-śāstra* or the *Nātya Śāstra* in the classical tradition.

The problematic for the political thinker in India, however, was due to considerations of a different order than those that troubled the legal thinkers, though the two were not entirely unrelated. The stage was again set by the varṇa theory, though this time in a different way. The Vedas, where the varṇa theory is supposed to have been propounded, had themselves compounded the problem by calling a particular varṇa both rājanya and kṣatriya. Now if rājanya is taken to mean 'king', then obviously it cannot be a varṇa, for most people cannot be kings. In a polity, there is generally only one king at a given time and by making a varṇa out of him, not much is gained for social or political thought, except perhaps to point out that the king forms a unique class by himself and cannot be assimilated into others. He is, of course, formally a member of the class of 'kings', but all the other members of his class belong to other societies and polities, potentially hostile to one another. The kṣatriya, on the other hand, refers to a large class of which there can be many members within the same society or polity and which are differentiated, at least at the theoretical level, by their functions and professions. These are supposed to be in contradistinction to professions engaged in by members of other varṇas, which collectively cover all the functions, through the joint and complementary performance of which a society maintains itself. The functions which a person who belongs to the kṣatriya varṇa is supposed to perform, of course, overlap many of those ascribed to the king also. But over and above these, the king is supposed to perform other functions which are connoted by the term 'daṇḍa', that is, the rightful exercise of ultimate coercive power which is another name for sovereignty. And, in this case, daṇḍa can be exercised, at least in the traditional context, only by one person, that is, the king. There is thus no question of kṣatriya and rājanya being coterminous, as the former are large in number even in the same society or polity, while the latter can, by definition, be only one.[6] The confusion, however, between the two has continued to plague Indian social and political thought throughout its history. The latest evidence of this is found in the very title of a book published some years back, called *Way of Life: King, Householder, Renouncer*. Now, kingship is *not* a way of life, though the life of a householder or a renouncer may be treated as such. The confusion here is between the āśrama and the varṇa viewpoints, though the king fits into neither. Kingship is neither a varṇa nor an āśrama even in the classical thought of India on the subject.

If the king does not fit into the varṇāśrama paradigm of Indian social thought, he at least raises a problem for the political theorists of the classical tradition. And this relates to the question of whether kṣatriyas alone were entitled to be kings. Thus, though every kṣatriya could not be a king, a king had to be a kṣatriya, for only a kṣatriya was entitled to hold that position. This would obviously be the orthodox position if one accepted the strict varṇa-centric picture of society. But the socio-political reality at the ground level did not conform to the ideal varṇa picture, and anyone with a combination of prowess, cunning and luck could become a ruler of some sort and even a king of some consequence if he had the backing of political skill and military strategy. Neither the Mauryas nor the Guptas were kṣatriyas, a fact political theorists could not ignore. Yet, the prevalent theory with regard to society did present a problem which theorists had to come to terms with.

The discussion basically revolves around the question of how the term rājanya or rājā is to be understood. The earliest answer to the question, as given in the *Nirukta*, is that one who rules is the king (*Rājā rājateh*).[7] The second definition given in the *Dharmakośa* shifts attention from what may be called the *functions* of the king to the formal ritual procedure which invests him with the authority and designation of a king. It says:

sa mūrdhābhiṣikto rājā bhavati.[8]

There is no awareness here of the issue which was to plague later thinkers, and the only interesting difference is the transition from a straight functional definition to a formal-ceremonial-legal one. The *Mahābhārata*, however, contains a discussion on 'being a king' and 'being a kṣatriya', as if it was important to come to a decision on this issue that had troubled thinkers down the ages. Yudhiṣṭhira pronounces as clearly and decisively as possible on this issue and says:

> *brāhmaṇo yadi vā vaiśyaḥ śūdro vā Rājasattama*
> *dasyubhyos'tha prajā rakṣeddaṇḍam dharmeṇa dhārayan.*[9]

The heading under which the discussion is given is even more telling. It says:

> *kṣatriyajātibāhyopi brāhmaṇo vaiśyaḥ śūdro vā yaḥ ko' pi*
> *prajāyā dharmeṇa rakṣakaḥ rājatvādhikṛtaḥ.*[10]

Yudhiṣṭhira's statement suggests that persons from these varṇas are the next best choice if a kṣatriya is not available or if, due to *varṇasaṅkara* or the mixing of varṇas, there are no pure kṣatriyas left.

The śloka says:

> *abhyutthite dasyubale kṣātrātrthe varṇasaṁkare.*
> *sampramūḍheṣu varṇeṣu yodyanyo'bhibhavedbalī.*[11]

But the notion of varṇasaṅkara in this context is gratuitous in the extreme, for it is difficult to believe that there is any varṇa that does not have some element of varṇasaṁkara in it. In fact, Yudhiṣṭhira seems to forget not only that the idea of varṇa is an ideal construction and that all existent, empirical exemplifications cannot but be departures from what the pure idea of varṇa may imply, but that he himself, along with the other Pāṇḍavas could not be supposed to have any varṇa at all. On the other hand, even if they are regarded as the sons of Pāṇḍu, they cannot escape being varṇasaṅkara as Pāṇḍu himself is supposed to have been born of a union between persons belonging to different varṇas.

The reference to the ascendancy of the power of the *dasyus* in the śloka raises problems of another sort. The dasyus do not have a separate varṇa of their own, and hence they can belong to any varṇa. Thus, a dasyu can be a brāhmaṇa, a kṣatriya, a vaiśya or a śūdra. But as he is a person who exercises violence and oppresses people, he is most likely to come from a varṇa which specializes in the exercise of power or means of violence. This can only be the kṣatriya varṇa. However, dasyus are those who exercise power only for adharmic ends while kṣatriyas, at least in the ideal classification, are those who exercise power for purposes that are in accordance with dharma alone. In the classical formulation, it is for the maintenance or perpetuation of dharma that the kṣatriya uses force. But who flouts dharma? He is of course the dasyu or the *rākṣasa* or, in other words, the kṣatriya in his negative aspect. It is surprising that no one has thought or written about the varṇa vyavasthā amongst the dasyus or rākṣasas. The latter are mainly known from the Rāmāyaṇa, and Rāvaṇa, a rākṣasa, is supposed to have been a brāhmaṇa. But it is obvious that all the rākṣasas in Laṅkā and elsewhere were not brāhmaṇas, and that if we treat Kaṁsa as a rākṣasa, he certainly was not a brāhmaṇa but a kṣatriya.

It is, of course, true that anyone can behave like a dasyu or a rākṣasa, but then anyone with the proper qualities can also do what the king is supposed to, that is, protect people against those who behave like rākṣasas or dasyus. Yudhiṣṭhira seems to take this stand, and in doing so changes the definition of 'king' from the formal-legal-ceremonial one given earlier into a functional one. A king is one who can protect his people, and anyone who can successfully do so may become a king. But the primacy accorded to the kṣatriya in the context of kingship that has come down from earlier times, as evident in the *Rājasūya Yajña* where even the brāhmaṇa sits below the king (B.U.1.4.11. D.K. vol. I. 354), has continued to plague thinkers. The many twists and turns in the debates may be seen in the arguments of the *nibandhakāras* or commentators on Manu who differ from the explicit position taken by Kulluka Bhaṭṭa that the word 'king' here has nothing to do with the kṣatriya varṇa but refers rather to a person who has been ritualistically consecrated and is capable of protecting his people, and is thus eminent among men.

> *rājaśabdo'pi nātra kṣatriyajātiparaḥ.*
> *kiṅtu abhiṣiktajanapadapālayitṛpuruṣarparaḥ.*[12]

Others have taken the orthodox position embodied in the *śruti*, particularly in the context of its description of the *rājasūya* sacrifice.[13] Jaimini, in fact, discusses this issue in his *Mīmāṁsā Sūtras* and opts for the position that the term rājanya is confined to the kṣatriya varṇa only. But, interestingly, most of the *ṭīkākāras* on Manu veer to the opposite view. Some of them argue that even if it is true that originally the term was applicable only to the kṣatriyas, its usage has now changed, and with a change in usage, there has been a change in meaning as well:

> *lokaprayogaeva śabdārthāvadhāraṇe pramāṇatṁ.*[14]

Some take recourse to *lakṣaṇā* or the metaphorical use of words and some even go so far as to deny the relevance of Vedic authority in this context:

> *na tāvadvaidiknirdeśādatra nirṇayaḥ śakyate.*

and

> *rājyakartri ca varṇāntare lākṣanikaḥ.*[15]

Both Medhātithi and Kulluka Bhaṭṭa reject the narrow interpretation in the clearest of terms. Medhātithi writes:

> *rājaśabdaśca neha kṣatriyajātivacanaḥ, kim tarhi? abhiṣekādhipatyādiguṇyogini puruṣe vartate.*[16]

And Kulluka Bhaṭṭa, as we have already noted, says:

> *rājaśabdo nātra kṣatriyajātivacanaḥ kintvabhiṣiktajanapada paripālanakartṛvacanaḥ.*[17]

Ultimately, therefore, whoever can perform the kingly function of protecting the people is worthy of being a king, and not just one who is born of kṣatriya parents and thus belongs to a varṇa whose members are usually capable of performing this function. At the ground level, of course, whoever usurped power became king and if he consolidated his position, was also recognized as a kṣatriya since he was exercising a preeminently kṣatriya function. Of course, he had to be consecrated, but then the brāhmaṇas could bargain or impose their conditions for anointing the person, as they are supposed to have done in the case of Shivaji. And, in this way, a new kṣatriya caste could be born.

But the reverse functional definition of varṇa could not be

confined to the issue of who could be a king, though discussions occur primarily in this context alone. Anyone who actually performs the functions assigned to a varṇa may be supposed to belong to that varṇa even though there may be a significant time-lag and generation-interval in the situation. The carrying out of the functions of most other varṇas did not require the important formal ceremony of *abhiṣeka* or consecration essential in the case of the king, except perhaps for the performance of certain priestly functions in the case of brāhmaṇas. But then, strangely, these functions were never rated highly even amongst the brāhmaṇas, let alone the general public. A knowledge of the Vedic rituals was, of course, rated more highly, but then the complicated Vedic yajñyas were performed infrequently and, in any case, it was *knowledge* of the Vedas that was prized more highly than knowledge possessed by the *yājñika.* Even amongst the mīmāṁsakas, the ones who could argue about the correct vidhi and refute pūrvapakṣas such as Jaimini or Śabara, were respected and taken more seriously than the ones who just knew how to perform Vedic rituals. Ultimately, it was the exercise of knowledge and the commitment and dedication to acquiring and using it that gave the brahmaṇ his status in society; this knowledge could belong to any field, whether spiritual or secular. Knowledge, however, had to be theoretical, that is, *śāstric* in character. There was, of course, a radical difference between the theoretical, śāstric knowledge of the Vedas, or what was regarded as śruti in the tradition, and all other knowledge, as access to the former was not 'open' even at the theoretical level, evident in the explicit positions taken by both Jaimini and Bādarāyaṇa on this subject. However, the proliferation of jātis even amongst brāhmaṇas who had a śāstric knowledge of the Vedas indicates that the strategy of closing access to the śruti did not succeed quite as much as wished for by its guardians in spite of the precautions taken and the penalties imposed. The situation, however, could always be saved by treating the successful violator as a brāhmaṇa, notwithstanding the fact that he was not considered on par with the other pre-existent jātis of brāhmaṇas and was treated as inferior to them. The strategy had already been adopted in the case of the non-kṣatriya king.

The wielders of knowledge and power were, of course, the

centre of attention of Indian social and political theorists, as in most other civilizations and cultures. But it is the vaiśya or trader who actually provides dynamic mobility to society by seeking his fortunes beyond the settled frontier. By trading in goods and services between different regions, like the wandering monk or the wandering scholar, the nomadic trader also helps to break down boundaries between civilizations. However, the brāhmaṇa, the kṣatriya and the wandering ascetic have not taken kindly to the activities of the vaiśya, even though both the king and the renouncer depend on him for the exercise of their functions. Both the Buddha and Mahāvīra were patronized by rich vaiśyas who supported the saṇgha but there is little in their preachings that show recognition of the importance of the function of the vaiśyas. The saints, it appears, never worried about the way wealth was earned, provided the wealthy supported their organizations. This was also their attitude towards the wielders of political power. Neither Mahāvīra nor Buddha tried to dissuade Ajātas'atru or Kūṇdika from attacking Vaiśālī nor did they deny him the status of a *śrāvaka* or an *upāsaka* of the sangha. The fact that he killed his father, the king, did not seem to have lessened their regard for him or stopped them from enjoying his patronage.

There is, however, sufficient evidence in the texts to indicate that the relationship between the wielder of political power with those who created wealth in society, specially through trade and commerce, was ambivalent in nature. On the one hand, the king was supposed to foster their interests and not tax them too severely as this could deter them from engaging in activities that proved to be hazardous or unprofitable. On the other hand, however, if the king was in dire need of money, he was advised to even confiscate their wealth on some pretext or the other. The king, or the polity, ultimately acquires wealth through taxes, and though both the peasant, that is, the agricultural producer and the persons engaged in trade and commerce pay taxes, it is the latter who not only pay a larger share of taxes, but also have more opportunities to evade them. Not only this, since the vaiśya deals in cash, the moment taxes are realized in cash, even the agricultural producer begins to depend upon him in his double role as distributor and financier. The prajā, in fact, has been defined as *karapradāḥ* since Vedic times:

agninā prajāh karpradāḥ kṛtāḥ.[18]

It is true that the term vaiśya is supposed to apply equally to the trader and the agricultural producer. But this creates confusion because it fails to distinguish between two economic activities which are radically different. In a sense, the same problem arises with other primary producers also, particularly with those engaged in different kinds of crafts who, strangely enough, are generally not considered vaiśyas, but rather śūdras. In fact, classification of the agricultural producer under 'vaiśyas' goes against the tradition's own characterization of the varṇa being different from all other varṇas. The vaiśya has what has been described as:

asaṁkhyātadhanalābhakāriṇī buddhiḥ.[19]

This is, of course, a description of one who is engaged in *vāṇijya*, that is, trade. But as one who is engaged in agricultural production has a totally different outlook the two cannot be, or rather ought not to be, put in the same category.

The diversity of professions is evident as early as in the Vedas themselves. The *Śukla Yajurveda* in its thirtieth *adhyāya* mentions a large number of professions and peoples whom it, strangely, characterizes as not only *abrāhmaṇāḥ*, but also as *aśūdrāḥ*. The *Dharmakośa*, vol. IV, part I gives a more detailed list collected from the *Saṁhitās*, the *Brāhmaṇas* and other texts (pp. 413–19). In the context of the king, however, the problem primarily relates to the collection of taxes from the various professional groups, and the problematic always consists in maximizing taxes without drying up the very source of tax collection. The two most picturesque models recommended to the ruler on how to collect taxes from his people are the way one milks a cow or the way a bee collects honey from flowers:

bhramarakṛtamadhudohaḥ dhenudohaḥ–jalaukārkṛtaharaṇa–vyāghrīputraharṇādivat mṛdūpāyena prajābhyaḥ karagrahaṇaṁ nyāyyam.[20]

However, as the text says, in case the treasury becomes depleted, even unrighteous means, including force, can be used for acquiring wealth from those who have it.[21] As everybody knows, situations of emergency never cease in the case of most polities and if the prospect of war is accepted as central to any polity, as does Indian political thought, the path of political action and the path of adharma become almost similar, if not identical. The use of the word 'adharma' in this context is revealing as normally no Indian thinker would like to be caught preaching adharma explicitly, even though he may intend to do so indirectly. In fact, if something is considered *āpaddharma*, how can it be adharma, except in an exceptional metaphorical sense? The idea of āpaddharma seems to point to a hierarchy of values which are related to each other in the way the 'stronger' and the 'weaker' values are related in Nicolai Hartmann's thought. The latter, according to him, cannot exist or come into being without the former which can be realized or actualized without the latter. The 'weaker' values, according to Hartmann, are also generally the 'higher' in the hierarchy of values, while those which are 'stronger' are usually the 'lower' ones. But, as far as I know, neither the idea of āpaddharma nor of dharmasaṁkaṭa has been analysed or theoretically reflected upon in the context of any generalized theory of values, or of puruṣārtha, in the Indian tradition.

The political theorist, however, seems to have a problem with respect to dharma which neither the social nor the legal thinker generally had. For the latter, the violation of whatever is regarded as dharma is undesirable *per se*, and institutions and practices are required to rectify the situation. But such a situation cannot obtain for the political thinker, as he cannot but see dharma as an instrument of power, for if power weakens or vanishes, everything else ceases. This becomes clear if the relation of a polity to other polities becomes the focus of attention. The political theorist in India saw quite clearly that the central fact about a polity was that it was always one amongst other polities with which it had potentially hostile relations. The concepts of *rāṣṭra* and *maṇḍala* are found as early as in the *Ṛgvedic* period in the provisions for the *rājasūya* and the *vājapeya* yajñas (see *Dharmakośa*, *Rājanīti kāṇḍa*, vol. I, p. 33). And, as victory in war and the expansion of one's kingdom were the main aims of these yajñas one can see how central were matters of war and victory to thinkers who were concerned with the science of politics.

The problem of the relationship between different polities introduces, however, a problematic of a different kind. The internal relationship of a king with his subjects may, at least theoretically, be regarded as ultimately governed by dharma. But how could the relations between different polities be regarded as governed by dharma? This is the realm where victory has to be ensured and defeat avoided at all costs, that is, even at the cost of dharma, and this not just for oneself, but for one's people also. This is the realm of diplomacy and deceit, where 'peace' is merely another name for 'waging war by other means', and where there are no 'real' friends or enemies. That is why rājanīti and rājadharma are two different things: the former relates to other polities, the latter to one's own subjects. It is not that there is no element of nīti in the king's behaviour towards his own subjects but, at least at the theoretical level, dharma is supposed to prevail over nīti in this context. I have already indicated the tensions and conflicts between the king and the brāhmaṇas on the one hand, and the king and the vaiśyas or the trading community, on the other. But as far as the political thinker was concerned, he was clear that, by and large, dharma should prevail in all such dealings, even though he allowed exceptions in some situations, as I have already noted.

The problematic of the political thinkers in India may thus be divided into two major parts: the first relating to the prajā or the residents in a polity, the second relating to other polities and to all those who were not subjects of the king and who thus had no mutual obligations. The two problematics posed problems of a different kind. The latter raises the problem of how to bring considerations of dharma into a realm which is essentially non-dharmic, if not anti-dharmic, in character. The former raised the problem of how to minimize questions of adharma in a context that was mainly dharmic in nature. The former, as we have seen, was primarily taken care of by formulating the notion of āpad-dharma, that is, action required under circumstances of acute emergency that were both exceptional in nature and temporary in duration. The latter was met with by attempting to formulate rules for the conduct of war, norms according to which war was to be fought, and the occasions which could justify it. In short, an attempt was made to bring the notion of dharma into matters relating to war and peace and thus create what has been called the idea of a *dharma-yuddha*. The Mahābhārata is a classic example of such an attempt, but this can be found in the works of other political thinkers also.

Polities, it should be remembered, were classified in order of ascending hierarchy, and it was the natural dharma or *svadharma* of a king to take his kingdom to the highest possible level in the hierarchy. This is the reason we have sacrifices like the rājasūya, the vājapeya and the aśvamedha prescribed in the Vedas, with the performance of which the king could attain the desired expansion and glory of his kingdom, no matter if it involved large scale violence, killing and the destitution of people. It was not the daily agnihotra that was the centre of the king's Vedic activity, but the activities just mentioned.

The most comprehensive classification of the forms of kingdom in this context is given in *Śukranīti* which calls them *sāmanta*, *māṇḍalika*, *rājā*, *svarāṭa*, *samrāṭa*, *virāṭa* and *sārvabhauma*. Earlier writers used only such terms as *samrāṭa* or *cakravartī* to denote a king or an emperor. The rest were either rājā or *adhīśvara*, depending on whether they were lowest in the hierarchy or somewhere in between (see *Dharmakośa*, *Rājanīti Kāṇḍa*, vol. IV, part II, pp. 834–6). The ideal of everyone at the lower level in the hierarchy was to move higher, and the usual means of achieving this were war, marriage and diplomacy. Waging war, it should be remembered, was regarded not only as something legitimate for a king, but also as something heroic, involving the virtues of valour and courage which were admirable in themselves. The great epics of all civilizations centre around battles where outstanding acts of sacrifice, heroism and courage are performed. The kṣatriya was the warrior *par excellence* and that is why he was supposed to be the best person to perform the functions of a king. In fact, he was defined as one who earned his livelihood by the use of arms. Also, till very recently the great conquerors of history were heroes and what are now called 'ministries of defence' were called 'ministries of war' without any feeling of compunction.

The task of the political thinker in such a situation was to try to reconcile the irreconcilable, that is, the desirability of waging war to expand one's dominion and the need for preserving and strengthening dharma to the best extent possible. He attempted this by distinguishing between the right or dharmic way of treating conquered kings and people and the wrong or adharmic way. This led to the distinction which in modern parlance is designated by the terms 'sovereignty' and 'suzerainty'. Ultimately, the idea was that if a defeated king accepted the conqueror's overlordship, he should be allowed to continue to rule, according to the customs and traditions prevailing in his society and polity. The recognition of overlordship could take many forms, some even purely symbolic as evident in the distinction between the two kinds of adhīśvara in the *Nārada Smṛti*, that is, those who paid tribute or taxes and those who did not. The terms used are *sakaraḥ* and *akaraḥ*.[22]

But even if overlordship was not accepted and the recalcitrant enemy had to be made to realize his lower status in the hierarchy, the ideal behaviour on the part of the conquering king was supposed to be the same–to restore the defeated king or his son or some close relative, and let him rule over his kingdom as before. Kauṭilya in his *Arthaśāstra* has described this kind of king as *dharmavijayin*, or the righteous conqueror, 'who makes conquests for the sake of glory and who is satisfied with mere submission by other kings'.[23] As against this, there are other kinds of conquerors, driven by greed or the desire to shed blood and kill. The *Arthaśāstra* calls them *lobhavijayin* and *asuravijayin* (12.1.10–16).[24] The former is one 'who makes conquests out of greed and is out to obtain land or money or both', while the latter is one 'who makes conquests like a demon and seizes land, money, sons and wives of the conquered king and takes his life'.[25] Such conquerors are, of course, adharmic in increasing degrees.

It is the first type of conqueror king alone who is called dharmavijayin as he follows the dictates of his dharma which, if he is a ruler, is to be a *vijigīṣu*, that is, desirous of conquering other territories. Yet, after he has secured the submission of a king and made him accept his overlordship, he should 'treat him with honour, unless he continues to harbour hostile intentions'.[26] Instead of the direct annexation of territory, the relationship established with the conquered king is 'that of a suzerain and a feudatory or vassal'.[27] But, as noted earlier, even this is not necessary, though as far as the author of the *Arthaśāstra* is concerned there seems no other possibility. The *Nārada Smṛti*, however, as pointed out earlier, conceives of the possibility of an *akaraḥ adhīśvaraḥ* who would not be regarded either as a vassal or as having a feudatory relationship with the conqueror.

The idea of an āsuric or demonic conqueror as contrasted with one who is considered dharmic brings into sharp relief both the problematic which the ideal of being a *vijigīṣu* involved in the context of normative political thought in India and the attempt at its solution. But Indian political thinkers do not seem to have seen the more fundamental problem involved in the ideal as it implied an essential plurality of polities on the basis of the theory of *maṇḍala*, while the ideal of the *sārvabhauma* or the *cakravartin* denied it in principle. It might be urged that the reconciliation was affected by formulating the non-annexationist ideal of the cakravartin or the sārvabhauma ruler whose suzerainty or overlordship was mostly symbolic in character, and which was at the apex of a kind of hierarchy which went down to the *sāmanta* level. But first, the king desirous of attaining the status of a sārvabhauma or cakravartin had to make others agree to his overlordship, and this could only be done by the exercise of force, the ultimate manifestation of which was war, resulting in the defeat of recalcitrant kings. Second, the annexationist ideal was never discounted or underplayed as an alternative ideal to be pursued by a king. In fact, the idea of a unified, centralized pan-Indian empire on the model of the one achieved by the Mauryas or the Guptas has haunted Indian rulers down the ages. And this, even though Kṛṣṇa in the Mahābhārata had squarely stood against the monopolistic ideal and went so far as to get Jarāsandha killed by unrighteous means as he was the arch-practitioner of that kind of ideal in his times.

At a deeper level still, the problem relates to the issue of how a plurality of actors could desire to wield absolute power without giving rise to that very situation which the institution of kingship was supposedly evolved to counter–a situation of utter anarchy involving 'the war of all against all' and 'the big fish eating the small fish'. Any equilibrium achieved in such a situation would be short-lived and illusory, as those who accept overlordship do so only under duress and are required by the theory to want to become lords themselves. The situation, of course, has been transposed from the level of the people to the domain of the competing circle of kings whose number is very much smaller than that of the people. Thus the institution of kingship may be said to have enabled people to enjoy the solution of their problems. The respite would be temporary in view of the certainty of war because the very nature of kingship defined by the political theorist in the Indian tradition, which was essentially pluralistic in nature, required each ruler to absolutize his power. The task of the science of polity, as defined by Kauṭilya, is to undertake 'a systematic study of the ways and means of the acquisition and protection of earth'. Here 'earth' also includes everything that grows on it and is sustained by it.[28]

The problem, in fact, is intrinsic in all analyses which postulate a plurality of independent actors, each trying to maximize his gains in terms of welfare, wealth or power, without caring for the consequences for others. Much of modern economic theory is based on a similar postulate which assumes that each person necessarily strives to maximize his share of scarce goods. All goods, of course, need not be scarce, nor all individuals be of such a nature. But the theory underwrites the primacy of such goods and such persons and thus of greed and lust, of aggrandizement and aggression, in human life.

The Indian social theorist, however, emphasized the primacy of dharma, and though aware of *asaṁkhyātalābhkāriṇī buddhi*, his emphasis was to minimize its impact on society by treating the man of renunciation as higher than the man of wealth or power or knowledge since at least the time of the Buddha and the Mahāvīra. Besides this, he also suggested that the proper use of these attributes was to maintain and augment dharma on the one hand and support those who pursued the renunciatory ideal, either individually or collectively, on the other. At a deeper level still, they emphasized the primacy of goods which did not share the basic characteristics of economic goods. The ideal of mokṣa may be understood in a similar way. It was an attempt to conceive of the ideal of freedom in such a way that its attainment by one did not hinder its realization by others nor did the attempt at its absolutization come in the way, even theoretically, of a multiplicity of 'absolute realizations' on the part of others. Not only this, the ideal is conceived of in such a way that its realization by one positively helps others to achieve the same goal.

Much has been made in recent thought of the distinction between 'freedom from' and 'freedom to', but it has not been seen that freedom, as conceived in the Indian tradition, is *distinct* from both. Also, there is an essential asymmetry between the two types of freedom in that 'freedom to' necessarily implies a limitation or restriction of others' 'freedom to' which is of equal value, while 'freedom from' does not involve any such restriction or limitation. Furthermore, freedom as a state of being, the way mokṣa is usually conceived of in the Indian tradition, is supposed to lead both to 'freedom from' and 'freedom to'. Most people mistakenly identify the Indian conception of freedom with the former. The other type of freedom is usually supposed to be absent from the Indian ideal, even though there is hardly any form of *sādhanā* in the Indian tradition which does not simultaneously promise and warn against all the *vibhūtis*, or supernatural powers, that accrue to one along the path of liberation and which tempt one to effectuate all that for which the so-called 'freedom to' is wanted.

The dilemmas of the political thinker, however, are of another sort. He is aware of the centrality of the political function for the realization of all values in a society, but he is also aware that a polity is always amongst other potentially hostile polities and thus the realization of dharma in that society may be jeopardized. The political good, in other words, was the sort of 'good' modern economics considers economic good to be, and one could neither conceive of any higher dharma to which it could be subordinated, as was attempted in the case of the pursuits of artha and kāma, nor of something akin to mokṣa in the political realm where each sovereign king could absolutize his sovereignty without jeopardizing the possible or actual absolute sovereignty of others. The problems faced by philosophers in conceiving of more than one ultimate reality were similar to the problems faced by the political theorist when he tried to conceive of the possibility of a plurality of sovereigns in the political realm. The rules formulated for the conduct of a dharmic war, as Bhīṣma attempted in the Mahābhārata, failed to be observed even in the battle of the Mahābhārata itself, while the attempt to distinguish between the three types of conquerors, the dharmic, the *lobhin* and the āsuric, seemed to have failed equally, as even the dharmic king had to engage in conquering, for that was supposed to be his dharma. Of course, once the conquest was over and the king's sovereignty or suzerainty established, dharma again held sway, for that was how the newly acquired territory was supposed to be governed. Yet, there was bound to be tension between the newly acquired subjects, particularly those who were loyal to the old king, and the new rulers. And there was the ever-present danger of the old, defeated king trying to regain his kingdom by any means. The sources of instability were always present and so also the temptation to let dharmic considerations take a backseat and let *real politik* prevail, at least for the moment.

The perspective of conquest, it should not be forgotten, is also the perspective of defeat. The Indian political theorist is very much aware of it. In fact, the distinction between the three types of conquerors is drawn in the context of discussions regarding the possible strategies that a weaker king should adopt to prevent being conquered by a stronger king. Thus, as far as the theorist is concerned he is neutral in his attitude and is only interested in building a śāstra which takes into account all the possibilities and spells out the various policy implications which follow from them, keeping in mind the maximum advantages that can be derived from a given situation.

Besides the problematic which arises from the fact that a polity is always amongst other polities as well as the problematic between the wielders of political power and the wielders of knowledge on the one hand and that between the former and the creators of wealth on the other, there is another problematic of a different kind deriving from two conflicting perspectives on the human situation as conceived and analysed in different traditions of Indian thought. Any thought which focuses attention on society and polity cannot but view men as essentially dependent upon one another, while any thought which sees man as primarily a spiritual being, tends to view him predominantly in relation to the transcendent rather than in relation to his fellow-men in the socio-political world. And, as the dominant strand in traditional Indian thought tended to see man not only as a spiritual being, but also as a *kevalin*, that is, alone in an ultimate or transcendental sense, a problem arose for the socio-political thinker who obviously could not accept this perspective. The dilemma is perhaps most clearly brought out in the interpretation of the theory of karma from the two perspectives. For thinkers following the strict spiritual traditions of India, one can only reap the fruit of one's own actions. It is a strictly Leibnitzian world with no God to create harmony. The socio-political thinker, on the other hand, has necessarily to think of action in an institutional context where one's action has consequences for others, and hence one is held responsible for them and punished or rewarded accordingly. The view of society or polity that emerges from this perspective is totally opposed to the monadic interpretation of the human situation and tilts towards an organic view in which the king is the linchpin of the whole system.

There are, in fact, a host of characterizations which seek to emphasize the interdependence between the king and his subjects, or between the rājā and his prajā. It should be remembered in this connection that the Indian thinker did not distinguish between citizens and non-citizens such as slaves or women, as was done in Greek thought. Rather, everyone was included under the term prajā and, in fact, the king was supposed to have special obligations towards those who were disabled or weak or deprived. Special mention is made of children, widows, old people and orphans as being his special responsibility.[29] Kauṭilya specifically states:

> *bālavṛddhavyādhitavyasanyanāthāṁśca rājā vibhūyāt*
> *striyamaprājātām prajātāyāśca putrāṇ.*[30]

Nārada goes even further and suggests that it is the duty of the king to protect and support all those women who have no one to support them.[31] Strangely, Bhavaswāmī in his bhāṣya on *Nāradīyamanusaṁhitā* interprets this to mean that the śāstra denies the right to a woman to be *svatantrā*.[32] Brahatpārāśara gives an even more positively oriented, modern sounding duty to the king. According to him, the king ought to employ all people in tasks which are in accordance and commensurate with their capacities and capabilities. The Sanskrit summary given by the editor of the *Dharmakośa* reads thus:

> *tattatkāryasamarthānāṁ tattatkaryeṣu niyojanam.*[33]

It is not however clear from the details mentioned there whether the principle is directly enunciated therein or just implied by the instances mentioned. Further, it is not clear whether the principle was supposed to be restricted to the appointments made directly by the king or to all appointments, or even whether the king was held responsible in any way for what is today called 'full employment' in the state. In any case, the formulation of it as a principle is interesting in itself and though obviously correct, it is seldom observed in practice, particularly at the political level. This was perhaps the reason why Pārāśara chose to emphasize it in the context of appointments at the king's level.

The so-called 'welfare-functions' of the state are taken by many thinkers to a point where failure to protect his subjects is supposed to entail an obligation on the part of the king to reimburse them for subsequent losses. Thus, it is repeatedly urged that it is the duty of the king to restore whatever has been stolen from a person if the thieves are not caught and the stolen property recovered from them. The *Viṣnudharmottara*, for example, goes so far as to suggest that even before the task of investigating the theft is undertaken, the king should reimburse the loss incurred from his own treasury. It is specifically mentioned that this should be done in the case of all the varṇas:

> *sarveṣāmeva varṇānāṁ caurairapahṛtaṁ dhanam.*
> *tatpramāṇaṁ svakātkośāddātvyamavicārayan.*

and

> *tatastu paścātkartavyaṁ caurānveṣaṇamanjasā.*[34]

The king's responsibility towards his subjects seems to be total. But there is a reciprocity in the relationship, conceived not just in the formal manner of the obligation on their part to pay taxes to the king. The latter, surprisingly, is supposed to share in whatever merit or demerit his subjects earn by performing dharmic or adharmic actions. According to Vālmīki in the Rāmāyaṇa the king is supposed to share in one-fourth of the merit or the demerit of the actions of his subjects.[35] However, in the very next śloka he is said to share in one-sixth of the merits of his subjects if he rules them according to dharma.[36] In fact, the *Manusmṛti* supports the one-sixth rather than the one-fourth version.[37]

The problem, obviously, is not whether the king's share should be one-sixth or one-fourth, but rather how this squares with the general hard-core theory of karma and dharma. According to this theory it is the individual who is responsible for his actions and to whom alone pāpa (demerit) or puṇya (merit) accrue on the basis of his dharmic or adharmic actions.

But in the view just propounded, the king is not only a co-sharer in the pāpa or puṇya earned by his subjects, but is also co-responsible for their dharmic or adharmic actions. The king is the one who is responsible for the fostering and protection of dharma amongst his subjects and is thus entitled to a share in the results. But this would imply that one's performance of dharma or adharma does not depend on oneself alone, but is facilitated or hindered by someone else's actions. Or, rather, as no generalized theory is being propounded, but only a special case regarding the king is being mentioned, it may be concluded that it is the proper exercise of the political function that alone ensures the performance of dharma by the people. This, while not entirely untrue, could create serious problems both for the theory of dharma and the theory of karma as propounded in the Indian tradition. Also, it would put a great strain on the exemplars of the śramaṇa tradition headed by Mahāvīra and Buddha who had tried to promulgate a different ideal of dharma in the Indian tradition.

Yet, for some reason, the theoretical problems posed by this political perspective on dharma and karma were never faced or discussed by the thinkers of either the arthaśāstra tradition or the smṛti tradition. Even the internal problems which arise from the formulations of political theorists do not seem to have been either seen or discussed. Take, for example, the commonly held idea that the king shares in the pāpa or puṇya of all his subjects to an extent of one-fourth or one-sixth. Does it mean that the king's formal responsibility for the performance of dharma or adharma is only to the tune of one-fourth or one-sixth? But if the 'sharing' itself is dependent on the king's performance of his duty of propagating and protecting dharma in his kingdom, how can he be said to share in the puṇya of his subjects if he is not doing his duty properly, or share in their pāpa if he is actually doing everything possible for the maintenance and pursuit of dharma in his kingdom? Furthermore, while it is true that the king is formally responsible for whatever happens in his kingdom, it is well known that no dharma can be fostered or maintained only by the king's activities. What is needed is a good, committed, dharmic administration all along the line. But, if this is so, puṇya or pāpa will have to be shared by all, and not just by the king alone. What is required in such a situation is for the theorist to develop a distributive theory of collective pāpa and puṇya on the basis of the assumption that the proper performance of dharma depends on the precondition that someone else performs his dharma properly. The non-performance of dharma by a person or even the performance of dharma by him is seen as a *consequence* of someone else's failure to perform his dharma.

There is, however, at least a seeming asymmetry in the situation. The performance of adharmic acts and their large scale spread in a polity indicate a failure by the king to protect dharma amongst his subjects, but it is not quite certain if the performance of dharma by the people would be taken as an indication of the king's dharmic activities. The reason for this perhaps lies in the fact that while the absence of adharmic or anti-dharmic activities is a necessary condition for dharmic activities in a society, it is not a sufficient condition. The person performing a dharmic activity requires *saṁkalpa* of his own to an extent that is absent in the case of adharmic actions, except perhaps in the case of asuras or rākṣasas, that is, persons, who wilfully indulge in evil practices. Also, it should be remembered that the performance of a dharmic act is more difficult when large-scale adharma prevails, as this requires greater saṁkalpa on the part of a person and hence deserves greater merit. Yet, on the basis of the thinking prevalent on this issue in the tradition of political thought in India, the king should not be entitled to any share in the merit acquired in such a situation. On the other hand, if the king is held responsible for the prevalence of adharma in a society, and if the extra merit earned by a dharmic act is due to this fact, it would not be illogical for the king also to share in this extra merit. This would, however, lead to the strange, paradoxical conclusion that those who make it difficult for a person to do the right act, whether directly or indirectly, are entitled to an extra share of puṇya which a person earns. The rākṣasas, by this logic, would get a share of the extra merit earned by the ṛṣis of the Rāmāyaṇa era by virtue of the fact that they were at least partly the cause of the ṛṣis earning this extra merit. And, by the same logic, Rāma would be responsible for the disappearance of this extra merit due to his having eliminated the rākṣasas.

The paradoxical nature of obstructions in the path of dharma and the willed resolve for their removal (saṁkalpa), as well as their relation to the calculus of pāpa and puṇya is difficult to determine. But if admitted, even ever so slightly, this paradox is bound to have strange consequences for many of the accepted parameters of classical Indian thought on these subjects. Take, for example, the theory of *yugas*. It is obvious that an act of dharma would be increasingly meritorious in successive yugas since adverse circumstances would increase progressively, becoming highest in Kaliyuga when it would be almost impossible to do the right action, not because of any fault in oneself, but because of the nature of the cosmic cycle in which one is born. The theorists seem to have been vaguely aware of this for otherwise they would not have said that just taking the name of the Lord was sufficient to attain mokṣa in this dark period of the cosmic cycle. But, if this is true, how can the helpless king reverse the strong downward current of the cosmic cycle, a feat continuously demanded of him by the political theorists of the tradition? On the other hand, how does the whole theory of cosmic cycles square with the law of karma, as it is inconceivable how the karmas of most people in the dark Kali Age could lead, by a sudden reversal, to the highest, pristine state where dharmic action is supposed to be the second nature of most human beings?

The theorists themselves are in utter confusion. On one side, they allow complete laxity on the path to mokṣa, while on the other, they *prohibit* actions permitted to men of the earlier cycles. *Kalivarjitaḥ* or 'prohibited in Kaliyuga' is the common recourse of the theoretician of dharma when faced with an unpalatable practice present in the texts he is not prepared to question. The fact of the matter is that the Indian thinker in the social and political fields did not envisage the problems he was creating for himself by incorporating ideas and hypotheses developed in other contexts into his thought system.

The relation of morality to adversity on the one hand and to temptation on the other, has usually not drawn the attention of most thinkers who have been concerned with ethical issues in the realm of philosophy. Nor has the role of the 'other', whether at the individual personal level or at the impersonal institutional level, been examined. In fact, the interrelations between theory-builders of dharma in the personal domain and those concerned with dharma in the public realm have been almost non-existent in most cultures. There has been a relatively serious attempt in this direction in the Indian tradition, particularly in the

Mahābhārata and the Rāmāyaṇa but, on the whole, the subject has not been pursued in a significant way by the systematic theoreticians of the culture. Kant had brought in considerations of wager in the field of epistemology, but failed to consider them in the case of morality. But if one begins to waver in one's belief in the efficacy of a statement if the negative stakes are indefinitely increased in the event of it turning out to be false, there is no reason why one's belief in the goodness of an action should not be affected the same way. The postulate of āpaddharma in the Indian tradition seems to take care of adversity in relation to morality, while the innumerable stories of the temptation of saints by celestial damsels points to the factor of temptation in testing the strength of morality. Surprisingly, the temptations are mostly sex-centric implying that there are no other significant temptations on the path of dharma. The temptations faced by the Buddha were, of course, more varied in nature, though they included erotic temptations also. The temptations in the case of Mahāvīra shared the common trait of producing extreme adversity, rather than holding out the promise of any pleasure, sensual or otherwise. The temptations of Christ do not seem to have a predominantly sexual character, though many of his temptations share the characteristics of those found in the stories of the Buddha and the Mahāvīra, particularly if we include the trial on the cross.

The stories of temptation in the Vedic-purāṇic tradition of India are, however, not only erotic but also male-centric. There are hardly any stories of women being tempted from the path of dharma by their male counterparts. In fact, there are hardly any stories of women performing acts of supernormal penance except that of Pārvatī who, instead of being tempted by Kāmadeva or his human or divine counterpart, is accosted by a male mendicant who tries to dissuade her from seeking Śiva as her husband, the sole purpose for which she is undergoing the penance. Male centredness is evident, as usually women are shown to worship or undergo penance in order to find a husband or, if married, to increase his life-span, as in the case of Sāvitrī.

But whatever the problems created by the doctrine of the king's share in the pāpa and puṇya of his subjects, there is little doubt that it created a powerful argument for the organic, interdependent view of the polity and was a great incentive for the king to foster and propagate dharma in his kingdom and himself act according to it. In fact, as there was no system of institutional checks and balances, as in a liberal democratic polity where there is a separation of power between the legislative, judicial and executive functions, the whole emphasis was on self-control by the king on the one hand, and a meticulous carefulness in the appointment of ministers on the other. This explains the importance given to *indriyajayaḥ* or self-control in the treatises on the subject. This also accounts for the detailed attention paid to the appointment of various important functionaries in the state to the extent that various strategies, including temptations, are suggested to test them before appointing them. In fact, it would be an interesting exercise to find out the various devices recommended and used to ensure the functioning of the polity in such a way that neither the king nor his functionaries misused their power and betrayed the trust of the people.

The moral problematic for the ruler in the self-conscious tradition of political thinking in India seems to extend in many directions. It is strange, for example, to find that the king is advised to be wary of almost everybody near him, including his wife and children. In fact, the latter are the first to be feared as they are emotionally the closest to him. Kauṭilya, in fact, places danger from sons first in his list of dangers to the king and calls them *janakabhakṣa* or those who may eat up even their father.[38] The various commentators found it difficult to decide what to recommend in such a situation, that is, whether the sons should be killed or imprisoned or given some other punishment. Similarly, there is warning of danger to the king's life from his wife and other women of the royal household.[39] How, in such a situation, can the king, who is supposed to provide freedom from fear to all his subjects, be himself free from fear?

The problematic basically arises in the context of dharma, for otherwise there is little problem if this perspective is forgotten. The Indian political thinker, however, as we have often had occasion to note, seems sensitive to considerations of dharma even with regard to issues that are primarily political in nature. In fact, he even tries to bring considerations of dharma and adharma in the context of war and attempts to distinguish between wars that are dharmic from those that are not dharmic in character.

The basic discussion regarding this occurs only in the Mahābhārata, though almost all the other texts seem to make this distinction in some form or another. All the references in discussions on this issue under the title *yuddhadharmādharmavicāraḥ* in the *Dharmakośa*, for example, are only from the Mahābhārata,[40] while those under the section entitled *dharmayuddha* are practically from all the usual texts cited in this work from Gautama onwards.[41] The Mahābhārata goes so far as to say:

adharmo'pi āpadi dharmaḥ
dharmo'pi āpadi adharmaḥ.[42]

Surprisingly, it is Yudhiṣṭhira, the son of Dharma, who says this. However, it is in the context of the dilemma faced by the Pāṅdavas after receiving Sanjaya's message from the other camp, that we should try to understand the import of what Yudhiṣṭhira is saying. On the other hand, even before the great and final battle, there had been other wars on a smaller scale and no one seems to have been concerned with the ethical issues involved. There was the battle with the Kauravas themselves in the *Virāṭa Parva* which involved warriors of such renown as Bhīṣma, Droṇa and Karṇa, later the heroes of the Mahābhārata war on the Kaurava side. But even earlier, Yudhiṣṭhira had performed the rājasūya yajña, and normally this yajña did presage war with those who refused to acknowledge one's suzerainty. Yet, even the Mahābhārata is not able to clarify what exactly a dharmayuddha is, or what its *vyāvartaka lakṣaṇa* is. Normally, it is the victor or rather the victory, which decides the issue, but justification by force is supposed to be no justification. Ultimately, war *is* the central issue in political thought, and though its disastrous consequences are known to everybody, it is seen as both inevitable and unavoidable. The chasm between war and welfare, and the external and internal imperatives to which the exercise of the political function is inextricably wedded, along with the tensions and the relationships between them, have been the actual stuff of politics in any society. There also exists the problem of the safety of the one who exercises the ruling function in any society. Yet, most political thinkers outside India have not treated them at all, or have done so in a marginal manner. Both Plato and Aristotle, and the major traditions of political thought deriving from them in the west, are fair examples of this. But the tradition of political thought in India squarely faces the tensions and problems and formulates them as one of the central concerns to be addressed if an understanding of the nature of political reality is to be reached. So also is the ambivalent relationship between power and knowledge and power and wealth, as pointed out earlier.

The deepest problematic, however, is the dilemma faced by the king, as he is a human being like others, and thus reacts according to the perspective inculcated in him by his cultural background. This perspective, at its most foundational level, does not value or give a high status to the political domain. The highest life is not that of the citizen, or one who is an active participant in the affairs of the polity, as in the Athenian thought of Plato and Aristotle which influenced western tradition so profoundly, but rather that of the 'renouncer' exemplified preeminently by the Mahāvīra and the Buddha. The society-centred thought of the *Dharmaśāstras* had as much problem with this ideal as the rājanīti or daṇḍanīti śāstras which were primarily concerned with the realm of the political; but the latter had special problems of their own as not only could the rājadharma not be everybody's dharma like the dharma of the *Dharmaśāstras*, but also the king could not be allowed, even theoretically, to become a 'renouncer' and leave the world as ordinary persons in society could.

The strategies adopted by the two sets of thinkers overlapped and were convergent as well. The first step in this direction was to develop the so-called āśrama theory of human life where renunciation was supposed to be practised at the end of life when man had presumably fulfilled all his social obligations. The other and more fundamental attempt was to argue about the co-ordinate and interdependent nature of all the four puruṣārthas, or ends of human life, so that any pursuit of the one at the expense of the others was essentially a violation of dharma and led to disaster. This, of course, went against both the letter and the spirit of what the great teachers of the śramaṇa tradition in India, the Buddha and the Mahāvīra, had preached and practised. In fact, they had renounced the responsibilities of kingship at a fairly young age, and had admitted persons of all ages and from all spheres of social and political life into their monastic order. Mahāvīra admitted even children into the order, and though Buddha declined to accept the very young into the saṇgha, he allowed exceptions to the rule under special circumstances. In any case, kāma and artha as puruṣārthas in their ordinary senses, were not only strictly forbidden to the monks, but even minor violations of rules had to be expiated by undergoing the prescribed prāyaścitta after confession in an open assembly of monks. This is evident from the minute details contained in the *Ṇisīha* text of the Jains and the *Vinaya piṭaka* of the Buddhists which deal with these matters at great length.

The socio-political thinkers could obviously not accept such a position and hence had to expressly prohibit the king from leaving his kingdom and going to the forest to seek salvation like the Mahāvīra or the Buddha. The Mahābhārata explicitly says:

na vànagamanam, na sannyāso vā.[43]

and

smṛteḥ kṣatriyasya mauṇḍayādikaṁ niṣiddham..[44]

The term kṣatriya here obviously refers only to a certain kind of kṣatriya and not to all the members of the kṣatriya varṇa, as is evident from detailed discussions in the *Dharmakośa* (pp. 1047–1048 of the *Rājanītikāṇḍa*, part II). The repeated refrain here is '*nāsli siddhirakarmaṇaḥ*'. The way out suggested by some that the king retires to the forest after bequeathing the kingdom to his son does not take into account the fact that the king is warned to be careful of his own son as the latter would probably not like to wait that long to ascend the throne.

The subtler and deeper alternative to achieve the ideal of becoming a sannyāsi would be to remain in the field of action, but act differently. The *Gītā* is the classic text which propounds this alternative and Janaka the ideal exemplar who is supposed to embody this alternative. But Kṛṣṇa himself would be a better example and the Mahābhārata the text in which his multifarious activities are dwelt upon. That he is not usually treated as the exemplar *par excellence* of the alternative path may be due to the fact that he is regarded as God incarnate and hence cannot exemplify a *human* ideal. Moreover, the message of the *Gītā* itself moves away from the centrality of action to the centrality of *total* surrender to the Lord at all levels including those of emotion, will and knowledge, mediated by the display of the cosmic vision of the Godhead which inevitably silences all discussion. And, Arjuna, in any case, was a kṣatriya, always willing to engage in battle, and did not need much persuading to do what by nature and training he was himself inclined towards. After all, earlier he *had* fought his kinsmen, without feeling for a moment the hesitation which had overwhelmed him at the beginning of the battle described in the great epic. But imagine Kṛṣṇa arguing the case with the Buddha or Mahāvīra before their *mahābhiniṣakramaṇa*? Would they not have treated it as another temptation, perhaps more subtle and sophisticated than all the others they had been subjected to earlier, and which they had resisted so successfully?

The idea is not so preposterous as may seem at first sight, for there is an analogue to it in the tradition itself. Śaṁkara did not interpret Kṛṣṇa's message as advocating socio-political action for everybody, but only for Arjuna because he was a kṣatriya, and hence was not entitled to renounce the world. Only a brāhmaṇa had the *adhikāra* or the right to renunciation.

Recourse to the varṇa theory by Śaṁkara to restrict the karma-centric interpretation of the *Gītā* to particular varṇas was, however, pre-empted by both the Mahāvīra and the Buddha through their rejection of the application of the theory to human beings. It may be remembered in this context that Śaṁkara himself had rejected the stages set out in the āśrama theory by deciding to become a sannyāsī without going through the grahastha and the vānaprastha stages.

The post-Śaṁkara, non-advaitic *ācāryas* were as averse to the karma-centric interpretation of the *Gītā* as was Śaṁkara. The difference was that they did not care much for *jñāna*, or at least for his version of it and opted for *bhakti*, that is, an emotional relationship with a personal God, conceived of in diverse ways. Surprisingly, some of them, particularly those who belonged to the Vallabha Saṁpradāya, chose to remain householders and rejected sannyāsa or renunciation. Not only this, they even adopted the practice of hereditary succession to the headship of the order founded by the original ācārya, thus giving up almost the last vestige of the śramaṇa tradition which had influenced the Vedic tradition in India.

The fascination with the śramaṇic ideal, however, never ceased, nor did the problematic which it created for the socio-political thinkers of India. Yudhiṣṭhira himself had nirveda *after* gaining victory in battle in the Mahābhārata and had to be dissuaded from renouncing the kingdom he had won and retiring to the forest. The Rāmāyaṇa, on the other hand, does not show Rāma suffering from nirveda either before or after the battle with Rāvaṇa, but the absence is more than compensated for in the *Yogavāsiṣṭha* which seems to have been written not only around nirveda, but to prove that Rāma could also have nirveda. The only hero around whom no serious story of nirveda has been woven is Śrī Kṛṣṇa. The detached zest for life and action is ever present in him, though even he has his moment of frustration at the utter fruitlessness of action as in the episode in the Mahābhārata when he tells Nārada of his total helplessness in managing the affairs of the *vṛṣnis* of whom he is supposed to be the chief. The Kṛṣṇa of the Mahābhārata, however, was overshadowed by the Kṛṣṇa of the *Śrīmad Bhāgavad* and the *Gītā Govinda* and has receded to the back of the consciousness of most Indians in spite of the attempts of Bankim Chandra Chatterjee to resuscitate him in the modern context. The attempts of Tilak and Gandhi to give a karma-centric interpretation to his teachings in the *Gītā* have met with the same fate. They show, however, in their diverse ways, that the problematic still continues, and that the socio-political thinker in India has to try to come to terms with a view of man that denies or denigrates or underplays the society and the polity in which he has not only to live, whether he likes it or not, but which also shapes, to a very large extent, the way he lives and the goals he seeks as a human being.

The distinctness of the problematic of a culture can only be understood and appreciated when contrasted with the problematic of other cultures and civilizations. But first one has to articulate the specific problematic of a particular culture and then see how it compares with those of others. The problematic, however, is embedded in concepts which give it a distinctive cognitive shape, a nuance and a flavour which distinguish it from those of other civilizations. The conceptual articulation of classical Indian thought about man, society and polity, therefore, is as essential to an understanding of the problematic as is the articulation of the problematic itself. I will now attempt to articulate and explore the conceptual mapping of Indian thought regarding man, society and polity as attempted by its own thinkers in the past.

Notes

1. Some scholars have disputed that there was an attempt by any group to claim that it belonged to the kṣatriya varṇa, but there are many examples in the older texts, including the *Upaniṣads*, of an individual or a group which identified itself quite self-consciously as kṣatriya and in fact, the conflict between the kṣatriyas and the brahmins for supremacy is well known.
2. It may be interesting in this connection to note that none of the jātis that belong to the śūdra varṇa conceive of themselves as part of that varṇa. Also, by and large, all castes generally try to trace their lineage, i.e. gotra, to a primeval ṛṣi who usually belonged to the brāhmaṇa varṇa. However, there are well known cases of ṛṣis who did not belong to the brāhmaṇa varṇa. Viśvāmitra is perhaps the most well-known example.
3. There was also the idea of a dharma pariṣad which consisted only of brahmins and which was supposed to determine the prāyaścitta along with other punishments to any transgressor if the case was brought before it. Perhaps different institutions rose at different times and the different smṛti texts refer to them depending on when they were written and the context in which they raised the issue.
4. *Dharmakośa*, *Vyavahārakāṇḍa*, vol. I, p. 593.
5. The concept of prāyaścitta, even an imposed one, by a dharma pariṣad or a pancāyat, is different, though analogous to the one imposed by the regular law courts of the king where it was in lieu of a punishment and was mandatory not in a social but a legal sense.
6. It is true that the term rājan was used indiscriminately for anyone who exercised the ruling authority at any level but this does not affect my contention that while theoretically anyone who was called rājan could be a kṣatriya, not everyone who was a kṣatriya was or could be a rājan.
7. *Rāja rājateh* (*Dharmakośa*, *Rājanītikāṇḍa*, vol. IV, p. 780).
8. Ibid., p. 780.
9. Ibid., p. 780.
10. Ibid., p. 780.
11. Ibid., p. 780.
12. Ibid., p. 782.
13. *Dharmakośa*, *Rājanītikāṇḍa*, pp. 781–6.
14. Ibid., p. 782.

15. Ibid., p. 782.
16. Ibid., p. 784.
17. Ibid., p. 784.
18. Ibid., p. 378.
19. Ibid., p. 390.
20. Ibid., p. 1318.
21. *kṣīṇe kośe adharmamārgeṇāpi balāt dhaninām̐ dhanaharaṇam āpaddharmaḥ*, ibid., p. 1320.
22. Ibid., p. 835.
23. Kangle, *Arthaśāstra*, vol. III, p. 255.
24. *Arthaśāstra*, 12, 1, 10–16.
25. Kangle, vol. III, p. 256.
26. Ibid., p. 255.
27. Ibid., p. 261.
28. *pṛthivyā lābhapālanopāyaḥ śastramarthaśāstramiti. Arthaśāstra*, 15, 1, 1–2.
29. See *Dharmakośa*, *Rājanītikāṇḍa*, vol. IV, pp. 1032, 1072 and 1106.
30. Ibid., p. 1105.
31. Ibid., p. 720.
32. *ubhayapakṣābhāve rājā vibhrayād rakṣecca na svatantrā kāryā*. Ibid., p. 720.
33. Ibid., p. 726.
34. Ibid., p. 744.
35. *rājā prajā kṛtasya pāpasya sukṛtasya ca caturthāṁaśabhāk*. Ibid., p. 666.
36. *ṣaṣthaṁ bhajati bhāgaṁ tu prajā dharmeṇa pālayan.*
ṣaḍbhāgasya ca bhoktā'sau; rakṣate na prajāḥ kathāṁ. Ibid., p 666.
37. *prajāyāḥ dharmasya adharmasya ca ṣaḍabhāgaḥ rājagāmi*. Ibid., p. 707.
or
sarvato dharmaṣaḍabhāgo rāgyo bhavati rakṣataḥ.
adharmādapi ṣaḍabhāgo bhavatyasya arakṣataḥ. Ibid., p. 707.
38. *karkaṭasadharmāṇo hi janakabhakṣā rājaputrāḥ*. Ibid., p. 969.
39. *patnītaḥ antaḥpurastrībhyaśca rājarakṣanam*. Ibid., p. 973.
40. Ibid., pp. 2422–51.
41. Ibid., pp. 2754–95.
42. Ibid., p. 2431.
43. Ibid., p. 1046.
44. Ibid., p. 1047.

PART II

CHAPTER V

The Conceptual Structure of Classical Indian Thought about Man, Society and Polity

The problematic of thought is embedded within concepts which a culture uses to articulate its apprehension of reality in a particular domain, as well as in those aspects it considers more important than others. As concepts do not function in isolation but are interrelated, there is always a specific structure through which a culture simultaneously apprehends and gives shape to reality. Concepts, however, do not form just one structure; they permit diverse structures, depending upon the importance given to a particular concept within a scheme. Thinkers of different sorts take advantage of this to build different structures even within the same conceptual tradition, depending upon the direction they wish to give to thought or action in their culture. Moreover these concepts, though ostensibly remaining the same, undergo subtle changes of meaning over a period of time; and thinkers further exploit these changes to carry thought in new directions. Development in conceptual structures over a period of time, however, raises problems of a different kind from those that arise with freshly articulated conceptual structures. The preliminary task is to articulate concepts in the classical Indian tradition in relation to the contemporary situation so that modern thinkers have easy access to them. Conceptual structures grow only when they are *used* in everyday life and in the context of thought and when contemporary thinkers in India begin to articulate their experiences about man, society and polity in terms of classical thought, a new direction will be given to concepts.

In a sense, Indian thinkers from the time of Ram Mohun Roy have been trying to do this, but the focus has mostly been on matters primarily non-intellectual and non-conceptual in nature. It is generally forgotten that a culture *thinks* about itself and embodies this thinking within concepts related to each other in diverse ways, and that the cognitive enterprise of man is as important as his various other enterprises in the field of art, spiritual awareness, sensitivity development and human relations. What is needed, therefore, is to make the manifest aspects of the tradition available at a relatively *self-conscious* level so that it encourages active thought in contemporary India and elsewhere.

The streams of thought about man, society and polity are not all of a piece, and hence any attempt at their formulation is bound to be tentative and multiple in character, suggesting that alternative conceptual constructions of the tradition are possible. The idea is to lay open an area for investigation which subsequent thinkers concerned with the vast and diverse intellectual traditions of India may alter or modify in the light of their own perception and understanding of it. As most conceptualization in the Indian tradition is in the Sanskrit language, I will retain the original Sanskrit terms for these concepts, keeping in mind the Jaina and the Buddhist traditions in Prākrit or Ardha-māgadhī and Pāli. An attempt at rendering the conceptual structures in English is also made, though the reader will have to make the necessary corrections in view not only of the differences in the shades and nuances of meaning, but also differences in associations which analogous terms have in different cultures.

The concepts relating to the study and understanding of man in the Indian tradition may be approached from many directions. One such approach is to consider the differentiating characteristic of man that sets him apart from all other living beings, particularly those of the animal kingdom with whom he shows such an obvious affinity. What, in other words, is his *vyāvartaka lakṣaṇa*? The most general answer is that it is dharma, the self-conscious awareness of the distinction between 'is' and 'ought', coupled with a consciousness that the 'ought' should be desired and willed, implying thereby that man has the capacity to effectuate what he perceives or apprehends as his dharma. A well-known utterance in this regard is:

> *dharmeṇa hīnāḥ pas'ubiḥ samānāḥ.*
> (Devoid of *dharma*, man is just like other animals.)

It is therefore not rationality, as in Aristotle, but morality that differentiated man from the animals.

But as the Indian tradition accepts a realm of the gods, and the gods presumably also follow dharma, the question arises as to what differentiates man from the gods. The question, in traditional thought, does not seem to have been raised in this form. But in another context a distinction has been drawn between men and the gods in terms of *bhoga-yoni* and *karma-yoni*. The former means a form of life in which one only reaps the fruits of one's actions, while the latter is a form of life in which one can initiate new action. This is an interesting distinction, but its implications do not seem to have been rigorously worked out in the tradition. The karma-yoni, for example, has been confined to the human being, but as even human beings are supposed to reap the fruits of past actions, it should be treated as both karma-yoni and bhoga-yoni. Furthermore, if except for the form of life at the human level, all are bhoga-yonis, then life at the human level should be both logically and temporally prior to the life of the gods. This, perhaps, is implied by the story of creation in the *Puruṣa Sūkta*, but since it does not speak of the creation of man, but of the four varṇas, and as the varṇas themselves are supposed to be the result of the past karmas of individuals, it could not be accepted as supporting the logical and temporal priority of the karma-yoni over all the bhoga-yonis. There is, of course, the added problem of distinguishing between different bhoga-yonis, particularly the gods from the animals.

There is another problem with the gods as they are supposed to live in a *loka* which is not characterized by mortality. Theirs is the land of the immortals. In contrast, the world of man is ruled by death. It is, therefore, called *mṛtyu-loka*, the loka where all living beings are destined to die. But the idea of other lokas or worlds where different forms of life other than those found in this loka prevail, can normally not be construed in the plural, since all of them would be characterized by the absence of mortality in contrast with this world where death reigns supreme. But, for some unknown reason, the Indian thinkers always postulated at least three lokas, if not more. There was *deva-loka* where the gods dwelt, and *pātāla-loka* or the netherworld where presumably the asuras or the daityas lived. But then, the denizens of the netherworld would be as immortal as the gods, and the gods would lose their unique distinction from the inhabitants of the mortal world. There would thus be more than one immortal world and prayers for the world of immortality would have no unique reference and would thus lose its unambiguous character. Furthermore, if mortality is denied to residents of any loka, that loka cannot be characterized as a bhoga-yoni, as human beings will have to be born in it to have a bhoga-yoni, and once birth is admitted, death will have to be admitted as well. In a sense, this is explained by theorists who say that after having reaped the fruit of one's good actions in heaven, one has again to come back to this earth, the abode of mortality, to begin the cycle once more. But if one has to enter the deva-loka and leave it after sometime, however long, it has to be seen as *mṛtyu-loka*, as both birth and death reign there too. Perhaps, the difference is that there is only happiness there while here there is both sorrow and happiness alternatively or even together. The netherworld, then, will have to be conceived of as a loka where there is only misery and nothing else, being the counter-pole to the deva-loka or the world of the gods, where only happiness reigns. However, death will reign there also, and the idea of a loka where immortals exist will have to be given up altogether.

The gods, the asuras and man all have different dharmas, and yet how can it be so if dharma is understood in the way it is in the context of human beings? The ambiguity in the meanings of the word dharma has been utilized by some thinkers to suggest that the dharma of the asuras is to do evil, while the dharma of the gods is to do good and the dharma of human beings is to be continuously involved in a choice between good and evil. Dharma is here used in the sense of *svabhāva* or nature, a sense in which everything has its own dharma, including inanimate objects. But this is to confuse between dharma in the moral sense with dharma in the sense of an essential, natural property. Perhaps, the characteristic of dharma as a property that distinguishes human beings from all other beings in the cosmos, points to the fact that it is their inescapable nature to be aware of both good and evil, dharma and adharma, and to have the freedom to pursue either. The definition of man as a moral being is not to characterize him as being essentially moral, but rather to suggest that he is a being who inevitably *judges* all actions, whether his own or those of others, as right or wrong, evil or virtuous, or that it would have been better if the 'right' action had been done rather than the 'wrong' one, and that this consciousness does not, and cannot ever leave him for it characterizes him as a special human being and not just as this or that person.

But how does he *know* what right or wrong is, or what dharma is? For, if dharma is the feature that distinguishes humans or from other living forms it is imperative that one finds what characterizes dharma and how it is known. The classical answer to the first question is that dharma consists of *vidhi* or *niṣedha*, that is, what should be done and what should not be done. *Kartavyatā* is at the heart of it, but as hypothetical imperatives are accepted as dharma, even in the context of the Vedas, conditionality is not excluded from the notion of dharma. Not only this, the notion of dharma varies in relation to varṇa, āśrama, jāti, kula, deśa, kāla, yuga and ultimately even with the individual person concerned. There is, of course, the notion of *sādhāraṇa dharma* which is binding upon all human beings, but between svadharma and sādhāraṇa dharma there are other dharmas that affect and modify both, sometimes in contradictory ways. As Yudhiṣṭhira, the very embodiment of dharma, says in a particular context in the Mahābhārata: 'There are times when doing what is regarded as dharma becomes an act of adharma, and doing what is considered adharma becomes the real dharmic act in the situation.' But whatever the problems about the specificities of dharma in a particular context or situation, its formal character remains the same, that is, it is always an injunction or a prohibition, a vidhi or a niṣedha.

As for the question of how dharma is to be known, the answer is that it cannot be known either by perception or inference, the normal sources of knowledge. Yet, if dharma is the distinguishing feature of man and if it cannot be known by the usual processes employed for acquiring knowledge, we have to postulate a distinctive source other than perception or inference. This is usually described in terms such as *śabda* and śruti in the tradition. But it would make for better understanding if the two were kept apart and not confused with each other. Śabda need not necessarily be *apauruṣeya*, as śruti is supposed to be; it can be a *pramāṇa* for believing in the veracity of ordinary, empirical descriptive statements which śruti, both in its Jaimini and Bādarāyaṇa interpretations, is not supposed to be.

Śruti, then, is different from śabda, and though, as we shall see, both are important for a knowledge of dharma, śruti is more basic and fundamental than śabda in its wider and generally accepted meaning. But what is śruti, and why is it supposed to give us knowledge of dharma? A new concept is introduced at this stage to characterize an aspect of dharma that makes it specifically fit to be known by śruti. This is the concept of *adṛṣṭa*, something that cannot be apprehendid by the senses or the reason. Dharma is supposed to have this character of adṛṣṭa in two senses; the first may be put in modern terminology and may appear to the modern mind as more fundamental. This is the non derivability of 'ought' from 'is'. If this is accepted, it will easily be seen why dharma which consists of 'do's' and 'don'ts', or vidhi and niṣedha, cannot be perceived, as it is not a sensible object or derived from it through any reasoning, unless there be somewhere in the premises at least one premise which itself is imperative in nature. Śruti, in this perspective, would be that foundational imperative or set of imperatives from which all other imperatives are derived. This is somewhat akin to the notion of *grundnorm* formulated by Kelsen, a status which is generally accorded to the constitution of a country in the constitutional law, or is regarded as natural law in the context of law in general.

The other aspect of adṛṣṭa relates to what may be called non-empirical causality, that is, where the assertion of *kāraṇatā* is of such a nature that it cannot, in principle, be verified in the usual way and yet whose postulation is required to make the world morally intelligible to actors who feel obliged to act according to the demands of dharma. This is the problem of the relation between 'morality' and 'happiness' in Kantian terms, or between *yajña* and *svarga* in the language of Jaimini. There are, of course, enormous, even radical, differences between the two, but unless one sees the basic similarity between them, one would miss the problem which the ancient thinker was trying to solve by bringing in the notions of adṛṣṭa and *apūrva* in this connection. Kant, along with many others before and after him, had to take recourse to the idea of God to solve the insoluble problem. Not so the hard-core mīmāṁsaka in the Indian tradition. He saw quite clearly that to bring in God would be to compromise the absolute unconditionality and primacy of dharma. This was literally confirmed by the Lord himself for, when revealing the last and highest secret to Arjuna, He advised him to give up *all* dharmas and take recourse in Him alone. The source of dharma, therefore, cannot be any human or divine authority for then that authority would become superior to dharma, whether or not it declares itself to be so.

Action, according to dharma, must lead to a *phala* or result which is acceptable to the 'moral sensibility' of man, even though dharma is not followed for the sake of that result, and in actual fact is seldom seen to be associated with it. The discussion in *Mīmāṁsā* mainly revolves around the connection between yajña and svarga, as it considers yajña to be the paradigm of all injunctive action. But as both svarga and the supposed causality which leads to it are both adṛṣṭa, that is, not obvious to either perception or reasoning, one has to accept it on other grounds which, according to it, is the śruti. The identification of the śruti with the Veda is a further step, the analytical separateness of which becomes obvious only when one moves to the āgamic traditions of India which argue for an *āgama-prāmaṇya* instead of the *śruti-prāmaṇya* of the Vedic tradition. Even within the orthodox *Mīmāṁsā* tradition, there is the problem of how to interpret the Vedic injunction of *svargakāmo yajeta*, that is, whether it should be treated as a hypothetical injunction or a categorical one. In other words, is one supposed to perform the relevant yajña if one desires to attain svarga, or ought one to desire to attain heaven and hence perform the yajña prescribed in the Vedic texts? But it is not clear whether one could attain svarga if one only observed the yama and the niyama and did not perform the yajña, or if one only performed the yajña without observing the yama and the niyama, which are supposed to be an important constituent of dharma. In fact, it is not clear what role the wider notion of dharma, including the yama and the niyama, plays in the *Mīmāṁsā* tradition and what relation it has to the notion of yajña. In other words, can one conceive of dharma without yajña, and if one can do so what role would śruti have in the determination of dharma.

Śruti, however, is regarded in the tradition as the *only* source of acquiring knowledge about dharma. Manu cites three other sources which he calls *smṛti*, *sadācāra* and *ātma-tuṣṭi*. There is some difference of opinion as to whether they should be taken in descending or ascending order of authority, or as co-ordinate in character. But whatever the difference of opinion in this regard, what is worthy of note is that something had to be *added* to the śruti for acquiring knowledge of dharma, and this included not only examples from the past and the present, but also one's own conscience or judgment or intuition regarding the matter. In fact, the tradition itself refers not only to śruti as the source of dharma, but also to something analogous to ātma-tuṣṭi in the well-known statement *dharmasya tattvaṃ nihitaṃ guhāyāṃ*, that is, the essence of dharma is contained in the heart of man himself. The term 'ātma-tuṣṭi' itself may be understood in three different senses. The first, and the obvious one, is that ultimately each individual has to judge and decide for himself what dharma really is. On the other hand, it may also be taken to mean that in order to discern what dharma is, a person has to ask himself if it fulfils his being in an essential sense or not. This is perhaps the direction that the author of the *Vaiśesika Śutras* wanted to give to the discussion by defining dharma as that which leads to both *abhyudaya* and *niḥśreyasa*. The well-known saying *atmārthe prithvīṁ tyajeta* points in the same direction.[1]

The source of knowledge of dharma, the distinguishing feature of man, may thus be found in some transcendental internality as ātma-tuṣṭi, but it may also be understood not in any specific context or as that which performs any specific function but as the consequence of the exercise of a faculty that enables discrimination between right and wrong, good and bad, dharma and adharma, that is, what ought to be done and what ought not to be done. *Viveka* is the name given to this faculty in the Indian tradition and the word usually means 'to discriminate' and refers to the faculty of discrimination which is a feature of buddhi or reason in man. But reason in the Indian tradition is primarily supposed to discriminate between *sat* and *asat*, or the real and the unreal, the true and the false, and not between dharma and adharma as is required in this context. The bringing in of the faculty of buddhi with the function of viveka into the picture, gives not only primacy to metaphysical issues over ethical ones, but also gives a radical reorientation to Indian thinking about dharma and adharma by linking them to considerations of what is real and what is unreal. This, however, establishes the primacy of knowledge over action, or of jñāna over karma and leads to the problem of the interrelation between the two.

To think of man as primarily functioning on the basis of knowledge takes us in a direction different from that to which the karma-centric thought about man takes a particular culture. The former leads to an exploration of the nature of perception and the jñānendriyas on which it is based along with the problem of error or illusion and hallucination on the one hand, and of memory, dream and śābda-bodha or verbal knowledge, on the other. There is also the co-ordinate problem of the ontological status of the object of erroneous cognition, particularly at the perceptual level. At a still deeper level, there is the problem of whether what is 'ultimately real' or 'really real' can be 'known' by ordinary processes of perception and inference, on the analogy of the answer to the question of what ought to be done, which cannot be found either through perception or inference. Alternatively, one may postulate a different faculty other than the usual ones of perception, memory and inference, for acquiring knowledge of that which is ultimately real and treat that knowledge as being radically different in man from all the other types of knowledge that he acquires through the usual faculties common to everybody.

Both these alternatives have been adopted in the jñāna-centric understanding of man in the Indian tradition. The Bādarāyaṇa tradition argues for the source of knowledge of the ultimately real to be in the śruti alone, the śruti being understood primarily as the *Upaniṣads*, while all traditions of spiritual sādhanā postulate, implicitly or explicitly, a faculty in man which, when aroused, apprehends that which is ultimately real. The apprehension may be simultaneous with an apprehension of the unreality of that which is known through the other faculties or may lend it a deeper, richer and fuller dimension, transforming it in the light of knowledge of that ultimate reality. The internal faculty hidden in the innermost recesses of one's being and the śruti revealing the ultimate truth about what is really real or what ought to be done may be seen as co-ordinate and it may be said that the latter can be understood only through the former, as the former is the real source of the latter. But then the possibility of new śrutis coming into being through the perennial source which lies in the very being of man would have to be admitted. The Indian tradition has not hesitated to draw this conclusion, but there has always been tension between those who have opted for the notion of a closed, external śruti in any form whatsoever, and those who have emphasized the innermost sources in the heart of man for the apprehension of what is real on the one hand and what should be regarded as right in one's conduct, on the other.

The apprehension of the 'really real' or the *satyasya satyam* and that which is known in the tradition as dharma, however, leads in different directions. Dharma is essentially concerned with action, while the apprehension of that which is ultimately real has little to do with action, except perhaps as a means of attaining that apprehension. The apprehension of dharma or the viveka between dharma and adharma results, however, in only a necessary condition of the dharmic action; it is not its sufficient condition. The well-known statement of Duryodhana in the Mahābhārata that though he knows what dharma is, he has no inclination towards it, and that though he knows that what he is doing is adharma, he cannot refrain from doing it, attests to this fact.[2] The terms used in this context are *pravṛtti* and *nivṛtti* which seem to emphasize habitual inclination or disinclination, rather than *saṁkalpa* (will) or *prayatna* (effort) on his part to avoid the latter and do the former. It is his svabhāva or nature that impels him to act thus, and as Kṛṣṇa said in the *Gita* :

> *prakṛtiṁ yānti bhūtāni, nigrah kiṁ karisyati.*[3]

But if *manusya-yoni* is to be treated as a karma-yoni, distinct from all others considered to be only bhoga-yonis, some freedom has to be granted to human beings to go against their pravṛtti or prakṛti, particularly if it leads them to do what is wrong and undesirable. The relation of viveka to saṁkalpa and prayatna, and of these to svātantrya or freedom have not been clearly formulated or discussed in the Indian tradition. But there can be little doubt that these are the contexts in which the capacity for free and independent decision has been denied to some on the ground that one is not able to determine what is right or wrong, that is, dharma or adharma, because to be swayed or ruled by desire is the very nature of one's being. In this context, Dr Mukund Lath has drawn our attention to the discussion about women in the tradition.[4] According to him, as a woman was regarded by her very nature to be *kāmopahatā*, that is, swayed by desire, by many Indian thinkers, she was not considered svatantrā, that is, capable of taking decisions on her own. Also, on this ground he denies her having any puruṣārtha of her own. Surprisingly, it was the *gaṇikā*, or the courtesan, who was regarded as svatantrā, according to Dr Lath. But even if she was not kāmopahatā, for she could not pursue her profession if she were that, she had to be *arthopahatā*, that is, swayed totally by considerations of acquiring wealth and this means being swayed as much by desire as by anything else. Perhaps, what Dr Lath wants to say is that she is not swayed by *moha* as she has no familial attachments, but then this would not distinguish women from men in any fundamental sense, as he wants to do. Man can be as *mohāndha*, that is, blinded by attachment, as women, and as far as the classical literary texts in Sanskrit are concerned, they have more examples of men being blinded by attachment and passion than women.

The denial of the independent pursuit of puruṣārtha to women, according to Dr Lath, is based on the ground that, except for the gaṇikā, they generally did not have an independent profession of their own. This is corroborated to some extent by the strange story in the *Nātyaśāstra* where a special class of women had to be created to dance the *Kaiśikī Vṛtti*, as it could not be danced by women of ordinary households or the daughters of sages. The flourishing of arts such as singing and dancing amongst the courtesans and *devadāsīs* seems to attest to this to a certain extent. But then artha would become the *parama* puruṣārtha which would ensure that independence without which no other puruṣārtha could be pursued at all. On the other hand, the tradition cannot be construed as having denied complete freedom or independence to women as it has prescribed *vidhi-niṣedha*, that is, injunctions and prohibitions for them. As Pandit Laxman Shastri Joshi pointed out to Dr Lath in a private discussion, one who is the subject of injunctions and prohibitions cannot but be regarded as free or independent in some sense or another.

The doctrine of puruṣārtha points to both the empirical and transcendental nature of man as it includes not only dharma and mokṣa as puruṣārthas, but also artha and kāma amongst the legitimate ends which man ought to pursue if he is to fulfil his nature as a human being. This empirical-transcendental nature of a human being leads to an analysis in terms of his body, mind, intellect and ego or the sense of 'I' on the one hand, and consciousness or self or puruṣa or ātman, on the other. There is a further division of *sthūla* and *sūkṣama* or gross and subtle at almost all levels from the body to the ego or the 'I', on the one hand, and between sāttvika, rājasika and tāmasika, deriving from the threefold *sāṁkhyan* classification of prakṛti, on the other. As for consciousness or *cit*, it can perhaps be characterized both in terms of sāttvika, rājasika and tāmasika, and sthūla and sūkṣama, even though in the strict sāṁkhyan sense it would not be correct to do so. But as we are not using the terms in their strict, system-specific sense, it may not be misleading to do so. In fact, the tradition itself is forced to make a distinction between the embodied self or the self in bondage and the self in its pure state, that is, when it is free or is established in its own nature. Many of the characteristics which apply to it in its former state do not and cannot apply to it in the latter state. But this introduces a strange ambivalence in the treatment, for while life at the human level is exalted above all others as it is the only yoni which is karma-yoni, the embodied state itself is regarded as a state of bondage. To be embodied is to be a *jīva*, and to be a jīva is, by definition, to be in a state characterized by avidyā which is supposed to be the cause of bondage.

The complex of cit, *ahaṁkāra* or the sense of ego, buddhi or intellect, manasa or mind, and the *indriyas* or the senses, constitutes the jīva or the embodied being which at the human level is differentiated by the capacity to discriminate between dharma and adharma, sat and asat, and *nitya* and *anitya*. It is born and it dies, like all beings in the world, and like other living beings is capable of feeling sukha and duhkha, that is, pleasure and pain, and like them, seeks the former and shuns the latter. But, unlike all other beings, the viveka that he alone has, coupled with the fact that he enjoys a karma-yoni which gives him the freedom to seek not only pleasure but that which is sat, nitya and dharmic in nature, gives him a unique status envied by all other beings in the universe. But there is a deep fundamental cleavage at the very centre of his being not only between the natural impulse to seek kāma or pleasure in all its forms, and the awareness of dharma and the necessary obligation to seek it even at the expense of kāma, but also between the consciousness of dharma with its obligations to all other beings in the universe and the awareness of that which alone is nitya and sat, and hence worthy of being continuously dwelt upon, adored, and being one with. There is little activity involved in the pursuit of the latter; rather, it is all a matter of consciousness, what one attends to or lives with. Most action can only be a distraction in such a situation.

* * *

The roster of concepts that I have drawn from the tradition and used until now for understanding and articulating human reality in classical Indian thought may be enumerated as follows:

(1) dharma (2) bhoga-yoni (3) karma-yoni (4) loka (5) karma (6) varṇa (7) deva-loka (8) mṛtyu-loka (9) pātāla-loka (10) svabhāva (11) adharma (12) vidhi (13) niṣedha (14) iti-kartavyatā (15) āśrama (16) jāti (17) kula (18) deśa (19) kāla (20) yuga (21) sādhāraṇa dharma (22) svadharma (23) śabda (24) śruti (25) apauruṣeya (26) adṛṣṭa (27) kāraṇatā (28) yajña (29) svarga (30) āgama (31) āgama-prāmāṇya (32) śruti-prāmāṇya (33) yama (34) niyama (35) smṛti (36) sadācāra (37) ātma-tuṣṭi (38) tattva (39) guhā (40) abhyudaya (41) niḥśreyasa (42) ātmā (43) buddhi (44) sat (45) asat (46) viveka (47) jñāna (48) jñānendriya (49) śābda-bodha (50) sādhanā (51) satyasya satyam (52) pravṛtti (53) nivṛtti (54) saṁkalpa (55) prayatna (56) svabhāva (57) nigraha (58) manuṣya-yoni (59) svātantrya (60) kāmopahatā (61) puruṣārtha (62) gaṇikā (63) arthopahatā (64) moha (65) mohāndha (66) kaiśikī-vṛtti (67) parama puruṣārtha (68) mokṣa (69) artha (70) puruṣa (71) sthūla (72) sūkṣama (73) sāttvika

(74) rājasika (75) tāmasika (76) prakṛti (77) jīva (78) avidyā (79) cit (80) ahaṁkāra (81) manas (82) indriya (83) nitya (84) anitya (85) sukha (86) duḥkha.

This is a long, formidable list of terms which have been used in the previous pages. They are not given in the order in which they have appeared in the discussion, nor has there been an attempt to impose any order in their listing. But now that we have all of them together, we can see patterns and interrelationships among them. For example, dharma, iti-kartavyatā, karma, adṛṣṭa, yama, niyama, sadācāra, saṅkalpa, prayatna, svātantrya, puruṣārtha, karmendriya and ahaṁkāra are closely related to each other. One may say that dharma in the sense of *iti-kartavyatā* is the central puruṣārtha as it is the vyāvartaka laksaṇa of human beings, and that it is inconceivable without svātantrya, saṁkalpa, prayatna, karmendriyas and ahaṁkāra in the sense that 'I have to do this' or 'I ought to do that'. Dharma in the sense of iti-kartavyatā, however, seems to be intrinsically and inalienably plural in character. Thus we have not only the sādhāraṇa dharma which is supposed to be binding on all human beings by virtue of the fact that they *are* human beings, but also yuga dharma, varṇa dharma, jāti dharma and ultimately svadharma. This may be taken as the concretization of what ought to be done by a particular person in a specific situation at a given place and time. This would be called 'casuistry' in the western intellectual tradition, but the Indian thinker never saw anything strange in the universal, the particular and the individual being indissolubly linked together at the level of action, though he was aware that ultimately it is the individual who has to decide and take the responsibility for what he does. The concept of svadharma and ātma-tuṣṭi not only emphasized this, but the very notion of karma-yoni itself would not be possible without postulating the locus of dharmic action in the individual. There are, of course, those who argue that svadharma is nothing else but varṇa dharma itself, but they forget that what concretely exists is not varṇa but jāti and the ascription of jātis to a particular varṇa is not only arbitrary and changes with time, but does not destroy the differences between these jāti dharmas even if they are considered to belong to the same varṇa. Furthermore, if svadharma were to mean the same as varṇa dharma its separate mention would be redundant.

It is, therefore, closer to svabhāva and in fact may be regarded as derived from it. Also, ātma-tuṣṭi as an independent criterion for knowing whether one is really pursuing dharma or not would, if the objection were correct, make no sense.

The feeling of svatva with respect to karma and the sense of ahaṁ for which the vidhi-niṣedha are meant and on whom the real *obligatoriness* rests and on whose saṁkalpa and prayatna, the fulfilment of dharma depends would, thus, be central in this way of seeing man. Dharma, in the case of human beings, would then not mean what it means in the case of all other beings; their very nature compels them to bring into being what is destined. Their *kāranatā* or causal potency or efficacy is, so to say, fixed. In man's case, on the other hand, there is no fixed kāraṇatā, as he has kartṛtva because he is in the karma-yoni. Yet, the svatva of this kartṛtva, or what is regarded as his iti-kartavyatā is determined not only by all the different dimensions of his being, denoted by the terms varṇa, jāti, kula, āśrama, deśa and kāla, but also by the yuga, that is, the cosmic cycle in which he happens to be born. The theory of the yugas seems central to the practice of dharma, as certain things, permitted in other yugas, are expressly prohibited in kali-yuga. Surprisingly, there is no attempt to give a list of activities which were prohibited in other yugas but are permitted in the kali-yuga.

Some of the concepts listed above show an intrinsic binary opposition, whereas others show a tripartite division which does not have anything intrinsic about it, while still others have a fourfold nature which appears to be as arbitrary as anything else. Dharma-adharma, for example, is such a binary pair and so also are nitya-anitya or sat-asat; sāttvika, rājasika and tāmasika form a tripartite division deriving from the sāṁkhyan classification of the guṇas of prakṛti. There are also three lokas: svarga-loka, mṛtyu-loka and pātāla-loka. The former two are also known as deva-loka and manuṣya-loka. As for the fourfold division, we have the four yugas, the four varṇas, the four āśramas, the four puruṣārthas, the four sources of the knowledge of dharma. The sources of ultimate authority regarding both what is dharma and what is sat or satyasya satyaṁ are supposed to be two, that is, śruti or nigama and āgama, and thus we have śruti-prāmāṇya and āgama-prāmāṇya. There is the two-fold distinction between bhoga-yoni and karma yoni, though the latter does not exclude the former. There is also the distinction between *pauruṣeya* and apauruṣeya, dṛṣṭa and adṛṣṭa, vidhi and niṣedha, yama and niyama, pravṛtti and nivṛtti, sthūla and sūkṣama, cit and acit, sukha and duḥkha, vidyā and avidyā.

The problem with respect to all binary divisions is whether they should be treated as clear-cut dichotomous divisions or as two poles of a continuum which are ideal limits, all the concrete existing examples sharing the characteristics of both, lying as they do somewhere in between. On the other hand, the problem with a tripartite or fourfold division is that one may ask as to why only three or four, and why not more? The problem or continuity versus discreteness would, of course, plague all divisions. There is the added problem of what has been called *lāghava* and *gaurava* in the Indian tradition, that is, the problem of parsimony or economy in thinking about things.

Yet another important question regarding these distinctions concerns the differences in the realms they relate to and whether they are primarily descriptive or explanatory in character. The distinction between dharma and adharma, for example, seems to primarily be in the realm of action, while that of nitya and anitya is in the realm of the objects cognized. The division between sukha and duḥkha relates neither to action nor to knowledge, but to the realm of feeling. But not all of these dichotomies seem to characterize our experience in the same way, nor can their existential status in our experience be regarded as identical. Pleasure and pain, or happiness and suffering seem equally to be facts of experience, but it will be difficult to say the same of nitya and anitya, or the permanent and the transitory. Nothing in experience seems to be nitya; in fact, not only does the content of consciousness, but also the act of consciousness or rather consciousness itself seems to fluctuate all the time. Kant grasped this aspect of consciousness in his doctrine of time as being a form of inner sensibility, for even if one were to accept the experienced fact of a dṛṣṭā, or witness consciousness, which Indian thought has emphasized all the time, the relation between that consciousness and the usual consciousness of objects would itself be perpetually fluctuating in character. Perhaps, they are not *two* consciousnesses as the two-bird image in the *Upaniṣads* and earlier in the Vedas themselves seems to imply, but only two aspects of the same consciousness. But even in the latter case, the problem of the relationship between the two aspects would remain.

The problematic nature of the concept of nitya and its apparent constructional character as against both sukha and duḥkha in the other dichotomy, gets even more complicated when contrasted with, say, the dharma-adharma dichotomy. Are dharma or adharma characteristics of experiences at all? And, if they are supposed to characterize action, one could ask in what sense they can be said to do so. Also, is adharma merely an *abhāva* of dharma, or is it something more than that? In case we choose the latter alternative, we will have a tripartite division consisting of dharma, dharmābhāva and adharma. Adharma would then be something as positive as dharma, though, of course, negative in character.

The use of abhāva as a negative operator on the analogy of 'not' in modern logic reveals whether the so-called binary division is really binary or not. Gadādhara, the famous Indian logician, had used the technique to show in his well-known work on *vyutpattivādaḥ* that *abheda* could not be understood as *bhedābhāva* or the abhāva of bheda. The reason he gives for the inadequacy of this translation is the impossibility of the absence of bheda or difference anywhere as, to use the nyāya technical terminology, it is *kevalānvayī*, that is, present everywhere. Gadādhara, however, did not realize the importance and implications of his argument. He was in such a hurry to understand and explicate the notion of *saṁsargatā* through which śābdabodha occurs, according to him, that he forgot that if abheda cannot be defined as bhedābhāva, there are not only two categories of bheda and abheda, but a third one which is neither bheda nor abheda. Nor did he see that in denying the correctness or adequacy of the translation of abheda as bhedābhāva he was establishing a powerful criterion for testing the correctness of all binary opposites.

In a sense, all finite classifications claiming exclusive disjunction may be tested for their adequacy in the same way; all of them can be treated as examples of binary opposition by bracketing all the other alternatives and treating them as single for logical purposes. Ultimately, the problem is of total exclusion and collective exhaustion that defines the logical nature of the relationship and not their number or particular specificity. But the presuppositions of total exclusion and collective exhaustion may be challenged by hypotheses of continuum and of intrinsic, inexhaustible, and infinite variety which would lead in a different, metaphysical direction. The objection could certainly be made that the two counter-hypotheses would make the cognitive enterprise impossible in principle, as no knowledge is possible if the principle of limited variety along with some sort of 'limited exclusion' is not accepted. But even if one were to accept such a contention, it would necessitate that the so-called transcendental preconditions of the cognitive enterprise be true of whatever is also 'real'. But epistemological conditions need not dictate or determine what 'is' in the world. Alternatively or concurrently, we may assume that there is a mode of apprehension inherent in man appropriate to all that is 'real' and that what escapes the conceptual, categorical mode of cognition is apprehended some other way. In any case, the continuum is not unknown to science, having been effectively taken care of since the invention of the differential calculus. As for the problem of 'infinite variety', at any given moment in space and time, this cannot but be finite in number; even the new 'specificities' are bound to be limited in number.

But whatever the problems at the theoretical level, there is no doubt that the Gadādhara strategy can be effectively applied to determine the adequacy of any classificatory division which a culture formulates to articulate its understanding of nature or society. Besides this, however, we also have to distinguish between the particular specificities which a culture formulates and the generalized category under which these specificities are supposed to obtain. The category of puruṣārtha, for example, is supposed to include dharma, artha, kāma and mokṣa. There is some dispute about whether or not there were originally only three puruṣārthas, and mokṣa as the fourth one was added later. That bhakti was added as another puruṣārtha still later, is seldom discussed by thinkers on the subject. Nor is its explicit conflict with mokṣa as a parama puruṣārtha ever mentioned. This, of course, suggests that the tradition was not averse to adding a new puruṣārtha to the already accepted list, if the older list did not contain new goals. The conflict between the new puruṣārtha and the old ones is evident in the history of Indian thought about puruṣārtha but has been suppressed, as the current consciousness is afraid of finding any deep-seated foundational conflict therein, for it would then be *forced* to think for itself and make choices, or even to consider anew the problem independently of the way the tradition tried to formulate or solve it.

We can thus conceive of a theory of puruṣārtha totally independent of the traditional classifications of dharma, artha, kāma, mokṣa and bhakti, challenging us to view afresh our own experiences and that of humanity in different cultures and civilizations to determine what makes life meaningful and what ends are really worthwhile for man to pursue. This can also be done with respect to the other major categorizations such as varṇa which need not be tied to the usual sub-divisions in terms of brāhmaṇa, kṣatriya, vaiśya and śūdra. The point obviously is that our thinking need not be constricted by the traditional formulations under these heads; we should feel free to add or subtract or even to draw up a totally different list which may have nothing to do with the old one accepted unquestioningly since very early times. There is, so to say, no analytical relationship between the idea of puruṣārtha and the specific puruṣārthas usually mentioned under it or varṇa and the varṇas included therein. Strangely, it is only the theorist who talks about varṇa in the Indian tradition, knowing full well that what actually exists are the jātis which are in constant struggle with one another. Why something similar has not happened with respect to the theory of puruṣārtha where everyone continues to talk of the four puruṣārthas and not of anything else even at the ground level, should be the subject of discussion and reflection.

In any case, before we exercise the freedom granted to us by the delinking of the generalized category from the specific ones generally included under it, or employ the Gadādhara strategy to test the adequacy of those usually accepted by thinkers in the tradition, it would be advisable to note the ones missing from our list. Even a cursory look at the list reveals that it does not contain such commonly known notions as *pāpa* and *puṇya*, *śubha* and *aśubha*, *śuddha* and *aśuddha*, *svarga* and *naraka*, *janma* and *maraṇa*, etc. These concepts take us into a different world where we talk not of dharma and adharma, but of pāpa and puṇya which translate the earlier concepts into an individual calculus of merit and demerit accumulated as in a bank account, whose fruit is svarga or naraka, that is, heaven or hell. Objects are pure or impure, that is, śuddha or aśuddha–a category tangential to the usual one of sāttvika, rājasika and tāmasika. The categories of śubha and aśubha take us in an entirely different direction. They seem to be concerned with the essential uncertainty of all action and the attempt to read the signs to determine which way the wind blows, or rather, is likely to blow.

We also do not have such terms as *ṛṇa* or debt, *ācāra* or conduct, *vicāra* or thought, *anubhava* or experience, *anugraha* or grace, bhakti or devotion, *ātmajñāna* or self-knowledge, gṛhastha or householder, sannyāsa or renunciation, *ihaloka* or this world, *paraloka* or the other world, prāyaścitta or penance, *preyasa* and *śreyasa*, *śakti*, *saṁskṛta*, tapas, *śraddhā*, *aśraddhā*, *tarpana*, *śuci*, *aśuci*, *dṛvya*, dakṣiṇā, yajamāna, *purohita*, etc. The list could obviously be extended, but as we are primarily interested in apprehending the conceptual structures which have shaped Indian thought about man, society and polity, there would be little point in doing so, unless we have really missed some crucial concepts which should be taken into account. We may thus attempt alternative arrangements of these concepts to see what different patterns emerge in classical Indian thought about man, and how we can take them further into the contemporary context to include man's rich and varied experiences in other cultures and civilizations.

We may start with, say, the centrality of the term puruṣa and see how it gives rise to, and is related to, other concepts in the tradition. The term puruṣa naturally gives rise to puruṣārtha. The realms of puruṣārtha may, however, be seen in terms of the analysis of the basic dimensions within which puruṣa is viewed. If we conceive of puruṣa as one who has an embodied existence and yet has a transcendent dimension, we will see two different types of puruṣārtha, one relating to vyavahāra and the other to *parmārtha*. The puruṣārtha relating to vyavahāra of the embodied self will be abhyudaya, while the one relating to parmārtha will be *apavarga* or niḥśreyasa. Surprisingly, it is only Kaṇāda who has said that dharma, in his sense of the term, incorporates both. Abhyudaya, however, is not all of a piece, and if the puruṣārtha of the embodied puruṣa is to be thought of, then the way embodiment is conceived of or analysed will determine how one would conceive of abhyudaya with respect to each of them as a puruṣārtha separately. And if abhyudaya and niḥśreyasa, or vyavahāra and parmārtha are seen as conflicting or contradictory, the puruṣārtha of each embodied aspect or level would also have to be seen in terms not only of its own abhyudaya and niḥśreyasa, but also in the way it contributes to the abhyudaya and niḥśreyasa of others and of the whole of which they all presumably form a part in an integrated manner.

To think of the puruṣārtha of each of the parts or aspects of an embodied puruṣa, and of them in interrelationship, raises the question of what these parts or aspects are in terms of which we analyse or conceive of the embodied puruṣa. The usual analysis is in terms of the body, mind, intellect or reason and ego. The question would then arise as to what the puruṣārtha of each of these separately is as well as in relationship with others. In other words, what is the puruṣārtha of the *śarīra*, the manas, the buddhi and the ahaṁkāra individually and in relationship to one another?

The puruṣārtha of the body may easily be regarded as health or *ārogya* and the science of medicine or *āyurveda* may be considered to help in its achievement. However, the analysis of the body itself may differ as well as the concept of the ideal puruṣārtha with respect to it. The puruṣārtha of a girl competing in a beauty contest can hardly be the same as that of a girl competing in a swimming or diving contest. The same holds true for men, and it is not only that bodily strength and skills are different from bodily health, but that the strength and the skills themselves are of different kinds. Even in the classical Indian thought on the subject, there is a difference between the way Suśruta or Caraka conceived of the body and the way *haṭha yoga* or *tantra yoga* conceived of it. If we think of Bharata's *Nāṭya-śāstra* we will understand how differently he conceives of each part of the body and all the possible combinations of movements it can make. Or we may think of the *Saṅgītaratnākara* of Śāraṅgadeva where he conceives of the body as a physical instrument for the production of sound and sound-combinations.

This may appear to be unnecessarily complicating a fairly simple thing, and in a certain sense it is. It would be fairly reasonable to assume that health is the primary or foundational puruṣārtha for the body, and that all the others are supervening or meant only for those who are striving to attain some specific skills of the body. But what, then, would the puruṣārthas of the mind be, and would they display the same distinction between mental health and the other skills of the mind? But the first, and perhaps the most difficult problem with the mind is to know what it is. For, unless we have some reasonable idea of what it is, how can we think about its puruṣārtha? On the one hand, it seems to be too tied to bodily states while, on the other, it seems to have a private life of its own. It is also so closely identified with consciousness and self-consciousness, on the one hand, and its usual tripartite division into knowing, feeling and willing, on the other, that it is difficult to dissociate it from these. But it is desirable for the sake of intellectual and existential clarity to do so. One has to distinguish consciousness, which is involved in very strange and complex ways at all levels of existence, from life-processes on the one hand and even inanimate matter, on the other. The relationship between consciousness and self-consciousness has also to be explored separately, and the problem of their puruṣārtha formulated independently from the one about the body or the mind or the buddhi or the ahaṁkāra. The problem of consciousness seems tangential to all these, though it certainly is more central and foundational. The problem of self-consciousness, on the other hand, appears to plunge one into the unfathomable and unsolvable mystery of Being itself which, though closest to one in a sense, seems farthest in another. The usual tripartite division into knowing, feeling and willing, on the other hand, seems more a characteristic of consciousness than of the mind, though they are ascribed to the latter when it is used in an omnibus sense to include everything under it except the material, as in Descartes. But in the context of the theory of puruṣārtha, the issue would be what the puruṣārtha of knowing or feeling or willing is, if we do accept these as legitimately distinguishable aspects of consciousness. But first it would be better to explore what we understand by mind or manas and what its possible puruṣārtha is if we understand it in a certain way.

Manas or mind may be regarded as desire when it is relatively free from its biological roots in the body and becomes a subject of elaboration by the imagination or fancy. This, I suggest, is the real meaning of kāma in the tradition which also explains to some extent its close relation to physical love as well as its transcendence over it. Another name for kāma is *manasija*, that is, one born of the mind or manas. This provides some justification for the meaning of manas that I have suggested. The world of desire, built from fancy and imagination, which makes man dream of and seek the elusive and the illusory in a sensuous world, is a world that the mind creates from experiences and sense-perceptions. It is this secondary world in which man usually lives and experiences happiness and frustrations.

What could the puruṣārtha of this kāma born of the mind be which creates a world of desires of such variegated hues, each more insistent, demanding and complex than the other? The psychology of the world of desire has been explored thoroughly in the Indian tradition, but it has mainly centred around its intrinsic instability and the way it essentially leads to bondage which is related to the illusion that the fulfilment of desire would lead to its cessation also. It is not clear, however, why one should want any desire to cease, or why desire should be fulfilled in such a way that it should never arise again. The desire for knowledge, for example, is unending where success normally leads to the raising of new questions and problems which demand their own answers and solutions. This situation is healthy and one would not have it otherwise. The same is true of creativity in the field of art or literature. No one would think it desirable, for example, if Kālidāsa had been satisfied with writing just one play or *kāvya*. In fact, we feel disappointed that, like Shakespeare, he did not write more plays than the three usually ascribed to him.

These are, of course, desires of a kind that belong to what are usually regarded as subtler levels of the personality. But even the grosser desires as mediated and transformed through the imaginative powers of the mind, have a sort of infinity, complexity and growth built into them which is indicated by the term '*abhyudaya*' in the tradition and which normally no one thinks or feels to be intrinsically undesirable. The desire for a higher state of consciousness or of a living relationship with nature or the transcendent, is perhaps too radically different to be ascribed to the mind, and to be thus grouped with these others in one category.

But while the puruṣārtha of manas may be said to be the world of desire with its infinite variety and complexity, there can be little doubt that there is an aspect of it which leads to psychic bondage of the worst kind. This occurs when one is driven by desire, or is obsessed by it, or cannot be free of it even when one wants to be. The word for such a state in the tradition is *tṛṣṇā*, and the puruṣārtha of manas would then be to ensure that kāma which is its product does not become tṛṣṇā, which is just the opposite. The *Gītā* sees this as the central issue in the phenomenon of desire and suggests a number of strategies to ensure that desire does not become the cause of bondage. Unfortunately, the thinking in the *Gītā* regarding this problem has been almost exclusively identified with niṣkāma karma usually interpreted as action undertaken without the desire for the fruits of action. The term, however, is misleading in more ways than one. First, it suggests that it is kāma which is at the root of the trouble and secondly, it suggests that there can be deliberate, willed, voluntary action which is not undertaken for the achievement of some particular specific result and thirdly, that the only relevant consideration in action is the effect it has on one's own-consciousness and not on anybody else's. These are not only questionable presuppositions but are also unnecessary in the context of what the *Gītā* has to say. Another word is in fact used which better conveys the meaning of niṣkāma. This word is *niḥsaṅga*, which does not connote that an action is not undertaken for the sake of the desired result, but only that if the result is not achieved, one is not unduly troubled or perturbed. In the sphere of action, it is the counterpart of a healthy, sceptical attitude to one's own opinions and hypotheses which is considered desirable in the field of knowledge. 'Non-attachment' in the field of action is thus the counterpart of 'non-attachment' in the field of knowledge which manifests itself in self-reflective doubt or scepticism which accompanies, or ought to accompany, all forms of knowledge.

At a deeper level, the concepts of non-involvement and non-attachment may be said to derive from the fact that the 'object' at all levels is really independent of the 'subject', and that there are a plurality of subjects, each as much a subject as the other. The non-attachment and non-involvement are thus a consequence of the recognition that the others are really other, that there are a plurality of real, independent actors in the situation and that one is only 'one' amongst the myriad factors affecting both knowledge and action. At a still deeper level, the very phenomenon of self-consciousness ensures, at least to a certain extent, that a certain kind of detachment occurs because of the fact that one 'observes' whatever one does or feels or perceives, even if the object of observation is intimately connected with the self, or rather is such an inalienable part of the self that one cannot disown it as not oneself. It is thus that which can neither be owned nor disowned completely. The *Gītā* is aware of this as it does not say that the *sthitprajña*, or the realized person, does not *feel* pleasure or pain, but only that he does not yearn for the continuance of pleasure, nor does he get unduly upset by pain. The exact words in the *Gītā* are *spṛhā* and *udvigna.*[5]

Much of what the *Gītā* says, thus, refers to this second level of consciousness, and not to the first level, as has been generally thought. Such terms as niṣkāma, niḥsaṅga and *nirāsakta* as well as their equivalents, therefore, do not refer to the first level at all and thus do not imply that one does not or should not have desires, but only how one should respond to desires and their consequences. Even the various strategies suggested at the end could be understood in some such way, though they also try to turn the purely negative way of conceiving puruṣārtha at this level in the sense of niḥsaṅga into a more positive state by basing detachment on an awareness of the Lord or the *Puruṣottama* who is the source of all that is real as well as the inner controller of all that happens in the universe.

That desire or kāma should not become tṛṣṇā or compulsive obsession is certainly a meaningful way of conceiving puruṣārtha at the level of manas, but it may be doubted that the only way of giving a positive turn to the conception is to take recourse to the idea of Īśvara or a personal God in the situation. It is, of course, true that recourse to the idea of God in any form whatsoever, always turns the negative into the positive, but for a theory of puruṣārtha at the *specific* level, some other strategy may be required. Perhaps a simple strategy would be to distinguish between the *types* of objects desired and the forms of desiring them. But the world of desires spawned by imagination based on the experience of sensuous satisfactions and delights is so vast and varied that little can be said about it except that perhaps the world of ideal objects is richer and more positive than the world of concrete, sensuous, empirical objects, and that desire for goods that are essentially competitive is less positive than desire for those that are non-competitive in nature. However, even such a broad formulation seems to demand obvious exceptions such as those that relate to the world of sport, or skills, or other such realms where competitive merit is involved. As for 'forms of desiring', one can only say that those that are desired for others, rather than for oneself, are relatively 'better', and even amongst the latter, the positive quality of 'desiring' seems to be inversely related to the degree of svatva involved in the desire. The refinement and elevation and subtilization of both the objects desired and the process of 'desiring' along with regard for the effect that any attempt at the fulfilment of desires may have on others, are perhaps the other two considerations in any serious thought regarding the puruṣārtha of manas so far as it is regarded as the root cause of desire at the human level.

If the problem of the puruṣārtha of manas seems difficult to articulate, it is not only because of the diversity and variety of desires at the human level, but also because the tradition has mostly seen desire in a negative way and has thus neglected this rich realm which constitutes human beings to a large extent. Even when it has paid attention to desire, it has done so primarily in the realm of sex, so much so that kāma as a puruṣārtha is supposed by many to be the subject of the Kāmaśūtra alone with which it has come to be identified totally both in the scholarly and the public mind. The world of desire created by the human mind, however, does not necessarily consist only of sex, even though it undoubtedly gets unbelievably complicated by sexual desires. Kāma, thus is neither what the texts on the Kāmaśūtra are about nor what the existential analysts of the human situation from the Buddha onwards have said about it. But in however narrow or negative a way kāma at least has been considered a puruṣārtha in the Indian tradition. This can hardly be said about buddhi or intellect whose puruṣārtha is hardly discussed and no known text is devoted to it.

The puruṣārtha of the buddhi is considered to consist in its being able to distinguish between nitya and anitya, or between the timeless and the eternal on the one hand, and the temporal and the transient, on the other. But this is not the same as the distinction between truth and falsity, though in one sense the two may be said to coincide. The *sat* in the sense of Being is, by definition, supposed to be that which can never not be, even though there are passages in the Vedas and the Upaniṣads which seem to suggest that Being arose out of Non-Being. The Parmenidean dilemma does not seem to have troubled Indian thinkers, at least not in the same way, even though one may see vague similarities between the Parmenidean and the Heraclitean pictures of reality on the one hand and the Upaniṣadic and the Buddhistic pictures of reality, on the other.

The puruṣārtha of the buddhi, however, cannot be confined only to the determination of truth or falsity, though this undoubtedly is one of its most important functions. It also discriminates and interrelates, questions the seemingly obvious and problematizes the unproblematic, provides the categories of thought and weaves conceptual structures which determine our perception of reality and gives us that objective criticality which leads to the distancing of the ego from itself, resulting in an attenuated ego, at least to some extent. Buddhi, however, does not merely do all this; it also tries to *understand* its own creations. The great tradition of commentaries in the Indian intellectual tradition is sufficient evidence of this. But, strangely, this tradition never reflected on the great puruṣārtha that was involved in such an enterprise. Nor did it reflect on why another commentary was needed if there already was a commentary on an ancient text. Did it imply that the earlier commentator had not understood the text or that he had misunderstood it? And why a chain of unending commentaries? Or why an auto-commentary by the author himself on his own work? It is, of course, true that Jaimini did try to formulate certain principles of textual interpretation, but though they were widely accepted did they really help matters?

This, it should be remembered, is not the pramāṇa-prameya vyāpāra which may be regarded as the specific function of buddhi and its proper field or domain to operate in. Nor is it *saṁśaya* and its *nivāraṇa* which may be considered the other great function of buddhi. Neither for that matter, is it concerned with the understanding of the world or reality, or that which is sat, in either its empirical or ontological sense. It is rather the understanding of somebody else's understanding as expressed and embodied in language. But, then, what is the relation of thought to language, or of consciousness to the medium through which it can express its intentions? Language, of course, is not the only medium, though most thinkers have ignored the other media. Deeper than these problems is the necessity of there being some medium or other for consciousness to embody or articulate itself. Husserl talked about the essential intentionality of all consciousness, but that is something different from this. Also, Husserl seems to have thought that intentionality was just pure and simple intentionality, without different modes or modalities. The relation between 'modes of intentionality' and what are called 'propositional attitudes', for example, has hardly been explored or investigated.

The construction of the House of Intellect is one of the puruṣārthas of buddhi and this is done by successive generations of intellects, each adding, modifying and even destroying some of the portions built earlier. There are, of course, what Yeats called 'monuments of unageing intellect' such as those which a Plato or a Śaṁkara represent, but there are also lesser intellects which build and contribute to the unending enterprise of understanding and knowledge which man has always pursued. In this, one inevitable step has always been to understand what others have tried to build. Thus, the perennial dialogue among intellects where each tries to understand, critically evaluate and creatively carry forward other thinkers' thought processes. The enterprise of buddhi or intellect, however, is not only to understand what it has built itself, whether on its own or with the help of another. Rather, its task is to understand what every faculty of man has tried to build and thus raise it to the level of self-consciousness without which man finds not only the world, but also all that he does, dark, opaque and alien.

The fact that the intellect builds an unending world of its own suggests that the other faculties of man must be doing the same, that is, creating a world of their own. In a sense, this is true, though we are not much aware of the 'constructional' character of other worlds. Manas, as we have seen, creates the world of desires and each of the senses may be said to create a world of its own. But, perhaps the most interesting worlds created are from the interrelationships between human beings. The terms 'society', 'culture', 'civilization' and 'polity' are usually used to describe these worlds, but the actual worlds created within these larger 'given' frameworks are those created by each man around his own self through continuous interaction and interrelationships. In this continuous creation of 'worlds' even animals and plants are drawn in, as everyone who has kept a pet or tended a garden knows well. The task of buddhi and thus its param puruṣārtha is to reflect and interrelate all these worlds that man creates so that they may become transparently intelligible to one's self-consciousness.

Buddhi, however, may do so in various ways. The *Gītā*, taking its cue from *Sāṁkhya*, has characterized buddhi as being sāttvika, rājasika and tāmasika (ślokas 30, 31 and 32 of the eighteenth chapter). Its characterization has centred around the distinctions between the knowledge of pravṛtti and nivṛtti, bandhana and mokṣa and dharma and adharma. Thus it is said that while the sāttvikī buddhi already knows the distinctions between these, the rājasikī does not seem to know about them quite properly (*ayathāvat*), while the tāmasika just turns the world topsy-turvy and thinks of dharma as adharma and adharma as dharma. The distinction between the rājasika and the tāmasika is not quite clear as the term 'ayathāvat' used in the context of the former can also be taken more naturally to mean 'not in accordance with facts'. Perhaps the situation could be saved by treating ayathāvat as indicating a state of doubt or hesitancy, while in the case of the tāmasika buddhi, there is no doubt about what is dharma and adharma, but only a totally inverted or topsy-turvy judgment about them. It considers dharma to be adharma, and adharma to be dharma. But this could be the result of a confusion which could possibly be clarified. And, in any case, if someone genuinely, but mistakenly, thinks he is following his dharma, he cannot be blamed for it. An alternative interpretation of tāmasika buddhi could be that it actually knows what dharma is and what adharma is but wilfully chooses to follow the latter course because it is evil. But this is the āsuric or the demonic will. There is another version of it, where though there is no confusion or indecision about what dharma is, there is just no inclination towards it. Duryodhana's well-known and oft-quoted statement is an apt illustration of this. But then one would have to accept that the source of the pravṛtti or the nivṛtti, to use Duryodhana's words, would be somewhere else and not in the buddhi. Also, there would be no real distinction between the sāttvika and the tāmasika buddhi, as both would *know* what dharma or adharma is, the difference lying not in their knowledge, but rather in the source which determines the *vṛtti* towards them. Such a source has been understood by the word 'will' in the western tradition but, as far as I know, there is no equivalent in the Indian tradition. The term '*dhṛti*' may perhaps perform this function, but the way it has been used in the *Gītā* (18.33–35) would preclude this, unless it is stretched to yield this or at least an analogous interpretation.

The problem, however, would then be compounded, for we would have to admit that a person may possess a sāttvikī buddhi but a tāmasika dhṛti which makes his knowledge of dharma ineffective in practice. In fact, the *Gītā*'s discussion of jñāna raises problems of an analogous kind. In śloka 18.20–22, the distinction between sāttvika, rājasika and tāmasika jñāna has been drawn. But here again the problem of the relationship between these three kinds of jñāna and the three kinds of buddhi elaborated later remains. The sequence is also a problem as normally one would assume that jñāna is a function of buddhi and would be of the same kind as the buddhi from which it has originated. Moreover, the characteristics that the *Gītā* ascribes to jñāna seem at least *prima facie* to belong more properly to the buddhi. The characterization, for example, of that jñāna as sāttvika which sees unity in all things, and rājasika as that which sees differences amongst them may more properly be considered characteristics primarily of the buddhi and only secondarily of the jñāna which may be regarded as its product.

But whether it is the classification and characterization of the buddhi or the jñāna, the author of the *Gītā* has not taken into account the fact that in the classical *Sāṁkhyan* sense, nothing can be purely sāttvika, rājasika or tāmasika, but can only be predominantly so and that too not for long. One, of course, need not accept the classical *Sāṁkhya* view on this matter and may even modify it. But one should at least declare that one is doing so. Alternatively, one may treat these descriptions as ideal types in the Weberian sense constructed for cognitive purposes, keeping in mind that the actual reality at the concrete level is a mixed phenomenon with one or the other usually predominating, at least for some length of time.

The incorporation of the threefold division from *Sāṁkhya* by the author of the *Gītā* into almost all domains suggests that all concepts relating to man, society and polity may be viewed in this threefold aspect. All possible combinations of concepts may also be conceived of in terms of sāttvika, rājasika and tāmasika taken from the classical *Sāṁkhya*. Or, if one finds the specific characterization of these *Sāṁkhya* guṇas inadequate or their number inadequate, one may add to, subtract from or modify them as required for theoretical purposes. The tradition itself has shown in such an authoritative work as the *Gītā* all that can be done in this regard. And once the buddhi is exposed to this possible way of looking at things, it may discover concepts and facts left untouched even in the tradition. The author of the *Gītā*, for example, has not said how the manas or the indriyas may be classified or characterized in terms of the threefold scheme taken from *Sāṁkhya*. Moreover, as the *Sāṁkhya* classification applies to all objects, whether animate or inanimate, one may ask whether the five gross and subtle elements, that is, earth, fire, water, air and ether, are sāttvika, rājasika or tāmasika in nature. This may also be asked about society, culture and polity, or even about the physical environment, as one may legitimately wonder whether one can be sāttvika in a physical or socio-cultural environment which is essentially non-sāttvika in character.

To ask these questions is to see both the potentiality and the limitations of the traditional scheme and to accept the challenge of widening it so as to make it more meaningful and relevant in today's context. However, as manas or buddhi do not encompass the entire human being, one has to ask about the other faculties of man, what the puruṣārtha of each of them is, and how the different puruṣārthas are to be interrelated and formed into a meaningful whole so that they are not at cross-purposes with each other.

According to the tradition, beyond the buddhi there is either the sense of egotism called *ahaṁkāra* between the self or the puruṣa and the buddhi, while in the *Gītā* there seems to be no such intervening term. But there is another term in the Indian tradition which is different and is beyond buddhi. This is denoted by the term prajñā which has also been used in the *Gītā* in its earlier part but forgotten later, as is shown by the fact that in the eighteenth chapter where a threefold classification of so many other concepts is attempted, '*prajñā*' is not mentioned at all. But it is a difficult term to translate, and perhaps the closest English equivalent to it is the word 'wisdom'. Yet, whether one accepts the equivalence or not, the question of the puruṣārtha of prajñā seems a little strange, for while one may think of buddhi or manas or even the indriyas as not functioning properly, or as having a hiatus between their 'is' and their 'ought', there does not seem to be any such thing with respect to prajñā or wisdom. It is either there or not there. Yet, the problem of a balance between the different puruṣārthas through a super-puruṣārtha remains, and it is not clear as to which faculty of man this function should be assigned. Perhaps it can only be the function of self-consciousness itself and not of any separate faculty, as the ultimate problem of a balanced co-ordination can only be solved by the self and not by any separate, differentiated faculty which would have a vested interest or value of its own.

The term prajñā in such a perspective may then be treated as that faculty in man which makes him aware of the transcendent and relates him to it in some way or the other. To a certain extent, buddhi does this and in this respect its function may be said to overlap with that of prajñā. There is an analogous distinction in the western philosophical tradition between understanding or intellect and reason, wherein the latter tries to grasp the totality while the former tries to grasp things in their limited, differentiated interrelationships. But the awareness of the transcendence is not the awareness of totality, though it may sometimes be so also. The prajñā in its usual traditional connotation, however, is not just awareness of the transcendent but also of the relation between the transcendent and all that is immanent and met with in experience at the level of the indriyas, the manas and the buddhi. Its puruṣārtha may, therefore, be viewed as consisting of seeking the most meaningful way in which this relationship may be conceived of and achieved in the human personality. The *Gītā*'s way of conceiving this puruṣārtha in its ideal of the sthitprajña is too negative and, in any case, is only one of the ways in which it may be conceived.

Beyond the manas, the buddhi and the prajñā, there is the ahaṁkāra or the sense of I-ness the puruṣārtha of which, though entangled in an essential sense with the puruṣārthas of all these, may yet be conceived of separately. To ask what the puruṣārtha of ahaṁkāra is may appear to be the same as to ask what the puruṣārtha of the embodied self or the jīva is. But a little reflection will show that the two are not the same, even though the sense of egoism or I-ness is a necessary precondition of the embodied self, as without it there can be no such thing as a distinctive self. The puruṣārtha of ahaṁkāra would then have to be distinct from the puruṣārtha of the embodied self or the jīva, even though it would have to be foundational in the sense that the puruṣārthas of all the other constituents of the embodied self may not be considered to be so. Perhaps a clue as to what the puruṣārtha of ahaṁkāra is may be found in what is definitely regarded as a perversion of the sense of I-ness which results in egoism on the one hand and a sense of pride and possessiveness, on the other. Ahaṁkāra normally connotes these negative qualities and is regarded as something undesirable. The puruṣārtha of ahaṁkāra, then, is avoidance of this perversion of itself or the achievement of a self-awareness which precludes possessiveness and pride. Thus, the puruṣārtha of ahaṁkāra would be a denial of svatva in its ontological as well as existential sense. It would be, so to say, an achievement of detachment at the most foundational level and an awareness that the ego is a shadowy accompaniment of self-consciousness without any reality of its own except to facilitate the organization of the empirical ego, that is, the jīva. The ahaṁkāra is ultimately the borderline which demarcates the ontological from the empirical self and hence has to realize itself as such.

Beyond the manas, the buddhi, the prajñā and the ahaṁkāra, there is the self or the existential centre of consciousness which has usually been designated as the ātman or puruṣa in the Indian tradition. Normally, the ātman or puruṣa in association with all these is called the jīva and its puruṣārtha is supposed to be to get rid of this entanglement and association in which it finds itself and become established in its own pristine, pure state which is called mokṣa, nirvāṇa or *kaivalya.* But this way of conceiving the puruṣārtha of the self *negates* all the other puruṣārthas in an essential sense. It does not transform or fulfil them, but rather sees them as obstacles and hindrances in the path of the real puruṣārtha which can be attained only by denying them at their very roots so that the illusory seekings that they generate may be apprehended for what they really are. But such a way of seeing the real puruṣārtha cannot but create insoluble problems for a culture, and the history of Indian civilization may be understood in terms of the various attempts made to come to terms with it.

However, even if one does not accept the traditional way of conceiving the puruṣārtha of the self, the question regarding this puruṣārtha and the relation it has to other puruṣārthas remains. What, in other words, is the puruṣārtha of the jīva or the embodied being, for that alone is how we know or experience it. As this is the puruṣārtha of the existential, embodied consciousness which is conscious of itself, it relates to the nature and quality of consciousness and the immanent ideal involved therein. The quality of consciousness that one habitually enjoys is perhaps the one most intimately known to a human being, as also the fact that most of the time one is dissatisfied with it and would like it to be different. There are times when one finds it to be different and more in accord with what one would like it to be, but these moments are too fleeting for one's satisfaction. Also, they are not always of the same type, nor do they display any uniform relationship with the world of objects and persons, either in terms of dependence on them or independence from them. The tradition has emphasized some of these feelings, perhaps even overemphasized them, but they need to be explored and articulated without commitment to any metaphysical position. Yet the qualities of peace, joy, clarity, enthusiasm and freedom are such that most would regard them as puruṣārthas specific to human consciousness. So also is the capacity to relate positively, to be other-centred in one's relationships and yet be able to withdraw, and to accept adversity if one cannot do anything about it.

The puruṣārtha of consciousness, however conceived, does not and should not override other puruṣārthas as has been the case in the tradition. True, it is closest to man and very central to him, but since man is an embodied being, that is, a body-mind-buddhi-prajñā-consciousness complex, he has to care for the puruṣārtha of each and interrelate it with the puruṣārthas of the other constituents of his being to the best possible extent. Man, however, is not only aware of all these aspects in his or her own being and the puruṣārthas of each, but also of other human beings who have their own puruṣārthas which need to be cared for and interrelated and integrated to some extent. This is what leads to a consideration of society and polity when considering the theory of puruṣārtha. To confine oneself to the individual alone is to not do justice to the notion of puruṣārtha. The idea of dharma in traditional thought in India tries to consider the puruṣārtha of society, but the very fact that it does not know how to deal with law and polity on the one hand, and mokṣa on the other, shows that it was not able to deal with the problem effectively. In fact, it did not even formulate the idea of a collective puruṣārtha without which the real problems of a plurality of jīvas who are aware of each other and who depend upon each other for the realization of their own puruṣārthas cannot even be formulated, let alone understood.

The delinking of the theory of puruṣārtha from the traditional formulation in terms of dharma, artha, kāma, mokṣa, and/or bhakti and relating it to the embodied self or jīva as we know it from our living, day-to-day experience, and extending it to include the relationship between the jīvas who are interdependent on one another and constitute the world as we know it, are the two priority tasks before any contemporary Indian thinker who takes classical Indian thought about man seriously and believes that puruṣārtha is the key concept around which classical thought was constructed. But it is not *necessary* to think in this way, as one need not accept puruṣārtha to be the central concept around which Indian thought about man was actually built; even if it were so, it need not be accepted by the contemporary thinker for constructing his own thoughts about man. There is no reason, for example, why concepts such as varṇa, karma, guṇa, saṁskāra or any of the others mentioned earlier should not serve the same function. But whatever the concept we choose as central, the approach would have to be the same: we would have to ask ourselves in what ways the traditional understanding of this concept is inadequate or incomplete, or even mistaken, and in what direction it has to be extended for it to become relevant or meaningful in the contemporary context.

Suppose, for example, we make karma the central concept for

understanding human reality, we will have to ask how the theory of karma in its strict sense is compatible with the *fact* of the interdependence of human beings, or how the svatva of karma is possible in a situation where jīvas, independent of one another, are inconceivable in principle. Or what is the karma of the śarīra or body, the manas or mind, the buddhi or intellect, the prajñā and the cit or consciousness? Alternatively, one could talk of individual and corporate or collective karma and try to distinguish between the two. It may be difficult to give an exact lakṣaṇa to distinguish between the two, but some criteria will have to be developed to demarcate the area of responsibilities arising out of acting on behalf of others and acting on behalf of oneself. A distinction between *svārtha* karma and *parārtha* karma will have to be drawn just as between *vaiyaktika* karma and *sāmūhika* karma. Once the idea of sāmūhika or corporate action is accepted, one would also have to accept the notion of a sāmūhika phala and its fair distribution among all those involved in such action.

A karma-centric view of man would also have to view the relationship of karma with jñāna or knowledge on the one hand, and with bhāva or feelings and emotions, on the other. Will these, in other words, be treated only as instrumental to karma and find their meaning and validity in terms of karma alone? What would it mean for karma to be performed intrinsically for itself, and not instrumentally, whether for the sake of another action or something else? Will it be like, say, dharma or doing one's duty for duty's sake? Or could we understand it as *līlā*, more analogous to play which itself could be conceived of in diverse ways. One could explore the diverse relationship between dharma and līlā as the two paradigmatic norms of conceiving action in the Indian tradition. The rich reservoir of thought in the classical traditions of India could be used for the purpose, though of course we need not feel bound by them in any way. To put it in traditional terminology, it is the dharma of the buddhi to have a *līlā-bhāva* with respect to the concepts it has inherited from the tradition and play with them in the best possible manner. But how would we distinguish between the māyā of buddhi and its līlā? Or for that matter between māyā and līlā of the senses, the mind, the prajñā and the cit or consciousness? Perhaps the distinction lies in freedom and bondage, in being obsessed or overcome by the object, or in being too involved with it as against being detached from it. But what about other persons? Can a līlā be līlā equally for all the participants in it? Or, as someone remarked, 'Kṛṣṇa's līlā is Rādhā's tears'. Is māyā, then, somebody else's līlā and is it māyā only because it has not become one's own līlā?

The relationship between dharma, māyā and līlā, concepts which have played such an important role in traditional Indian thought about action, seems interesting and worth exploring and developing further. But so are the other concepts that have evolved over millennia to understand man, society and polity in its long intellectual history. Take, for example, the concepts of guṇa and varṇa which could also be made central to the understanding of man instead of puruṣārtha or karma. If we accept the *Sāṁkhyan* categorization of guṇas, then human beings will have necessarily to be understood as sāttvika, rājasika or tāmasika. But we will then face the problem of how to understand this classification. Are they like the three primary colours from whose various combinations all the other colours arise? Or should we understand them as *Sāṁkhya* seems to understand them, that is, in terms of dominance and recessiveness where everything is a mixture of all the three in various proportions and where there is a continuous interaction between them, resulting in a change in their relative dominance over a period of time? Then, not only will there be nothing as purely sāttvika or rājasika or tāmasika, but also nothing would retain the dominance of any one guṇa over a long period of time. It would be somewhat like the theory of the yugas where each yuga, however good or bad, has to give rise to another. The theory of cosmic cycles has not been much thought about, but taking a cue from *Sāṁkhya*, one could think of them in a different way and claim that there is no such thing as a pure satya, tretā, dvāpara or kaliyuga but that all are intermixed and that the characterization is because of the dominance of one set of qualities over others which are not totally absent, but are present in a subservient or recessive form.

However, the *Sāṁkhyan* perspective, though interesting from many points of view, gives rise to serious difficulties in as much as even the predominance of the sattva in individuals and society over a long period of time will not ensure its continuance or further deepening as it is bound to be overtaken by the recessive elements of rajas and tamas. Perhaps the difficulty arises because of the close association these terms have had with virtues and values of a positive or negative kind in the traditional thought. It may be better if we dissociate them from the moral and spiritual discourse altogether and treat them as analogous to elements or constituents of health in Āyurveda where the preponderance of any one over the others signifies disease rather than health. The theory of health rooted in the equilibrium model would then imply that each is equally necessary both at the individual and the social level, though the equilibrium itself need not be conceived of in purely static terms or just at one level only. The dynamic model of a shifting equilibrium explored in modern economic theory could perhaps be of some help in this connection.

Any move in this direction however, will undermine the close relationship between the theory of guṇas and the theory of values with which it has been so closely associated till now. The hierarchical versus the equi-importance model would, in fact, appear in all conceptualizations of Indian thought. The theories of varṇa āśrama and puruṣārtha would all have the same immanent strains taking them in different directions. The varṇa-centric interpretation of man would see him primarily in social terms, while the āśrama-centric view would see him in terms of the biological cycle in which all living beings are inevitably involved, with suitable modifications to accommodate individual psychic differences. The varṇic interpretation, however, may be done at either the individual or the social level, while the āśramic interpretation has to be confined to the individual level alone. The varṇic conceptualization views man either on the mixed model of the guṇas or on their pure model. The individual will thus have the characteristics of all the varṇas but be characterized by one or the other on the basis of the preponderance of any one of them, but that too not permanently. Also more varṇas may be needed in the classificatory scheme than the usual four traditionally associated with it, just as we may need more puruṣārthas or guṇas than the ones generally accepted. Not only this, value associations with the term śūdra will have to be given up, just as in the case of the term *tamas* in the context of the theory of the guṇas.

The theories relating to each of these concepts, however, are not isolated in character, but form an interrelated network just as the concepts themselves form a cluster where thought on each affects and is affected by thought about others. Any radical change, therefore, which affects thought and theory about one is bound to also affect all the others. Changing interactions between concepts and theories built around them, along with new dimensions in the meanings of old concepts, provide a continuity of thought which often mask radical innovations and sometimes even substantive discontinuities in the tradition. The preferred intellectual style of putting across fresh ideas by writing a commentary on an older text has added to this impression. So also has the widely prevalent practice of what Rājaśekhara called *svīkaraṇa* and which Dr Lath has recently brought to scholarly attention through concrete examples of what is actually meant by this term and the way it was practised.[6] Traditional thought was creatively integrated with contemporary views by self-consciously and *openly* borrowing things from past masters and modifying the material by adding to it or subtracting from it. The reverse of this process, perhaps, was when one ascribed to past masters what one wrote oneself, provided it conformed in spirit to what they had said in the original. Much of the bhakti literature seems to have grown this way and given rise to the increasing corpus of writing by Mīrā, Sūra, Kabīra and others which has created insoluble problems for those who have tried to search for the so-called Ur-text of these writers. One reason, amongst many others mentioned by Winaud Callewart and Mukund Lath who have engaged in this exercise with respect to the work of the earlier saint-poet Nāmadev, is that these songs were meant to be sung and that each singer freely introduced the changes he felt were necessary keeping in view the mood of the audience.[7] But as Dr Mukund Lath has himself argued, this could not be the only reason, for the tradition accepted it in non-musical contexts also.[8] Perhaps one should distinguish between what the tradition thought should be preserved unchanged in its texts and what could be creatively added to, modified or changed according to the genius of the innovator and the demands of the time. In any case, the conceptual and theoretical corpus of the past is there, and it is the task of thinkers in present-day India to see how this can be shaped to meet the intellectual and practical needs of a society which is being increasingly shaped by innovative trends in science, technology and economy at the global level.

There are many ways of interweaving classical concepts and theories into contemporary thought, and the theoretical and practical consequences of such attempts are determined by diverse considerations and factors. The basic attitude of the persons engaged in this activity should be one of involvement in an on-going enterprise that tries to carry forward the unpursued cognitive endeavours of the past. Much of the work done in this domain has lacked something vital because those who have tried to study and understand *living* cultures and civilizations have done so without being a part of the living present themselves. They want to *understand* something as an *object*, finished, final and completed, when it is not an object at all, but rather a part of the lived experience of a people, and like everything living, either growing or decaying, with which all who are involved are *actively* concerned. The non-participant or pseudo-participant student of cultures and civilizations is always afraid of going wrong, of being mistaken, of having misunderstood, while those who see themselves as inheritors of this rich theoretical and conceptual legacy of the past realize its unactualized potentialities and ask themselves how they can enrich it further to help shape a more meaningful present and future for man, society and polity. Even the recent attempt by Marriott to view the classical Indian conceptualization about man, nature and society in an interrelated manner suffers from this defect.[9] He has tried to correlate the four puruṣārthas, the three guṇas, the Āyurvedic elements constituting the body and the five *mahābhūtas* comprising nature. But he does not mention the elementary fact that both the theory of elements (earth, air, fire, water and ether) and the theory of humours (wind, bile and phlegm) are not peculiar to classical Indian thought alone, as with some minor modifications or variations they are found in Greece and China also. One may also find the correlates of at least the three puruṣārthas (dharma, artha and kāma) amongst them, leaving only the last, that is mokṣa, as specific to India along with the theory of the three guṇas, that is, the sattva, the rajasa and the tamasa. He is obviously not aware of the inclusion of bhakti as a separate, or even as a fifth puruṣārtha or of the problems this raises for his interrelational scheme.

Of greater magnitude than all these deficiencies, however, is not only the utter neglect of the diversity and development in the meanings of these various concepts or their replacement by others as in the case of those following the Āyurveda, but what can only be called a smug acceptance of these concepts and their formulations, something one never does with the concepts of one's own culture except in the context of a textual or historical investigation. But in spite of these deficiencies there can be little doubt that Marriott's attempt carries us a step forward and opens the way to a broader, more flexible interrelational conceptual structure of classical Indian thought and its development in the contemporary context, not only as an ethno-sociological tool for understanding Indian society, but also as an *alternative* conceptual structure for apprehending and understanding any social reality whatsoever.

But, strangely, though Marriott is a cultural anthropologist by profession and is 'constructing' an 'ethno-*sociology*' which, according to him, is specifically and exclusively Indian in character, the concepts he has picked up from the vast reservoir of concepts in the Indian tradition all apply *primarily* to the individual and only secondarily and derivatively, if at all, to society with which sociology is presumably concerned. The conceptual structure of classical Indian thought about society is hardly touched upon by Marriott, except indirectly in the first three puruṣārthas mentioned by him, but even there the focus is on the individual and not on society. The social theorists of classical India have been done a grave injustice by Marriott through his tacit assumption that there was no such thought in India, and that he is the first one to construct it, and that too on the basis of concepts which primarily apply to man as an individual being and not as a member of society or as a social being. I will try to articulate the conceptual structure of Indian thought about society in the next chapter.

Notes

1. There is also the concept of *sadācāra* besides that of ātma-tuṣṭi in the texts as a source of dharma, but there can be little doubt that the choice of the exemplar is ultimately one's own as there are multiple and even conflicting exemplars of sadācāra in the tradition and while in the objective

domain Śruti may be fundamental, in the realm of the moral experience, judgment regarding what ought to be done cannot but ultimately lie in ātma-tuṣṭi the 'ātma' being interpreted in the transcendental sense.

2. *jānāmi dharmaṁ, na ca me pravṛttiḥ. jānāmyadharmaṁ, na ca me nivṛttiḥ.*
3. *Gītā*, 3.33.
4. Mukund Lath, 'Svatantrā Strī', *Unmīlana*, 5, 2 July.
5. *Duḥkhesyanudvignamanāḥ sukheṣu vigatspṛhaḥ. Gītā*, 2.56.
6. Mukund Lath, 'Svīkaraṇa'.
7. Winand, M. Callewart and Mukund Lath, *The Hindi Padāvalī of Nāmadeva*, Delhi, Motilal Banarasidass, 1989.
8. Mukund Lath, 'Svīkarana'.
9. McKim Marriott, 'Constructing an Indian Ethno-Sociology' in *Contributions to Indian Sociology* (n.s.), 23, 1, 1989.

CHAPTER VI

The Conceptual Structure of Classical Indian Thought about Society

Social theorists in India have concretized social reality through a number of concepts related on the one hand to the individual and, on the other, to groups, classes and organizations which form an integral part of society. Thus concepts at the individual level and at the social level are bound to overlap. There are overlapping concepts at the social and political levels too, though each realm does have concepts specific to it alone.

The key concepts around which much of classical thought in India regarding society has been woven are: (1) dharma (2) vyavahāra (3) saṁskāra (4) varṇa (5) jāti (6) kula (7) *śreṇī* (8) *pūga* (9) ṛṇa (10) dāna (11) *dayā* (12) *maitrī* (13) *karuṇā* (14) *lokasaṁgraha* (15) *sarvabhūtahita* (16) *lokakalyāṇa* (17) *samabhāva* (18) *samatva* (19) *samāja* (20) *sāmājika* (21) *nāgarika* (22) vyavasthā (23) *saṁbandha* (24) saṅgha (25) *samaṣṭi* (26) *para* (27) *paraspara* (28) paraṁparā (29) *rūḍhi* (30) *varga* (31) *viś* and (32) *janapada*.

The most obvious and interesting fact that emerges from even a cursory glance at these concepts is that there is no single equivalent of the word 'society' in the Indian conceptual repertoire relating to this domain. The terms that come closest to 'society' are samāja, loka and samaṣṭi. But samāja was traditionally not used in the sense that it has come to acquire in Hindi these days. This is clearly indicated by the way the term sāmājika was used in the tradition. It was closer to what was conveyed by the word *nāgarika*, that is, cultured or civilized, than what is understood by the term 'social' today. Similarly, the word '*loka*' refers to the world as a whole and not just to society. Moreover, in the concept of loka, as developed in the tradition, this is only one loka amongst many other lokas and it is distinguished from them by the fact that death reigns here or that it is possibly the only world where one can act freely. The term *samaṣṭi*, though opposed to *vyakti* which connotes an individual, still does not specifically convey what is meant by 'society'. Rather it connotes any whole or group which is seen in its totality and not in terms of the individuals composing it. There is also the word '*janapada*' which connotes a socio-political formation and which has been used in the tradition.

This is perhaps because what we call society today was not a natural unit, but an artificial, logical construction from existing groups for which there were a myriad names. The terms varṇa, jāti, kula, saṅgha, śreṇī, gaṇa, pūga, vrāṭ, *naigam*, *samūha*, *pariṣad*, *caraṇa* found in the *Smṛti* literature of India refer to actually existing and functioning organizations which deal with familial, commercial, civic, craft and administrative functions. The idea of something overarching all these and interrelating them was indicated by such concepts as *loka*, *paraṁparā*, *dharma vyavahāra* (in the sense of law) and *rājya*. Thus, it was tradition on the one hand, and law, morality and polity on the other that together constituted the idea of what we today generally mean by the term 'society'. This is as it should be; for what else is society but legal, moral and political institutions in the public realm and all that is bequeathed in terms of cultural heritage? The idea of loka incorporates both the cosmic and the transcendental dimensions, as the society in which we live is not only related to the past, but is also part of the cosmos which includes worlds other than our own and beings other than those familiar to us. The idea of dharma was supposed to have brought the transcendental dimension into the understanding of society as it was usually held that dharma cannot be known either by perception or inference or any of the usual means of knowledge available to man. However, the idea of loka makes an addition of a different kind. It suggests that what happens in this world of ours, or is enacted in it, is intimately related to worlds other than this one. We do not live in a world which is the only world in the universe or with which we have no interrelationship whatsoever. This loka is only one of the many lokas above and below, which sometimes were collectively designated as the three lokas, the one comprising all the worlds above, and the other comprising all the worlds below, while the world we live in is the world in between.

The individual human being was related to all these worlds both visibly and invisibly not only because he was supposed to be a microcosm mirroring the macrocosm but also by virtue of the web that was woven through the actions he performed and the consequences he had to face. The doctrine of karma articulated the intricate web one was supposed to weave and wind and unwind perennially, getting caught and then freed. The drama of karma, however, is played by an individual mostly in relation to other beings, who are primarily human in nature. Society may thus be understood as the net or web that men collectively weave for one another and for succeeding generations.

The transcendental or rather the trans-empirical nature of society is evident not only in the theory of karma where individual destinies are woven through interaction with others, but also in the way society itself is supposed to have come into being as seen in Indian thought. The sacrifice of the primeval cosmic Being resulting in the creation of separate varṇas may be understood in the way we understand the contractual or the covenant theory of society. What is being suggested by such originative mythologies is that society may be logically understood in some such way. The contractual theory, it is true, was propounded in the context of the emergence of the state and not of society, but the problem of finding reasons for the origin of society is the same, and so also is the problem of subordination of one's freedom to someone else's authority. The Indian theory regarding the emergence of the state is similar, though if the Indian theorist had taken his theory of the emergence of society seriously, he would have perhaps seen that he could not legitimately propound the thesis about the origin of the state or kingship, or hold the two together.

Indian myth about the origin of society is that an original unity has been divided on the basis of functional differentiations, embodied in different varṇas which, therefore, *together* now constitute the unity, that is, society. Society, thus, is the primeval cosmic puruṣa which has sacrificed itself to constitute its plurality and multiplicity. But the plurality into which the original cosmic person divided itself was not just the plurality of society, but rather the plurality of the cosmos itself. Moreover, it is explicitly stated that only one-fourth of it is manifest in this world, while three-fourths remains unmanifested. Thus society is not only a part of the cosmos, but also shares in the transcendental, unmanifested reality which underlies everything manifest and visible.

There is, of course, a problem in conceiving of the cosmic puruṣa with parts; or even if it is granted that he did have parts, with which parts did he create the other parts of the cosmos besides the varṇas which constitute society? However, as the whole thing is a myth and has to be understood metaphorically, such questions need not be pressed too far. But if the myth is to be taken seriously even as a myth, the varṇa theory of society will have to be treated as a universal theory for all societies, and not be confined only to the region of the *āryavarta*, as the theorists generally tend to do. It would have no place for the idea of *mlecchas* (foreigners) or any other varṇa as so many of the other societies tend to have. Though the theory only tries to describe what an ideal society should consist of, the myth is too factual and positive to be construed this way, and even the ideal interpretation could not permit more than four varṇas, though it might allow for less.

The concept of varṇas, however, need not be grounded in the myth, which is usually the case, nor need we feel bound by the specific idiosyncrasies of the Indian theorist who was continuously busy trying to accommodate the various existing jātis into these varṇas, or even accept only the four varṇas in the concept, as pointed out earlier. Even if we take the concept in its traditional formulation and assume the necessity of the four varṇas in every society, we may ask which varṇa, or function corresponding to it, is given priority and importance in a society. There may then be brahmanical societies in which the brāhmaṇa varṇa, and the function corresponding to it, is most valued and given the highest prestige in terms of status and honour. On the other hand, we may similarly have kṣatriya, vaiśya or śūdra societies, that is, societies in which functions ascribed to these varṇas are given primacy in terms of status, privileges and honour. A kṣatriya society will give the highest place in its hierarchy of values to heroic virtues, valourous deeds, skills in the art of warfare and the readiness to engage and die in battle. The literature of such a society will extol such virtues and sing the praises of heroes locked in mortal combat or engaged in preparing for battle. Most classical literature is of this type, and the epics and ballads are full of tales of heroes who receive coveted weapons from the gods and win or die with honour on the battlefield, which alone is considered an honourable death. The Rāmāyaṇa and the Mahābhārata are, in this respect, no different from the epics of other cultures and may thus be regarded more as representing a society which is not brahmanical, but rather kṣatriya in nature. If one takes the battle scenes away, little of interest would be left for the reader.

A vaiśya society, on the other hand, would give primacy to the virtues of thrift, prudence, and the acquisition of wealth through trade and commerce. A wealthy man would be considered higher in status and more important than men engaged in the pursuit of knowledge or skilled in the art of warfare. The so-called capitalist societies are vaiśya societies *par excellence*, even though there were civilizations in the past, such as the Phoenician, which are described in those terms and can easily be characterized as such. Buying and selling, and the whole structure of habits, institutions and values that they presuppose and imply, predominate in such a culture. Even brahmanical and kṣatriya values are seen as instrumental to them. Everything is seen in terms of a cost-benefit aṇalysis, and one always determines what one can get out of a transaction, not whether it is right or wrong, or true or false.

In contrast to the idea of a brahmanical, kṣatriya or vaiśya society whose ideal types one may build if one so desires, it is difficult to easily conceive what a śūdra society would be. Normally, the śūdra function is identified with *sevā* or service, that is, with those whose primary task is to serve others. But the term 'sevā' or service is itself generally confined to the performance of activities which cater only to the physical needs of others. The services of a teacher, for example, have never been regarded as part of the śūdra function in any society. Nor have the services rendered by shopkeepers or traders or soldiers ever been regarded as those performed by śūdras in the Indian texts on the subject. Thus, though in one sense service is rendered by everyone to someone or the other, no one is regarded as a śūdra unless he or she performs only a certain kind or class of service. The services generally relate to the performance of those activities which one would not like to do oneself. They are mainly concerned with facilitating the day-to-day business of living and thus provide an opportunity to those who are relieved from them to pursue other things.

A śūdra society, therefore, can only be conceived of as one in which the basic activity of living is regarded as being the highest in importance, and all other activities as instrumental or subservient to it. There is perhaps no society which can conceive of itself in such a way, as to be human is to conceive of oneself as more than just a biological being. No human society can be conceived of without the culture which is integral to it, and which distinguishes it from the realm of the biological in which it is embedded. It is thus the cultural values that are accorded primacy in any society, and it is difficult to see how these may be conceived of in purely biological terms.

The Marxian theory and vision may seem an exception, as they not only ground all values in the physical productivity of human labour, but also see them, in all their variegated forms, as instrumental to it. But even if we ignore the systematic ambiguities involved in the notions of 'labour' and 'production' which play such a key role in Marxian theory, it is obvious that the vision of a 'non-exploitative' society conceived in Marxian terms *frees* the cultural 'superstructure' of its instrumental character and restores to it the autonomy which rightfully belongs to it. In fact, the replacement of human labour by machines will be the ideal in such a society so that man may become free of the *necessity* of performing physical labour for sheer survival. And though Marx could not have anticipated the revolutions wrought by developments in the field of electronic computers and artificial intelligence, the trend was apparent even then.

The functions that one would prefer to have performed by someone else, whether by a human being, an animal or a machine, may then be regarded as śūdra functions. In fact, the successive replacement of the labour of human beings by animals and machines may provide a clue to what is to be regarded as a śūdra function. But as an activity may be engaged in by a person even when it can be done by another person, or an animal or a machine, the distinction may be said to lie in conditions with respect to which one is not free at all and those in which one is free to choose to undertake the activity. It is a distinction between what Marx called the 'realm of necessity' versus 'the realm of freedom'. The śūdra functions would then be those that belong to the realm of necessity, and the brahmanical, kṣatriya and vaiśya functions those that belong, at least relatively, to the realm of freedom in which one exercises choice. These functions will themselves have sub-functions which may belong more to the realm of necessity than to the realm of freedom. There may then be a hierarchy of functions which may be arranged in terms of greater or lesser freedom of choice.

The notion of a śūdra function seen in this way will permeate every other function and form a necessary component of it, though it would never coincide with it completely. The realms of freedom and necessity will thus intersect at every level, and the quantity and quality of freedom involved in the function will determine its value and status in the hierarchy of functions. But as freedom itself has been seen in two different ways, the points of intersection would also be different according to the precedence given to a particular view of freedom in the paraṁparā of any culture. The usual formulations have been in terms of 'freedom to' and 'freedom from', the one generally conceived of as control over the means of realizing one's ends, and the other as independence from, or not dependence on anything whatever. The first presupposes a realm of desire for the fulfilment of which one has all the means at one's disposal, both human and non-human, with no obstruction or hindrance in the fulfilment of desires. The idea of omnipotence in the context of a divine being epitomizes this notion of freedom, though at the empirical level, the king or the ruler has usually been seen as its paradigmatic exemplar. The second concept of freedom, on the other hand, sees the world of desire itself as the cause of one's dependence on others and its ideal is the renouncer who minimizes his needs to the greatest possible extent, reaching its extreme in the paradigmatic example of the Jain monk who performs *santhārā*, that is, gives up all food and drink and waits quietly for death. There is thus a cessation of bodily functions which are themselves seen as being the cause of dependence in the most basic sense of the term and may be regarded as the paradigmatic example of the realm of necessity to which everyone is subject, whether a saint or a sinner.

The linkage of the śūdra functions to the realm of necessity in either of the two ways leads to an extended application of the term at the level of the individual person where all that binds him to the wheel of life, all that is necessary to keep the wheel turning may be regarded as śūdra in character. It should be noted, however, that these are functions that cannot be performed by anyone else or be taken over by machines because of their very nature. Each individual will then be condemned to perform the śūdra functions by the very fact that he is a living being with the material underpinnings of all other levels which not only presuppose the reasonably efficient functioning of the body, but also the requisite learned skills for their own performance. The realms of freedom are embedded in the realms of necessity, and except for the theoretically postulated realms at the lowest and the highest level, there is no realm which may be regarded as either that of pure necessity or of pure freedom. All the realms in between, and they are the only ones we really know of, share characteristics of both, being freer in relation to those in which they are embedded, and more bound in relation to those which are embedded in them. There will thus be a śūdra and a non-śūdra function intermixed at every level, except at the very extremities postulated for theoretical purposes. It would be the task of the discerning consciousness to distinguish between them and neither demean the śūdra functions nor think very highly of the non-śūdra ones, for the former provide the very base for the successful functioning of the latter, and the latter themselves are śūdra in character in respect to the other functions which are freer and for which they, in turn, provide the necessary foundation.

None of these formulations, however, helps us in conceiving of an ideal society in which the śūdra function is given primacy in terms of prestige, honour and status. It is, of course, true that we have tried to explain the notion of a śūdra function in terms of the basic biological functions of the body which, though belonging to the realm of necessity, cannot, in principle, be delegated to any 'other' as they can be performed only by oneself. The common point between the two obviously is that they both belong to the realm of necessity, but this realm has a very peculiar characteristic which has generally not been paid much attention to until now. This peculiarity is that it is the realm of necessity which provides the necessary precondition for the realm of freedom to arise, and which it facilitates by its relatively efficient functioning. It is the śūdra functions, therefore, that make possible the performance of all other functions, whether of the brāhmaṇa, the kṣatriya or the vaiśya, even if we confine ourselves to the traditional classification of the varṇa theory in India. The performers of all the other functions should thus be grateful to those who perform the śūdra functions and not feel superior to them, as without the latter they would not be able to perform their own functions, just as in the realm of their own body they do not regard its healthy functioning as being less important or inferior to anything else. Perhaps this was what was sought to be conveyed by the *Puruṣa Sūkta* when it said that the śūdras were born out of the feet of the Lord, for on them stood everything else, and if they grew weak or tottered or fell, everything would fall with them. The message, however, has not been understood down the ages. Nor is it likely to be heard in the future.

There is, however, another strand in the traditional notion of the śūdra function which, if interpreted in a certain way, might provide the ideal type of śūdra society where this very function is regarded as pivotal and accorded the highest status, at least theoretically if not practically in all cases. This is the notion of sevā or service in terms of which the function has been primarily understood in the tradition. Normally the traditional interpretation is in terms of the service that members of one varṇa render to members of all the other varṇas, and not in terms of the attitude with which members of all the varṇas perform their functions. The basic śūdra attitude of serving others may, or rather ought, to permeate the performance of all functions and not just those that are usually performed by members of a certain varṇa. It is not so much the content of what is done as the attitude with which it is done that matters and is considered of central importance. A brāhmaṇa, for example, is supposed to learn the Vedas and teach them, or, extending the idea of the said function, to pursue any kind of knowledge and impart it to others. But the preservation, advancement and transmission of knowledge are important functions in any society and may be seen as 'serving' the community and therefore performed consciously with that attitude. As a matter of fact, we have greater regard for those persons who are thus motivated. This is also true for the performance of what is usually called the kṣatriya and vaiśya functions in the tradition. They ought to be performed with the attitude of serving society or the community.

The idea of a society where everyone is motivated by the idea or the ideal of serving others is not unknown in the classical Indian tradition of thought, though it has perhaps never been thought of or presented in a focussed manner. The closest analogue, of course, is the idea of dharma, but then it is too much like 'duty for duty's sake', where the 'other' functions only in a tangential manner. The other claimant is the idea of niṣkāma karma so forcefully propounded in the *Gītā*, but this is also concerned with one's own consciousness and with the so-called fruits or consequences of action, rather than with 'others' either at the individual or at the societal level. The concept of 'social welfare' of the Benthamite kind may be said to come closest to it, but it is too tied to the hedonistic calculus of the quantitative kind to capture the attitude we are talking about. There is also the idea of being 'an instrument of the divine' so well epitomized in the *Gītā*'s well-known phrase *nimittamātraṃ bhava savyasācin*, but then it is not *concerned* with others at all, let alone with the idea of serving them. There are, besides these, the notions of karunā in Buddhism, 'charity' in Christianity and the modern idea of 'public service', but they all assume and imply a basic superiority of the person who bestows his 'services' on another, or behaves towards them in such a manner, while the śūdra notion of sevā or service implies just the opposite attitude.

A śūdra society would then extol the idea of having the 'other' at the centre of one's consciousness and the impulse to serve all living beings in every way so that they grow and develop. The *Gītā* expresses this in the phrase *parasparaṃ bhāvayantaḥ śreyaḥ* but it primarily concerns the relations between the gods and men; the *śreya* or the good is supposed to exclude, and even be opposed to, the *preya*, that is, what is dear to the senses and the heart. The ideal śūdra society will, however, not only emphasize relations between men, or rather between man and all living beings, but also include the preya in the śreya without confining the latter to the former alone and thus carry relations between the gods and men into the world inhabited by men and other living beings together.

But what, then, of the world of the gods and its relation to the world of men? Or, in other words, what should be the relation of the world of the transcendent to the world of men, which is constituted by 'self-consciousness', that is, reflective self-awareness which is conscious both of itself and the 'other' and the relations between them and the various 'demands' on oneself arising from them? The claim of the 'world of gods' would perhaps be seen in such a world in terms of the immanent ideals, demands and norms apprehended in all the varied dimensions of the relationship between the self and the 'other' on the one hand, and the self and itself, on the other. The idea of the 'indwelling god' or the god immanent in a particular domain or realm is not unknown to the Indian tradition. In fact, it is generally known as *adhiṣṭhātrī devatā*, particularly in the Tāntric tradition and may be invoked for the fulfilment of any desire or aspiration related to that realm. Our formulation, then, is only a translation of the traditional formulation into a modern idiom, though it certainly has shades and nuances of meaning which are somewhat different from those associated with the old terminology. But, then, any translation is bound to have some such difference, particularly if it is into a language rooted in a cultural matrix different from the one in which the terms that are translated are rooted in.

The sketch of an ideal śūdra society which I have tried to give is, of course, not present in the tradition. Nor has it ever been attempted to be explored therein. Yet, it is equally true that there *are* strands of thought, particularly in certain forms of Vaiṣṇavism, which lean in that direction. In fact, the *Svādhyāya* movement in contemporary India may be said to have drawn its inspiration from this and may be seen as an interpretation of it in the modern Indian context.

The alternative ideal constructions of different societies based on the classical notion of varṇa show the dynamic possibilities inherent in the notion when it is freed from its traditional moorings and allowed to float freely in the context of contemporary thought. This holds true for all the other concepts as well. Concepts have both a static and a dynamic aspect, though normally thinkers who try to *understand* a culture or a civilization, study only the static aspect or that aspect of a culture that has been thought about and formulated until then. They tend to treat the civilization as if the possibilities and potentialities inherent in it are exhausted. But this is an illusion, structurally projected by the very enterprise of 'understanding', where the concept is only 'mentioned' and not 'used', where one is interested only in discerning the ways in which it was used in the past and not using it oneself in the active, dynamic process of 'thinking', which is closely akin to the activity of an artist who also does not know exactly what he is going to create or what exactly will emerge from his activity. Collingwood has made an interesting distinction between art and craft in this connection. He has argued that while in craft one knows what one is going to produce, in art there is no such pre-existing idea which the artist is trying to actualize. Rather, one knows what one is trying to produce only when one has produced or created something. 'Using' a concept would be something like the creative act of thinking, while 'understanding' a concept would be more akin to engaging in a craft-like activity. The distinction, of course, is not as clear-cut as Collingwood would like it to be. It may, for example, not be easily applicable to architecture or portrait painting. But whatever the limitations, it does point to an important distinction and is perhaps even more relevant in the field of thinking. The distinction between the creative use of concepts and their continuous modification in the process of thinking, and the attempt to understand the way the concepts were used in the past in their pristine purity, are central to all living traditions where the impulse to present the past as it was, always comes into conflict with the other, equally important, demand to develop it and make it relevant in the contemporary context.

The concept of varṇa thus seems to occupy a central place in the conceptual structure of the Indian social theorist's thought about society. But that was not the only concept around which his thought revolved. First, it was well known that the varṇa was an ideal construct, and that social reality at the ground level consisted of jāti and kula on the one hand and various functional and regional associations at the village and town level, on the other. The concept that wove them together in an interactive social fabric was dharma, both at the level of *sādhāraṇa* dharma, that is, dharma which is supposed to be obligatory for every individual by virtue of the fact that he is a human being, and at the level of other *viśiṣṭa* dharmas which are obligatory because he happens to belong to a particular group. The conflict between sādhāraṇa dharma and viśiṣṭa dharma and the different viśiṣṭa dharmas resulting from the fact that one does not belong to just one group but to many groups simultaneously, has been the staple of both classical Indian literature and the Indian thinker's moral reflection on the human social situation.

Beyond such primary groups as the kula or the extended family and the various functional and regional associations to which one belongs by virtue of the fact that one practices a certain profession or engages in a certain craft or resides in a certain area, there are also certain larger associations of which one is sometimes a member in a representative capacity, that is, as representing one's family or caste or village or profession. The idea of a hierarchy of increasingly larger groups, the interests of which were considered superior to those of smaller groups, was thus present in Indian thought about society. This implied an awareness of the larger socio-political unit of which one was a member and which could demand one's loyalty over and above loyalty to the group one directly belonged to and to which one felt more intensely and persistently obligated most of the time. But it is the public functionary, and ultimately those exercising the ruling function, who are more acutely aware of the need and the demand for the overriding obligatory function, and not the ordinary person engaged in the everyday business of life. Even the public functionary or the ruling elite are aware of this need and demand only in the case of 'others', and seldom, if ever, in their own case. In fact, in the dharma of the king, or of one who exercises the ruling function, this awareness is at its maximum, at least in the way it is ideally conceived. The well-known references to this in the Mahābhārata, (1.107.32, 2.55.10, 5.37.16, 5.126.48) and the *Manusmṛti* (VII. 212, 213) are all in the context of the dharma of the king but they have a generalized application also. The last line *ātmārthe pṛathvīm tyajeta*, though specially applicable to the king, is also applicable to others. In the case of the king, it merely means that in times of dire necessity, he may even leave his kingdom or the realm he rules over, as there is always a chance of his returning to it or reconquering it with the help of others. In the case of ordinary mortals, it may again mean that in times of distress, one's first duty is to oneself as the preservation of the self can alone ensure the pursuit of any dharma whatsoever. Surprisingly, even the Jains have put forth similar arguments, though their own ideal is the performance of *santhārā*. In case the saying is interpreted transcendentally, it would again apply to everyone equally. The ātman in this perspective, is interpreted to mean the ultimate transcendental Self, and the injunction only means that for its sake all other obligations, including those to the empirical world, should be given up. It is, in fact, dharma versus mokṣa, the brahmanical versus the śramaṇa ideals once again. But whatever the interpretation, it applies equally to both the king and the commoner.

The obligations, however, always had an aspect of 'mutuality' without which no social fabric can be built or conceived. The roots of these feelings of mutual obligations lie, as in most other cases in the Indian tradition, in the relations between the yajamāna and the ṛtviks on the one hand, and between men and gods, on the other. Both these relationships were centred around the yajña or the ritual sacrifice, which was performed on behalf of the yajamāna by the ṛtviks on payment of a prescribed fee, wherein the oblations poured were for the gods who, in turn, were obliged to fulfil those desires for which the yajña had been performed. On a different level, the performance of the yajña was supposed to maintain the cosmic order which is generally known as ṛta. The ṛtvik, in later decades, became the purohita, but the relationship, though still confined mainly to the sphere of religious rituals, seems to have become far more stable and permanent than the one which prevailed between the yajamāna and the ṛtviks in Vedic times. Later still, the relationship between the yajamāna and those who performed the yajñas for him seems to have become more tenuous, and secularized. The trend in this direction seems to have proceeded so far that almost every exchange of goods and services, particularly in commercial contexts at the village level, came to be subsumed under it.

The intermeshing of the obligatory relations and the creation of a societal network under the yajamānī system have been noticed but the fact that they are rooted in the earlier relationship between the yajamāna and the ṛtvik in Vedic times has been almost totally missed.[1] The web of obligations that wove the social fabric into an interrelated and interdependent unity was articulated through a number of concepts, the most important of which were dharma and ṛṇa. The latter was extended to cover almost all obligations, including those owed not only to parents and teachers, but also to gods and even to one's own transcendental self. However, as the notion of *ṛṇa* or debt gives too restricted a perspective to social relations, it was supplemented by other concepts such as *dāna*, *dayā* and *karuṇā*, which went beyond the idea of the repayment of a debt incurred earlier. Society was conceived of as consisting of members overflowing with generosity or with feelings of 'giving' for the sake of the good of another. The highest gift that could be offered to another was the gift of enlightenment, and that is why Buddhism specifically formulated the ideal of *bodhisattva* to embody this vision. Even the imparting of knowledge has been seen in terms of dāna and in fact has been designated as vidyā dāna in the tradition. The paradigmatic exemplars of this ideal have been persons like Śivi and Dadhīci who gave their lives for the protection of someone, or Raghu, the king after whom the dynasty into which Rāma, the hero of the Rāmāyaṇa was born, was named, and who renounced all that he had, including his kingship. Strangely, neither the bodhisattvas nor the other exemplars from the non-Buddhistic traditions seem to exemplify to many of the contemporary western students of Indian society, what dāna means or the role it plays in knitting society together and making people less egocentric. For example, Gloria Raheja sees the paradigmatic example of such virtue in the relationship between the yajamāna and his predetermined and preordained clients, and that too only for getting rid of the evil effects of one's bad karmas.[2] Such an observation is too narrow, for even if it were correct, it could perhaps be asked if these were the *only* exemplifications of the concept, and whether they could exhaustively convey the core content of the concept's meaning. Furthermore, even if this were accepted as the *typal* meaning of the concept, the *positive* counterparts of the example should also be determined and located in the texts as well as in the lives of the people, for if the undesirable effects of bad karmas can be transferred, so can the good effects of righteous karmas. Good karmas of the past lead to benefits in the present. Gloria Raheja would have found positive counterparts of her negative examples in the texts, particularly in the *Māhātmaya* section. The reading of a sacred scripture or a pilgrimage to a holy place or the observation of various fasts undertaken would also have been enlightening. The empirical evidence confirming this would be more difficult to find, but a thorough search would have most probably revealed at least some instances. These generally occur in the context of a serious illness of a very close relative, or a dear one, or even one's teacher. Sometimes it is also ritually performed by a priest who conducts special religious rites, the beneficial fruits of which are *renounced* by him for the sake of the person for whom the sacred ritual has been performed. The prototype of all these activities is the Vedic yajña where the ṛtviks are supposed to perform the sacrifice for the yajamāna to whom the fruit accrues if the yajña is done properly. How far all this accords with the theory of karma is, of course, another question which I have discussed elsewhere.[3] But even within the perspective that Raheja has chosen to understand the notion of dāna in the Indian tradition, she has no justification for treating only the negative instances as exemplifying its meaning to the exclusion of the positive ones.

Dāna as an outflow and overflow of the other-centred impulse contributes much more to the creation of a trans-individual notion of society than does the notion of ṛṇa or debt or the notion of reciprocal obligation which are ultimately too calculating and economic in nature. In fact, traditional society tried to minimize or even deny the supremacy of the economic aspect of even those transactions which were essentially economic, such as the buying or selling of goods for daily consumption. The usual technique adopted to deny the strictly economic character of the transaction was always to give something *extra* over and above required by the transaction, and if the exchange took the form of a barter, the buyer was also expected to act in the same way as the seller.

Besides dāna, there are the concepts of compassion and welfare, karuṇā and *hita* which encompass all beings and are not confined to human beings only. This results in the widening of the concept of society to include all living beings entitled to receive munificence, compassion and kindness. The community of human beings was seen as part of the larger community of living beings where each supported the other, and the human beings who were self-conscious felt responsible for the whole.

One of the key concepts which provided an underpinning for all these was saṁskāra or ritualistic ceremonies which, besides having many other meanings, referred to all the rituals that transformed the natural, biological person into a socio-cultural being from the moment of his conception. But as the act of conception presupposes the coming together of two beings of the opposite sex, this act itself has to be transformed from the realm of the biological into the socio-cultural through the performance of a ritualistic ceremony or saṁskāra, usually designated as 'marriage'. Perhaps it is for this reason that the *Saṁskāra kāṇḍa* of Pandit Laxman Shastri Joshi's monumental *Dharmakośa* starts with ritualistic ceremonies related to marriage and not to the birth of a child, as one would have normally expected. In fact, the first three parts of the *Saṁskāra kāṇḍa* of the *Dharmakośa*, consisting of 2281 pages, deal exclusively with saṁskāras related only to marriage. This assumes added importance if one remembers that the *Kosa* volume on the saṁskāras consists of five parts, the sixth one being an index. To have three out of five parts devoted exclusively to marriage speaks for itself. The fourth begins with *garbhādhāna* or the act of conceiving and ends with the ritual ceremonies at the time the child is introduced to a normal human diet. The ceremony is called *anna prāśana* and occurs even today in most Hindu households in India.

The saṁskāras related to marriage, then, hold a central place in classical thought on society in India as it is within this pivotal social institution that the individual is born and socialized into the culture. The cycle of the saṁskāras is completed as the child grows and his period of formal education begins either as a day-scholar or as an *antevāsin*, that is, one who resides with the teacher. The main saṁskāra ceremony in this period is that of *upanayana*, a ceremony that affects the transition from boyhood to studenthood. The saṁskāra which is performed after completing one's education is called *samāvartana*.

The ritualistic ceremonies symbolize the socialization of an individual at all the crucial stages of the human life-cycle, not only transforming a biological being into a socio-cultural being, but also making him a bearer of legal rights and duties. These are what he can claim from others and what others can claim from him. The whole legal system or vyavahāra, as it is technically known, consists of this and *Smṛti* literature is full of references to it. What is *prāpya* for one is *deya* for another, as the term *dāyabhāga* for one traditional system of legal rules attests to in this regard. The term adhikāra could perhaps also be seen in this light. Normally, the term is used in connection with *adhikārī bheda* where one's spiritual or karmic development entitles one to a particular kind of spiritual practice, or even to a particular kind of sādhanā. But the notion of entitlement could be extended to the worldly realm of vyavahāra also, and the term adhikāra used to cover both the spiritual and the worldly realms. Adhikāra would thus mean what is deya to one from others as well as what one may reasonably do to attain spiritual growth.

The conceptual structure within which the classical Indian thinker tried to comprehend social reality, thus, revolved around ṛṇa, dāna, dayā, karuṇā, sevā, dharma, adhikāra, prāpya, deya, saṁskāra, loka, hita, varṇa, jāti, kula, śreṇī, pūga, grāma, nagara, *pura*, sāmājika, nāgarika, kulīna, sabhā, sabhya, rāṣṭra, vyavahāra, *maryādā*, rakṣā, *pālana*, *paropakāra*, *pārasparikatā*, *parāśritatā*, paramparā, *lokakalyāṇa*, *lokasaṅgraha*, *lokahita*, etc. Some of these concepts have been discussed in detail and their potentiality explored for being used and developed in the contemporary context. Others can be handled in the same way; still others may be found and their untapped potentiality discovered. Many of them overlap with those that are primarily concerned with the individual, while others overlap with those that predominately relate to law and polity. This is as it should be, for the realms are essentially intermixed, though as we shall see, the concepts related to the fields of law and polity are far more specialized and specific than those related to society, mainly because the realms themselves are far better demarcated and segregated than society, even in principle, can ever be.

Notes

1. There is of course a radical difference between the *yajamāna-ṛtvik* relation in the context of the Vedic yajña and the so-called jajamānī system which became prevalent later in society where obligatory service relations obtained among certain castes or among certain individuals. The latter were generally of a more permanent and hereditary nature and though they happened to prevail between the upper castes and the lower castes, it was not always so, for sometimes, as in the case of the class of *paṇḍās* at holy places, they themselves were generally brahmins by caste though they engaged in jajamānī relations with persons of other castes, including non-brahmins. Perhaps, the most radical difference between the yajamāna-ṛtvik relation and the later jajamānī relation is not so much that the ṛtviks were always brahmins and that in the latter case jajamāna could also be from the lower castes, but that the ṛtviks were hired and their respective fees decided by the śruti. However, there is a continuity between the two in that the fruits of somebody's action were enjoyed by someone else and that there was a fixed relation of reciprocity in the situation. The yajamāna-ṛtvik relation has continued in other forms which are not included in the jajamānī system where somebody else, usually a brahmin, is paid to perform ritualistic ceremonies whose fruits he gives up through a saṅkalpa to the person who has hired him to perform the ritual on his behalf.
2. Gloria Goodwin Raheja, 1989, 'Centrality, Mutuality and Hierarchy: Shifting Aspects of Inter-caste Relationships in North India', *Contributions to Indian Sociology* (n.s.), 23, 1, 79–101.
3. Daya Krishna, 'Yajña and the Doctrine of Karma', in *Journal of Indian Council of Philosophical Research*, VI, 2, January–April, 1989.

CHAPTER VII

The Conceptual Structure of Classical Indian Thought about Polity

The concepts concretizing classical Indian political thought are far more differentiated and specific than those relating to society. The concepts are clustered around three different areas. The first relates to the functions a polity is supposed to perform. The second relates to the question of what constitutes a polity, or what the elements are that are necessary to constitute a functioning political system. The third set of concepts relates to the problems of war and peace or to the relations which a polity can have with other polities. As the second issue seems to be central to both the first and the third, it may be best to begin with the concepts relating to it.

The technical term used for describing the essential nature of what constitutes a polity is *prakṛti*. It is supposed to consist of *svāmī*, *amātya*, *mantrī*, *pradhāna mantrī*, *mitra*, *kośa*, *rāṣtra*, *durga* and *bala*. To these are sometimes added *janapada*, *daṇḍa* and *pura*. The basic idea seems to be that a polity cannot be constituted of the king alone, or of one who exercises the ruling function. In order for the ruling function to be exercised at all, there have to be, in addition to the king, a chief executive, an advisory council along with a chief adviser, friends, a treasury, a kingdom, a fort and an army. Some thinkers add to the list the people or those who are ruled and for whose sake the ruling function is exercised. Still others add notions of sovereignty or ultimate coercive power and the capacity to exercise it. The concepts of daṇḍa and bala may best be understood this way. A capital city, which some thinkers added to the notion of a fort, was obviously an explication or extension of it.

The polity was thus conceived of as a complex relational structure which included such diverse elements as a fortified city, the people, land, treasury, army, advisers, chief executive and the ultimate centre of authority and power, that is, the ruler or the king. The inclusion of mitra or friends of the king amongst the constitutive elements of the polity appears to be *prima facie* strange, but as friends tend to become extra-constitutional centres of authority and, in any case, function as informal advisers, it may have been perceptive of political thinkers of classical India to have formally included them in the system. They may thus be classed with the formal council of advisers, including the chief adviser or the *pradhāna mantrī.* The difference between the functions of the amātya and those of the *mantrī-pariṣad* including the pradhāna mantrī seems to be an attempt to demarcate the advisory functions and the executive functions in a polity. These are now called the legislative and the executive functions. The advisory function exercised by the mantrī-pariṣad was, of course, not exactly legislative in the modern sense of the term as it had to be accepted by the king in order to assume that character. But even in modern times, residual traces of this classical distinction may be found, particularly in constitutions where the legislature formally puts before the President for adoption what it legislates, and in the fact that it is not regarded as formally enacted till it is signed by the President or the highest formal authority in that constitution. The difference between deliberation, decision-making and execution, the segregation of these functions and their association with different kinds of functionaries, thus, appears to be reflected in the distinction between what the Indian thinkers concerned with polity called mantrī, swāmī and amātya respectively. The swamī in this schema could obviously only be one while the mantrīs and the amātyas could be many. In fact, the term for mantrī is used in the plural in the text, that is, *mantriṇaḥ*, and the separate specific mention of pradhāna mantrī confirms this. However, though the term 'amātya' has been used in the plural, there is no separate mention of pradhāna amātya in the list.

The terms 'kośa' and 'bala', indicating the two essential

constituents of any polity, do not create any problems as it is difficult to conceive of a polity without a treasury and an army. The two, however, share a relationship of mutual dependence. There cannot be armed forces without money in the treasury to pay for them, and often, at least in the past, military campaigns were launched to augment the treasury. In fact, in the absence of what is called 'deficit financing' these days, it is difficult to think of any other quick means of replenishing and augmenting the treasury than of waging war for loot and booty. The close interdependent relationship between kośa and bala thus accounts, to a large extent, for the imperative of engaging in war till very recent times. Also, what good is an army if it cannot meet its own expenses and accumulate some extra wealth for keeping the soldiers well-fed, well-clothed and well armed in peace time? A large army adds glory to a kingdom on formal occasions and is useful for suppressing revolts against the state, though its main function is supposed to be to defend the state in times of war.

A cost-benefit analysis has usually not been applied to the large expenditure on military forces incurred by modern states, even when all the members of the United Nations have formally renounced the use of war for settling differences among themselves. It may be argued that the upkeep of such a large number of soldiers and armaments has a positive effect on the economy. And even if war brings destruction it may prove beneficial to those who conquer. Perhaps all great civilizations have basically been imperialistic and not only the more recent ones which are designated by that term. On the other hand, they may also arouse a creative response even in those who have 'iron in their soul' because of the defeat they have suffered.

In fact, the necessity of war, whether for augmenting a depleted treasury or for keeping the soldiers engaged in work for which they are paid or for forestalling possible attacks, leads to the second cluster of concepts about polity which classical Indian political thought developed. These were divided into concepts which dealt with diplomacy or the art of managing relations with other states and those that dealt with the actual engagement in war. The concepts in the first category are sāma, dāma, bheda, daṇḍa, *upekṣā*, māyā and *indrajāla*, while those in the latter category are *sandhi*, *vigraha*, *yānam*, *āsanam*, *dvaidhībhāva* and *saṃśryaḥ*. It is obvious that the former set of strategies is as relevant in dealing with internal trouble-makers or those opposed to the policies of the king as it is with dealing with external friends or enemies or neutral parties. The latter set of concepts, on the other hand, relates specifically to the different stages in the preparation and conduct of war, once it has been decided that war has to be fought.

The concepts related to the problems of war and peace with neighbouring kingdoms and those related to the native people of the kingdom belong to two different worlds with little relationship between them. The concepts related to the latter are basically centred around lokakalyāṇa and lokarakṣā. Such terms as *lokamaryādā*, *lokasthāpanaṁ*, *prajāpālanaṁ*, *dharmarakṣaṇam*, *jīvalokadhārakaṁ*, *lokasaṁsthāpakaṁ*, *lokadhārṇārathaṁ*, *prajāhitarata*, *dharmaniṣṭha*, *lokasaṅgraha*, *prajāsukhkartavyatā*, etc. obviously relate to public welfare and public protection, and could easily be applicable to all societies and polities. The distinctive feature of classical political thought in India seems to be its linkage with the *varṇāśrama dharma* on the one hand and the theory of puruṣārtha on the other. As these were generally accepted by social theorists, political thinkers had to come to terms with them and hence there was a continuous tendency for political thinkers to conceive of the ruler's duty as being the maintenance of the *varṇadharma* and encouragement to the people to pursue all the puruṣārthas. There was, however, an inherent dilemma in the situation as the political thinker was aware of the realities of *real politik* at the ground level to be carried away by the palpably unrealistic contentions of the social theorist in this regard. Some of these dilemmas, as I have noted earlier, related to the acceptance of mokṣa as the highest end of human seeking and the renunciation of worldly life as the best means to it, making sannyāsa the highest āśrama to which an individual should aspire. The Indian political thinker obviously could not accept this unreservedly, nor could he ignore or reject it as it was accepted by the culture to a large extent. Thus he tried, as did many others who were seriously concerned with other cognitive enterprises in the tradition, to adopt different strategies to counter or minimize or even blunt the hard core thrust of the contention. The first move in the direction was to present an integral theory of the puruṣārthas rather than a strictly hierarchical one with mokṣa at the apex, as was usually done in the tradition. The second was to remove mokṣa from its high pedestal and treat it as irrelevant in the political domain, or even as inimical to it. The third was to argue for the primacy of the gṛahastha āśrama over all the others and thus reduce or underplay the importance of the sannyāsa āśrama in the socio-political life of the people.

Discussions on the puruṣārthas in literature related to politics, for example, take special care not to talk about mokṣa at all, as it is of little help to bring it into the discussion. The Mahābhārata, for example, is not unaware of mokṣa and yet talks only of dharma, artha and kāma in the context of politics. And it talks of their *ucit samuccaya* or in an even more telling phrase, of their *anyonyānubandha* and *anyonyāśarayaḥ.*[1] Similarly, Kauṭilya talks of the mutual compatibility of the *trivarga*, that is, dharma, artha and kāma, and ignores mokṣa in the discussion.[2] The *Viṣṇu-dharmottara Purāṇa* describes them as *anyonyāśrita* or dependent on each other.[3]

Such statements are found in almost every text on the subject. The mention of mokṣa as a puruṣārtha is studiously avoided and the relationship between the three puruṣārthas is rendered stronger by the use of such words as anyonyānubandhaḥ and anyonyāśrita. Normally, only those artha and kāma were approved of that were not opposed to dharma, thus giving it a primacy over others. But in the context of a discussion on polity, even the term *parasparāvirodhena* does not necessarily entail the primacy of dharma, but only an avoidance of mutual incompatibility. In fact, just after talking of *paraspara avirodha*, Kauṭilya gives explicit primacy to artha amongst the three puruṣārthas by saying *trivarge arthaprādhānyam.*[4] As for the fourth puruṣārtha, it is not only not mentioned, but at one place he explicitly recommends that it be avoided. The *Kālikāpurāṇa* is supposed to clearly say, at least in the case of the appointment of an amātya: '*mumukṣuḥ amātyo varjayaḥ*'.[5] The importance of this may by judged by the fact that the Mahābhārata considers amātya to be only second in importance in its fivefold classification of bala.[6] As for the primacy of the gṛahastha āśrama and the gṛahastha vṛtti, the *Dharmakośa* quotes only the Mahābhārata in this context, but it can also be found in other places, albeit in other contexts.[7]

The classical Indian political thinker thus cleverly bypassed the problems created for him by the supervening importance given by other theorists to the renunciatory ideals embodied in mokṣa as the param puruṣārtha and sannyāsa as the highest āśrama. The advocates of the ideals of mokṣa and sannyāsa, on the other hand, made their task easier by drawing a radical distinction between vyavahāra and parmārtha and by segregating the two realms and confining their supervening ideals to the latter realm alone. The vyavahāric thinkers, thus, could either think about the problems pertaining to their realms without paying much attention to the values and the ideals involved in the paramārthic perspective on human life or merely pay lip service to them.

There were, of course, both vyavahāric and parmārthic thinkers who have tried to reconcile the conflicting perspectives of vyavahāra and paramārtha in their thought. They have attempted this through the mediating concept of dharma which provides a bridge between the two. In fact, it would be interesting to view the classical Indian thinkers' way of dealing with different realms of vyavahāra in this light and see if they are really concerned with mokṣa as a puruṣārtha and sannyāsa as a way of life and, if so, to what extent. Thinkers who grant greater autonomy to the realm and treat it in its own context may then be distinguished from those who do not. One may also try to discern the significant differences between them along with the differential weightage given to the concepts commonly used. It may also be discerned if there are any concepts used by one type of thinker and not by the other.

The dichotomy between vyavahāra and paramārtha has a peculiarity which makes it distinctive from other dichotomies, though this has usually not been noticed. The peculiarity is that it is simultaneously both an axiological and an ontological dichotomy. The paramārtha is not only that which is ultimately and absolutely real, but also the param puruṣārtha, that is, that which is, or ought to be, the object of man's ultimate, or even only, pursuit. On the other hand, vyavahāra is not only ultimately unreal, but is also the realm where nothing is, or can be, worth pursuing. Yet, what we know or can know in the usual sense of the term is the realm of vyavahāra only, and only in this realm can anything be pursued, including even mokṣa which is said to be the param puruṣārtha by many. This is as true of *Sāṁkhya* as of the *Advaita Vedānta*. The world of vyavahāra may be transformed if it is seen as an arena for doing service to the Lord or seen as His līlā. However, this retrieval of the vyavahāric world, and that too primarily in the context of the worship and adoration of the Lord or the primeval, omnipotent power, that is śakti, came too late to affect vyavahāric thinkers in any substantive manner, particularly as thought in these fields was formulated and developed when the Buddhist, Jain and *Sāṁkhya* traditions were predominantly prevalent in the culture.

The vyavahāric thought in the political domain, however, had to deal with an issue which normally does not engage the attention of thinkers concerned with other vyavahāric domains. This is the problem of war and peace with neighbouring kingdoms. Moreover, as this is a crucial problem for any polity since it involves its very survival, the political thinker cannot but centre his attention on it and evolve concepts around it. The political theorist in India was aware of the centrality of the issue and was perhaps the first to see it in geo-political terms. This resulted in the well-known maṇḍala theory, or the concentric theory of political relationships where political friendship and hostility are primarily determined by geographical location. Since a polity is located amongst other polities, inimical, friendly, middling or indifferent relationships are bound to develop. The terms used in classical literature to denote these relationships are *śatru*, *mitra*, *madhyama* and *udāsina*. However, the basic contention is that such relationships are determined primarily by geo-political factors, rather than by ideological, psychological or valuational considerations, as is usually presupposed. This structural perspective appears to be a unique characteristic of classical Indian political thought, but it seems to be determined by the notion of a *vijīgiṣu*, that is, one who is desirous of conquering. But then the fact that one's immediate neighbour is an enemy follows analytically from this, for if one really wants to conquer and extend one's domains, the nearest neighbour is the first logical target. The neighbouring polity would, in its turn, consider the adjoining state its enemy because the latter would inevitably resist its expansionist policies. The relationship of structural enmity is thus always symmetrical between two neighbouring polities, though not transitive, unless the third polity's boundaries also touch one's own. If not, as is usually the case, the third polity which is the neighbour of the adjoining polity, will be a potential friend as it will be the natural enemy of one's enemy. It follows that the enemy of one's enemy is a friend, and thus the cycle can be extended further indefinitely.

The problem of the contiguity of one's frontiers with other states is however not so simple, as the boundaries of the kingdom of the neighbouring king's neighbour may touch one's own at some point, and hence the same polity will have to be conceived of as both a friend, because it is the enemy of one's enemy, and as enemy because it is contiguous with one's own boundaries. The situation can be further complicated if one so desires, though, to my knowledge, the classical thinkers do not seem to have discussed these complications. In any case, it is obvious that the theory of concentric circles based on geo-political considerations should not be taken too literally. Rather, it should be treated only as broadly indicative of the dominant influence exercised by geographical factors in the relationship between polities.

The perspective of the vijīgiṣu or the king desirous of conquest or of expanding his kingdom, seems to have unduly restricted the thinking of the Indian political theorist on this issue. Also, the concept of 'conquering' and 'expansion' have been too confined to the political realm alone. The realms of economy and culture seem to have been completely excluded from thought in this context, even though they constituted important facets of life. And though the concept of dharma-cakravartitva was known, it did not form the subject matter of discussion in this context. Perhaps the reason for neglect in these fields, where expansion was deemed to be equally desirable, was that they depended in an important sense on the protection and patronage of the king, and his successes or failures in the enterprise of political expansion inevitably affected expansionist enterprises in the realms of economy and culture. There is a pithy saying in India's political literature which summarises this in a pre-eminent manner: '*rājā kālasya kāraṇam*'. Roughly translated, it means that the character of the times one lives in is determined by, or is a function of, the character of the king, or the characteristic way in which the political function is being exercised in those times.

But even in the tradition, the perspective of the vijīgiṣu is not the only one contained in the political thought of those times. The Mahābhārata, for example, has the concept of the *ātatāyī* or the tyrant who has crossed all bounds of arbitrary cruelty and oppression and therefore deserves to be fought and eliminated. The concept not only introduces a restriction on when one may engage in battle but also provides a justification for it, if fought against an ātatāyī. But strangely, neither Duryodhana nor Rāvaṇa has been shown as an ātatāyī in the two great epics that have depicted heroic battles in the Indian tradition. It is, of course, true that in both strenuous efforts are made to avoid war and that it is engaged in only as a last resort and that grievous wrong is done to the parties concerned; but there is little evidence in the texts to show that they were not reasonably good rulers in their own domains or that they had unduly harassed or ravaged other kingdoms. Kaṁsa and Jarāsaṅdha may qualify for being considered ātatāyīs but then the former hardly appears in the Mahābhārata and the latter is only a minor character there. As for the Rāmāyaṇa, perhaps only Tāḍaka and Subāhu would qualify for the appellation, but they too are minor characters in the epic. In spite of these shortcomings, however, the perspective of the ātatāyīn deserves to be explored and developed further, though it is as susceptible to being misused and abused as the proverbial story of the lamb and the wolf.

The concepts of the *madhyastha* and the *udāsīna* in the concentric circle of the polities surrounding one's polity, are not as unambiguous as may appear at first sight. The texts themselves suggest that a madhyastha polity may have this character either because it helps both the sides in some way or the other to reap advantages from whoever wins in the struggle or because it tries to mediate between the two and helps them to avoid a conflict. Similarly, the polity which is described as udāsīna or as being indifferent in the situation, may be so either because it is too weak to matter much or too strong to care who wins in the struggle for power.

The problem of a conflict of interests generated by the space the contending parties occupy is far wider and applies to many other fields besides those that are strictly political. The concepts evolved by Indian political theorists to describe the geo-political relations between polities may therefore be applicable with suitable modifications to other domains also. In fact even in the context of the political realm they need not be accepted in the form presented by classical thinkers, and may be modified to suit the purpose of contemporary thinkers. Not only this, the theoretical postulations of the past theoreticians may be contrasted with the actual relations between polities in modern times to determine how far they actually accord with those predicted by the theory. Such an empirical testing of the theoretical insights of past Indian political thinkers would have an added importance as modern polities are generally unaware of traditional thought and hence have never been influenced by it, as may have been the case with Indian polities in past decades. In fact the impact such thought may have actually had on the conduct of polities in classical India has rarely been the subject of study, even though it is well known that princes in India were acquainted with the classics of political science and their ministers and advisers proficient in them.

There is, of course, a problem with knowledge of this kind as it is available to all the parties concerned and hence does not give an added advantage to any one party. But then this is true of most competitive knowledge and not just of that which pertains to politics alone. Moreover, not everyone desires to possess a vast amount of knowledge or to adapt it to continuously changing circumstances. However, it would be interesting to discover whether the classical political theorists in India paid any attention to this aspect of the matter.

The conceptual repertoire of Indian political thought encompasses four different concerns. These relate to (1) the structural constituents of the polity, or what minimally constitutes a political structure; (2) the functions that a polity is supposed to perform for its people, by the fulfilment of which it justifies itself in their eyes as well as in its own; (3) the relations within the concentric circle of polities with which it is surrounded; and (4) the conduct of war and diplomacy. The relevance of these concerns for any exhaustive, coherent thought on politics is evident and it would be interesting to compare them with the conceptual schemes of both contemporary political thinkers and those of other cultures. Ultimately, it is the art of war and peace that defines a polity, as well as the conduct of policy, both at home and abroad. Yet, the ultimate justification and function of any polity can only be lokarakṣā and lokakalyāṇa and *prajāsukha-kartavyatā*, which means protecting the people and fostering their welfare and happiness. But while there can be little dispute about these and other cognate concepts, the emphasis on dharma through which they were to be continuously interpreted, and which itself was usually conceived of in a narrow and restricted sense, can hardly be acceptable to most contemporary thinkers concerned with society and polity. What is needed is a more dynamic interpretation of dharma in which the concepts of an ideal society and polity are continuously reformulated in the light of experience and new knowledge. Though it is evident that the classical thinkers did struggle over the various theoretical and practical problems of their times, there is scant evidence that the very concept of dharma, as traditionally formulated, was subjected to a searching critique by them. In fact, even the concept of dharmasaṅkaṭa, so prominent in the Mahābhārata, did not lead to any reflection on the adequacy of the notion as traditionally conceived. Yudhiṣṭhira, for example, though regarded as the embodiment of dharma, did not question whether it is the dharmic duty of a king to accept another king's invitation to play dice and to gamble, especially since he had experienced the disastrous consequences of observing this 'duty' just a short while earlier. Nor did Rāma, considered to be the incarnation of Viṣṇu, suffer any doubts as to what his dharma was when in its socially existent form it impelled him to renounce his pregnant wife, Sītā, or to kill Saṁbūka for doing a penance which was forbidden to him because he was a śūdra. The protagonists of the epics, as well as the numerous commentators and innumerable readers do not question the notion of dharma as embodied in these examples, or see in them graphic illustrations of what dharma is not. Even Kṛṣṇa, who was far more flexible in his attitude to moral codes than these heroes of antiquity, apparently did not feel that it was not part of his 'duty' to commit the whole of his army to the cause of fighting an unrighteous war by promising Duryodhana the army and himself aiding the Pandavas in battle just because it was impossible for him to refuse aid to anyone who came personally to request for it. There are manifold examples of the deep cleavage between dharma as an ideal norm of human behaviour and dharma as it is actually understood in a particular society at a definite point in time. The former is as much a matter of continuous exploration as any other ideal that man seeks. The *Manusmṛti*'s enumeration of the four sources of knowledge of dharma, that is, *śruti*, *smṛti*, *sadācāra* and *ātmatuṣṭi* opens up avenues for exploration in this direction. But, as far as I know, no one seems to have availed himself of it. The theoreticians perhaps remain as constrained by what is regarded as 'right' and 'wrong' in the social conditions prevailing in society as are most other people. Perhaps the attitude of theoreticians has been determined not only by habituation to what has been done all along, but also by constraints in physical and social technology available at the time.

Most societies in the past have been as, or even more, conservative in their thought and behaviour than Indian society. Yet, whatever the reasons may have been in the past, there is nothing to prevent a dynamic re-interpretation of traditional concepts in the light of new insights except intellectual inertia or the idea that the thought processes of the past should be left unsullied in their pristine purity. The latter have, in a very real sense, strengthened the former as the traditional pandit-scholar and the modern Indologist have both, in their different ways, staunchly upheld the teachings of Manu or Saṅkara or one of the hundreds of thinkers of the past and on that basis have refused to accept new interpretations of traditional thought.

But if it is not accepted that classical Indian intellectual thought is dead—and no Indian who is intellectually alive and aware of the multiple ways in which India's intellectual traditions have developed in the past can accept this—the way is clear for looking at the Indian intellectual heritage in a new light. This new way of looking at classical literature will clearly distinguish between what a particular concept or set of concepts meant in the past and how these traditions of thought are to be carried forward in the contemporary context, just as they were earlier developed and carried on by thinkers in past decades. The two tasks are not opposed to each other, for an understanding of concepts as they were used and as they functioned in the thought of earlier thinkers, reveals both their defects and potentialities. The two, therefore, are complementary in character, and this is how it should be in any living tradition.

Notes

1. *Dharmakośa*, IV, pp. 538, 557.
2. Ibid., p. 680.
3. Ibid., p. 744.
4. Ibid., p. 680.
5. Ibid., p. 1230.
6. *pancavidhabalānām dvitīyaṁ balaṁ amātyāḥ*. Ibid., p. 1208.
7. Ibid. See slokas under *Grahasthāśramasya śresṭhtā*, p. 584.

CHAPTER VIII

Epilogue

The search for the problematic lying at the roots of the Indian civilization and the conceptual structures in which it is embodied in classical Indian thought about man, society and polity have been explored and articulated in all their various dimensions. The intellectual and the existential problematics are closely linked though they bifurcate in different directions, for the articulation of a problematic is an intellectual exercise and thus raises problems which immanently belong to the realm of the intellect itself. However, by a strange logic, the self-consciousness of the problematic at the conceptual level sets problems not only for the intellect but also for the existential life of man as it makes demands on him to realize the immanent possibilities apprehended as possible ideals which are brought to the fore by the act of articulation itself.

An awareness of the problematic in its diverse dimensions thus creates a two-fold movement, each of which develops independently and yet continuously interacts at many levels. The history of the Indian civilization, as I have tried to apprehend it, is thus the story of this problematic as it first appeared rooted in the self-consciousness embodied in the Vedas and as it later developed, after an encounter with the great Śramaṇic traditions embodied in the Buddhistic, Jain, Sāṁkhya and Yogic traditions. This is evident in the internal developments in Vedic thought itself, resulting in the declaration of Vedic knowledge as *aparā*, that is, lower than *parā* which was the highest form of knowledge, as well as increasing dissatisfaction with the idea of yajña, taken in its narrow, literal, ritualistic sense and seen as largely linked to the achievement of ends desired by man. The increasing emphasis on a symbolic and metaphorical interpretation of the notion of yajña as well as its internalization in mental and spiritual terms, along with the development of the notion of action undertaken not for the sake of any desire, provide further evidence of this. The replacement of the idea of swarga with that of mokṣa or nirvāṇa also indicates this gradual shift from a yajña-centric view to one centred more on knowledge and meditation. The fact that swarga ceased to be mentioned even as one of the puruṣārthas, indicates the deep change within the culture as the theory of the puruṣārthas may be seen as central to an understanding of any civilization.

This change is reflected in the new interpretation of the notion of dharma which, in the Vedic context, was interpreted, at least by Jaimini, as concerned with the observance of Vedic injunctions alone. Dharma, as the centre of the moral life of man which, at least at one plane, is essentially social in character, thus took the place of yajña in post-Vedic thought. Here, as in the Mahābhārata and the Rāmāyaṇa, it was seen not only as intrinsically indeterminable in principle but also as essentially pluralistic in nature in that it necessarily led to dharmasaṁkaṭa from which there was no real escape, for some dharma or the other was bound to be violated. The well known statement '*dharmasya tattvam nihitam guhāyāṁ*' articulates this insight in a pithy manner just as the fourfold sources of the knowledge of dharma–śruti, smṛti, sadācāra and ātma-tuṣṭi–given in the *Manusmṛti* and elsewhere confirm this. The contrast will be even clearer and more telling if we remember that the details of the Vedic yajña were clearly laid down and were determined as precisely as possible in the *Brāhmaṇas*. Jaimini, in his *Mīmāṁsā Sūtra*, is also primarily concerned with accounting for the apparent discrepancies in the authoritative texts regarding yajñas and hardly any of the issues that he tries to resolve are of deep moral import such as those contained in the Mahābhārata or the Rāmāyaṇa or even encountered in everyday life.

However, just as the conflict between dharma, as understood in the social and moral context, and yajña, as understood in the *Mīmāṁsā* context, define one of the basic conflicts in the tradition as it developed in post-Vedic times, so also does the conflict between dharma in the social and moral sense of the term and mokṣa or nirvāṇa understood as the realization of the most fundamental and real state of one's being. In fact dharma, concretely formulated in the ideal norms of behaviour articulated as ahiṁsā, satya, asteya, brahmacarya and aparigraha in the Vedic tradition and the various *śīlas* in the Buddhist tradition, was interpreted in such a way as to make its moral import only secondary in nature and see it as primarily instrumental in achieving that state of consciousness which was supposed to be the primary purpose of every human existence. It was of course argued that only from such a state could righteous conduct follow naturally. However it was not discerned that a circularity was involved in the contention as moral conduct was considered fundamental for the realization of that ultimate consciousness which was valued for itself, while, at the same time, this state of consciousness was valued highly because it provided the necessary ground for moral conduct which was also considered worthwhile by them. Moreover, it was not noticed that in many of the descriptions of this ultimate state of consciousness, action was not supposed to be a constituent of it. Not only this, the whole notion of dharma-saṁkaṭa in such a perspective made no sense, for if moral action was integrally rooted in such a consciousness and could only flow from it then there could, in principle, be no such thing as a conflict between different duties or between legitimate claims made on oneself by others.

The conflict between yajña and dharma and between dharma and mokṣa led directly to what may be called the Indian version of the conflict between the individual and society and thus it was the social and political theorists, along with theorists concerned with matters pertaining to law, who had directly to deal with issues at the heart of this controversy. The concepts through which the issues were formulated and discussed become increasingly different as the discussion moves from the individual to society, to law and ultimately to considerations which centre on the political realm, the realm of power *par excellence*.

Many of these issues are perennial in that they concern all human beings and all societies and polities irrespective of the place or time in which they are situated. However, only a comparative study of civilizations from this perspective will reveal what the areas of emphasis were in this regard and what the foundational conflicts were that were given importance by the people of different civilizations. It will also be of significance to determine whether the transcendental dimension of human life played the same role in other civilizations and, if so, how the transcendent itself was conceived of in these civilizations as well as in its relation to the different immanent dimensions of life. It would be of equal interest to discover the conceptual structures of other civilizations within which were articulated dimensions of these different realms and the problematics therein and compare these with the ones delineated in the foregoing chapters. But as I have repeatedly insisted, the cognitive enterprises of the Indian civilization are not closed and their traditional formulation need not become an intellectual prison-house for us. We can use the insights gained in a creative way to meet the challenges of our own times, just as thinkers in past decades also did. One must distinguish between the *use* of a concept and talk *about* it. The latter has been the job of those who, to use a currently fashionable phrase from Foucault, do the archaeology of knowledge. Such theorists comprise all those for whom other civilizations except the modern western one are dead and hence only a subject matter of historical study. But for those who treat these civilizations as still alive, their intellectual self-formulations are not just objects of study but theoretical and experiential insights which *demand* to be developed further. It is in this *use* of past conceptual structures that their living future lies and hence, as I have repeatedly emphasized, we should, while learning from past discussions on various issues that concern man, society and polity, not feel bound by them, but rather treat them as providing a firm foothold to walk cognitively into the future.

Index